ISBN 978-0-332-48007-7
PIBN 10264577

English
Français
Deutsche
Italiano
Español
Português

www.forgottenbooks.com

Mythology Photography **Fiction**
Fishing Christianity **Art** Cooking
Essays Buddhism Freemasonry
Medicine **Biology** Music **Ancient
Egypt** Evolution Carpentry Physics
Dance Geology **Mathematics** Fitness
Shakespeare **Folklore** Yoga Marketing
Confidence Immortality Biographies
Poetry **Psychology** Witchcraft
Electronics Chemistry History **Law**
Accounting **Philosophy** Anthropology
Alchemy Drama Quantum Mechanics
Atheism Sexual Health **Ancient History**
Entrepreneurship Languages Sport
Paleontology Needlework Islam
Metaphysics Investment Archaeology
Parenting Statistics Criminology
Motivational

BARODA
ADMINISTRATION REPORT
1904-05.

*Compiled under the orders of His Highness
the Maharaja Gaekwar.*

BY

ROMESH C. DUTT, C.I.E.,
Revenue Minister of Baroda.

PRINTED AT
THE BRITISH INDIA PRINTING WORKS,
BOMBAY.

1906.

TO HIS HIGHNESS
THE MAHARAJA GAEKWAR.

May it please Your Highness,

I have the honour to submit the accompanying Administration Report of Baroda for the year 1904-05. The official year begins in August; and the period covered by this report is, therefore, from August 1st, 1904, to July 31st, 1905.

The year, unfortunately, was a year of famine in many parts of the State; and the distress, coming after a series of bad years, required prompt and extensive relief operations. Relief works were opened in different parts of the State, and Your Highness was also pleased to give substantial help to the cultivators in the afflicted districts by a liberal remission of the Land Revenue, current and arrear, to the extent of 29 lacs of rupees, or nearly £ 2,00,000. The collection of large portions of the Revenue Demand, not covered by this remission, was also suspended, and large advances were made to the cultivators to sink irrigation wells. These generous and considerate measures had an excellent effect. They enabled the agricultural population to follow their avocations in their own villages and fields, instead of crowding to our relief centres in large numbers; and they have considerably lightened the burden of debt from which the cultivators have suffered for years.

Other measures, equally wise and benevolent, were sanctioned during the year under review, and are briefly noted below. And, on the whole,

Your Highness's Government can look back on the year with legitimate satisfaction, as a year of progress and reforms.

Foremost among the useful measures, introduced within the year under report, was the formation of an Executive Council by Your Highness, early in the year. The Council assisted Your Highness in preparing the Programme of our Famine Relief operations, aud has, since Your Highness's departure for Europe, directed and controlled the administration of the State in all departments of work. It meets twice in the month, and each session generally lasts for three or four days. It is gratifying to record that, while every Member of the Council acts and votes with perfect independence according to his own judgment, the deliberations of the Council have been uniformly marked by harmony and mutual courtesy. (Chapter I.)

Two Legislative Measures of special importance came into force during the past year. One of them was for the Prevention of Infant Marriages; and the other vested the State with some control and supervision over Religious and Charitable Institutions. Both the measures excited some public feeling at first; but the modifications which were made in the Bills in deference to public opinion, and the moderation with which the measures have been worked, have allayed these feelings, and, to a great extent, reconciled the people to these very necessary measures of reform. (Chapter II.)

In the Judicial Department the separation of Judicial and Executive Duties was virtually com-

pleted in the past year; and Your Highness has also taken measures for the prompt disposal of judicial work in all Courts of the State. The experiment of having petty Civil and Criminal disputes disposed of by village authorities has also been continued with success. (Chapter III.)

The Decentralisation of the vast Revenue Department, ordered by Your Highness, was carried out early in the year. The Department is now divided into five Sections; a responsible officer is placed in immediate charge of each Section; and the experience of the past twelve months goes to shew that more attention is paid to every branch of work under this system than could be done under the old arrangement. The most important reform, effected in the first Section of the Revenue Department, was a revision of the direct taxes. Over two hundred different kinds of taxes, levied on the different professions and castes, were swept away under Your Highness's orders; and an Income Tax on a uniform scale, exempting the poorest classes, was introduced throughout the State. A further reform, raising the minimum limit of taxable incomes, has been ordered by Your Highness, and will come into force from the next year. (Chapter IV.)

Arrangements have been made for the proper supervision of Religious Institutions over which the State has assumed control by the new Act. The management of Wards' Estates and the education of Minors are receiving adequate attention. And steps have been taken for the prompt payment of compensation in Land Acquisition Cases. (Chapter V.)

We are somewhat backward still in industries and enterprise, and it must be admitted that Baroda does not yet take rank with Ahmedabad and Surat and other industrial centres in Western India. Progress in this direction must be a work of years, but signs of improvement are already perceptible. Foremost among the measures, adopted for the encouragement of trades and industries, were two successive revisions of the tariff, which were sanctioned by Your Highness in the last year. Large classes of goods were exempted, and only a small number of paying articles remained subject to duties. A third fiscal reform, abolishing all duties levied in petty towns, and making a further reduction in the number of articles subject to frontier duties, comes into force from the next year. The hand-loom industry received a great impetus in the last year, a new and simple loom, called the Sayaji Loom, has been invented in our Weaving School, the number of hand-looms at work has doubled in Petlad and Vaso towns, and a hand-loom Weaving Company has been formed at Mehsana. Mill industry shewed an equally satisfactory progress in the last year, and the transfer of the State Spinning and Weaving Mill at Baroda to private hands has given an impetus to private enterprise. Two new mills have been commenced at Baroda, and a ginning factory with weaving apparatus has been established at Kadi. It may be added that the dying factory at Petlad is shewing continued progress; the chocolate factory at Billimora has been re-opened in the current year; the State sugar factory at Gandevi has been transferred to private hands; and the valuable concession made to the cultivators of these parts, by bestowing on them the ownership of all date trees growing on their holdings, is likely to help the sugar industry. Students were sent last year to Europe, America, and Japan, to learn mechanical engineering and other useful professions; the services of a silk-expert were borrowed from the Bengal Government in the current year for the extension of sericulture in this State; and the pearl-fishery of the Dwarka sea-coast is under investigation by an expert whose services have been lent by the Ceylon Government. (Chapter VI.)

Not the least important reform, introduced in the last year, was the organization of a complete system of Self-Government throughout the State. The old Village Communities were re-organized and invested with powers of Village Administration; groups of them were formed into electorates and returned members to the Taluka Boards; and the Taluka Boards returned members to the four District Boards, to which a handsome allotment of Rs. 4,45,000 has been made in the current year for carrying out the duties imposed on them by the Act. The larger towns of the State have also been formed into Self-Governing Municipalities, and specific grants and sources of income have been alloted to them for the discharge of the duties imposed on them by another Act. (Chapter VII.)

The organization of the Forest Department on modern principles has now been completed after the labour of years, and working plans have been prepared for the preservation of forests and the sale of trees by rotation. The transfer of the management of unreserved forests to the Revenue Department proper will save the people from a dual control and consequent harassment; and Your Highness has made a valuable concession by bestowing on the cultivators of Songadh the ownership of all trees growing on their own holdings,—a concession made before to the tenants of other parts of the State. (Chapter VIII.)

Land Settlement, according to the Bombay principles, was introduced in this State over twenty years ago; and the Baroda land system has all the merits and all the faults of the Bombay Ryotwari system. The services of a Bombay Civilian were lent to this State, last year, to revise the Settlement of the Talukas where a revision had become due. A satisfactory Settlement of the difficult Petlad Taluka was the first result of his careful and sympathetic labours; and Your Highness was pleased to sanction an abatement of over half a lac of rupees from the previous Revenue Demand of this Taluka, in consideration of its present condition. (Chapter IX.)

The administration of Finance was beset with exceptional difficulties in a year of famine and large remissions and suspensions of the Land Revenue. But the work has been performed by our able and experienced Accountant General with care, foresight, and success. (Chapter X.)

Over six lacs of rupees were spent last year, as in preceding years, on Education in a State the population of which is under twenty lacs; and nearly one half the boys of the school going age were actually under instruction, a result which is seen in few places in India. The Baroda College continues to be one of the most successful institutions affiliated to the Bombay University; our Technical School continues to teach useful industries to students; and a proposal to extend Compulsory Education throughout the State is under consideration. (Chapter XI.)

Forty hospitals and dispensaries gave relief to nearly two hundred thousand new patients, i. e. not counting the same patient more than once. The number represents one-tenth the entire population of the State, and shews the popularity of the institutions. (Chapter XII.)

Great endeavours were made in past years to construct large and useful Irrigation Works, but it must be confessed that our success has not been commensurate with our endeavours. It may be on account of the deficient rainfall of the last seven or eight years, or it may be from other causes, that our expectations have not in all cases been fulfilled. The perennial supply of rivers which was reckoned upon has failed, and the catchment areas secured for large reservoirs have not brought in the quantity of water that was expected. The duty of revising old plans and estimates, and in some cases of altering works already constructed to suit the present circumstances, has devolved on the present Chief Engineer, who has already distinguished himself by the construction of large and successful Irriga . tion Works in Mysore. On the other hand, our Railway

Systems have paid fairly well, and new extensions are under consideration. (Chapter XIII.)

A revision in the scale of salaries, paid to the inferior officers, has been effected in the different Departments. A better scale of pay has attracted better men in the Jail Department and the Police, and the administration of both these Departments was marked by some reforms in the last year. (Chapter XIV and XV.)

Relief operations were organized and supervised with foresight and care by the Famine Commissioner, and were completely successful. Nearly three lacs of rupees were spent on Relief Works, and over six lacs were disbursed in advances to cultivators and others. There was no epidemic disease in our relief camps, no increase in the death-rate of the year, and no loss of life from famine. (Chapter XVI.)

Your Highness's faithful servant,

R. C. DUTT.

BARODA, }
April, 1906. }

CONTENTS.

I.—POLITICAL.

(a)—The State and its Ruler.

Area and Population.—The State of Baroda, as stated in previous Reports, is divided into four distinct blocks quite apart from each other. The southern district of Naosari lies near the mouth of the Tapti river and is interlaced with British territory. To the north of the Narbada river is the central district of Baroda, in which the capital city is situated. Further up, and to the north of Ahmedabad, lies the rich district of Kadi with its busy towns and many industries. And far to the west, in the peninsula of Kathiawar, lie tracts of land, isolated and separated from each other, which comprise the district of Amreli. The area of the State in round numbers is eight thousand square miles, and the population is two millions.

The area and population of the four districts vary considerably, and are shown in the following table:-

District.	Area in square miles.	Population.	No. of towns.	No. of villages.
Baroda	1,887	6,44,071	14	924
Kadi	3,015	8,34,744	16	1,187
Naosari..........	1,952	8,00,441	5	979
Amreli	1,245	1,73,436	6	310
Total	8,099	19,52,692	41	3,400

Baroda, with its capital town, is the most thickly populated district, having an average population of over 340 per square mile. And the scattered district of Amreli is the most thinly populated, having scarcely 140 people to the square mile.

Over three-fourths of the entire population, or 15,46,992, are Hindus. The Musalmans number 1,65,014 or a little over one-tenth of the Hindus. Tribes or castes, low in civilisation, and returned as " Animistic," number 1,76,250. The Jains are 48,290 in number, forming less than one-thirtieth of the Hindu population. There are also 8,409 Parsees or Zoroastrians, and 7,691 Christians.

In his very interesting chapter on occupations, the Superintendent of the Census of 1901 classes the population of Baroda thus:—

Government Service	4·1	per cent.
Pasture and Agriculture	51·14	,,
Personal Services	4·98	,,
Suppliers of Materials	14·2	,,
Commerce and Storage....	3·5	,,
Professions....	2·86	,,
Unskilled Non-agricultural Labour	13·34	,,
Independent of Occupation	2·87	,,

Among the people engaged in professions, those dealing with textile-fabrics are 68,213, workers in metals 25,029, workers in earthenware and stoneware 26,284, and workers in wood, cane, &c., 19,364. Commerce of various kinds, not including storage, support 61,080 persons.

History.—The State of Baroda has a very interesting history which stretches back through twelve centuries. When the famous Chinese traveller Houen Tsang visited India in the seventh century after Christ, he found the whole of Gujrat a very flourishing country, ruled by the Valabhis, who had their capital at Valabhipura. In the following century, the power of the Valabhis was broken and the Chauda Rajputs ruled over Northern Gujrat from the eighth century to the middle of the tenth.

In 941 A.-D., the Chaudas were in turn supplanted by the Chalukya or Solanki Rajputs; and Mularaj, the first king of the new dynasty, extended his conquests to the south of the Narbada river. One of his successors, Bhimadeva, was ruling at Anhilwara-Pattan, then the capital of Gujrat, when Mahmud of Ghazni came on his famous expedition against Somanath Pattan. Mahmud took Anhilwara on his way, and drove out its young king ; but Bhimadeva soon collected his forces, and fell upon the Mahomedan army with such effect as to endanger its safety. In the following year Mahmud took Somanath, again defeated Bhimadeva, and then withdrew to Ghazni; and Bhimadeva continued to rule till 1063. His successor Jai Sinha was the greatest prince of the race, and was also one of the greatest builders; and during a rule of fifty years, from 1093 to 1143, largely enriched and developed the Gujrat style of architecture, which was subsequently copied by the Mahomedans at Ahmedabad. Jai Sinha was succeeded by his cousin's son, Kumara Pala, who reigned in great splendour for thirty years, from 1143 to 1173, and greatly favoured the Jains ; and the Jains of Baroda State assign many of their religious edifices and other public works and gifts to this munificent prince. Within seventy years after Kumara Pala's death, the Chalukya or Solanki dynasty came to an end in 1244.

The Vaghela dynasty then succeeded, and Visala-deva, the first king, united all Gujrat under his rule which lasted from 1244 to 1261. One of his successors, Karna Vaghela, ruled from 1296 to 1298, and was the last Hindu King of Gujrat.

Alla-ud-din Khilji then conquered the country from the Hindus, and the story of the beautiful Princesses Kamala Devi and Devala Devi, who became the wives of Alla-ud-din and his son, is one of the romances of Indian history. For some centuries Pattan continued to be the capital of Gujrat under the Mahomedan rulers; but the seat of Government was eventually removed to Ahme-dabad. Gujrat threw off the yoke of Delhi, and became an independent Mahomedan kingdom, in the fourteenth century, but was once more brought under Northern India by Akbar the Great in the sixteenth century. Aurangzeb's mad bigotry wrecked the Mogul empire which Akbar had built up, and in the eighteenth century the Mahrattas spread over Gujrat as over other parts of India. Pilaji Rao Gaekwar and his comrades in arms firmly established themselves in Baroda in 1723 ; and the present ruling family has therefore a dynastic record of nearly two centuries.

The present Ruler.—Events which took place during the rule of Maharaja Malhar Rao led to his deposition in 1875, and the present ruler, Maharaja Sayaji Rao Gaekwar, then a young boy, was chosen for the throne of Baroda. On attainment of his majority His Highness assumed the reins of Government in 1881, and has, since then, personally directed, regulated, and supervised the administration in all departments. His Government is modelled after the system followed in British India; but modifications, required by the peculiar conditions of this State, are introduced both in legislation and in administration. The heads of the different departments deal with all matters relating to their respective work, and take the orders of His Highness on all important questions. Similarly, officers entrusted with the duty of drafting laws receive their instructions from the Maharaja, publish the first drafts in the State Gazette called the *Ajna Patrika* to invite public criticism, revise the drafts in accordance with such criticism, and finally receive the sanction of His Highness to the revised drafts before they are passed into law.

Reforms and changes in laws and administration, suggested by the officers of the State, receive the Maharaja's careful consideration ; but in the majority of cases they are initiated by himself. A system of personal Government, carried on during more than twenty years, has made him familiar with every detail of administration ; and his frequent visits to the interior of the State enable him to keep himself in close touch with District and Taluka Officers, and with the actual working of laws and administration. The needs of the State in regard to railways and irrigation, schools and hospitals, municipalities and local institutions,

manufacture and agriculture, are thus made known
to him. He also keeps himself well informed with
what passes outside his own territory—both in
British India and in Europe,—and is quick in
adopting new ideas and introducing new reforms
among his own people. Some of these changes
have proved beneficial to his State, while some
have not yet been attended with success. The
following pages will be found to be an impartial
record of our failures as well as of our successes.

The Diwan.—The Diwan is the principal officer
of the State under the Maharaja. Early in 1904,
owing to the retirement of Diwan Bahadur Dham-
naskar through ill-health, Mr. Kersaspji Rustamji
Dadachanji, M.A. and LL.B. of the Bombay
University, was appointed Diwan of Baroda. Mr.
Kersaspji has served this State during thirty years
in various capacities,—as District Officer, as Settlement Commissioner, as Revenue Commissioner,
and as Chief Justice, and thus brings a ripe
experience and a mature judgment to the performance of his high duties. As Chief Officer of the
State, he is primarily responsible to the Maharaja
for good administration.

Officers appointed in 1904-05.—Some account of
the other high officers, presiding over different
departments, will be found in the subsequent
Chapters of this Report. It is necessary in this
place only to refer to some new appointments
which were made within the year under report.

In the first month of the year, *i.e.*, in August
1904, His Highness the Maharaja invited

Mr. R. C. Dutt, C.I.E., to accept office in the State. Mr. Dutt had been called to the Bar, and had also entered the Indian Civil Service, in 1871, and, after his retirement from that service in 1897, had continued his enquiries into Indian administration, and also his studies in Indian History and Literature. The Maharaja placed Mr. Dutt, under the title of Amatya, in special and independent charge of the Revenue, Finance, and Land Settlement departments, and desired him to pay his special attention to the fiscal policy, and the agricultural, industrial and commercial advancement of the State. As the monsoon failed, and the prospects of the year darkened, it became necessary to organise famine relief operation towards the close of 1904; and Mr. Dutt was placed in charge of those operations in addition to his other duties.

A younger member of the Indian Civil Service, Mr. C. N. Seddon, returned from furlough in November 1904, and joined the State as Survey and Settlement Commissioner. Mr. Seddon belongs to the Bombay Civil Service, and was Assistant Resident of Baroda before he went on furlough; and his services have now been lent to His Highness the Gaekwar for the Settlement of some Talukas in the State. His knowledge of the State, its people and its language, combined with his experience in administrative work, eminently befits him for the duties now entrusted to him. The nature of these duties, too, keeps him generally in the villages in the interior, and the information he is thus able to gather from personal observation, regarding the condition of the people and their systems of cultivation and irrigation, is greatly valued by the Maharaja, and is highly useful to general administration.

On the retirement of Mr. G. R. Lynn after fourteen years service in this State, Mr. Chunilal Dalal L. C. E. was appointed Chief Engineer. He rendered long and distinguished service in Mysore, for some years as Executive Engineer, and subsequently as Superintending Engineer ; and the famous Marikanave Dam, forming one of the largest irrigation reservoirs in the world, was constructed under his supervision. The title of Raj-Sabha-Bhushana was conferred upon him by the Mysore Government in recognition of his services. Mr. Chunilal Dalal joined his appointment in this State in March 1905.

The Council.—An important reform in the method of administration was introduced within the year under report. His Highness the Maharaja has formed an *Executive Council*, consisting of the principal officers of the State ; and many important questions were referred to this Council for discussion and opinion during the closing months of 1904. The state of the Maharaja's health compelled His Highness to leave India on April 1, 1905, for change and rest in Europe ; and the Council has worked efficiently, harmoniously and well since, and transacted all the important business of the State.

(b)—THE PALACE.

His Highness Maharaja Sayaji Rao Gaekwar is blessed with four sons and one daughter. His first wife gave birth to Srimant Yuvaraj Fateh Singh Rao in 1883, and died shortly after. His Highness then wedded the present Maharani, and she has presented him with three sons and a daughter.

His Highness went to Darjeeling in the month of September, 1904, with Her Highness the Maharani and Srimant Dhairyashil Rao. On his way to Darjeeling the Maharaja halted at Allahabad, where the notables of the city gave him a cordial reception, and presented him with a public address. His Highness returned from Darjeeling in the month of November. On his way back, he halted at Calcutta, where he was cordially received by all classes of people, and was the guest of Maharaja Sir Jotindra Mohan Tagore. A public address was presented to His Highness by the citizens. The Maharaja then visited Jagannath-Puri, before returning to Baroda.

In December, 1904, the Maharaja presided at the Social Conference of the Indian National Congress, held at Bombay, and delivered an eloquent presidential address on Social Reform. Her Highness the Maharani was also present there on the occasion. His Highness then proceeded to Gondal, having been invited there by His Highness the Thakore Saheb on the occasion of his son's marriage. The Revenue Minister and the Revenue Commissioner, Mr. R. C. Dutt and Mr. V. M. Samarth were also present on the occasion.

The Maharaja then went on tour in Amreli and Kadi Districts, with the officers named above, to see the state of the crops and the condition of the people, and returned to Baroda in the month of February.

His Highness subsequently went to Tilakwada, and a Darbar was held there. All the surrounding Mewasi Thakurs presented themselves, and offered customary Nazaranas, and in return His Highness presented them with dresses of honour.

The Maharaja's health was impaired by continuous hard work, and he was advised to go to Europe for a change. All the necessary arrangements were made. Their Highnesses left Baroda on the 31st of March, and sailed to Europe per S. S. Arabia of P. & O. Company on the 1st of April, accompanied by Srimant Shivaji Rao, Srimati Indira Raja and Srimant Dhairyashil Rao.

Household.—Yuvaraj Fateh Sinh Rao was initiated in the work of the Palace Department, and he showed keen interest in the work. In the month of January, he went to England, with Srimant Jayasinh Rao, to join the Cambridge University to complete his course there. Srimant Jayasinh Rao, who is studying in the Harrow School, had come to India here in the month of January during the winter vacation, with Mr. and Mrs. Elliot.

Srimant Shivaji Rao and Srimati Indira Raja joined the Eastbourne School while they were in England. Srimant Dhairyashil Rao was for a few months in France for the benefit of his health.

The notable event in this year is that Yuvarani Padmavati Bai Saheb gave birth to a daughter on the 23rd of June.

Mr. Harding was Khangi Karbari or Officer in charge of the Palace till the middle of February. Srimant Sampat Rao Gaekwar succeeded him.

The expenditure of this Department during the last two years is shown in the following table:—

Items.	1903-04.	1904-05.
	Rs.	Rs.
Household	11,13,698	7,50,803
Karkhanas	4,96,778	6,12,037
Devasthans	18,597	*Nil.*
Gardens	1,39,104	*Nil.*
Donations	1,09,273	66,618
Miscellaneous	1,14,161	1,05,219
Total	19,91,611	15,34,677

The decrease in the first item in the last year is mainly due to the fact that the marriage of Yuvaraj Fateh Singh Rao had swelled the figure for the preceding year.

The increase in the second item is due to the fact that the expenses of the Palace lights and gardens are transferred to this head.

In the third and fourth items there are no expenses at all. As stated in the last year's report the Devasthans are transferred to the Settlement Department; and the gardens are transferred to the head of Karkhanas as mentioned in the last paragraph.

The fifth and sixth items show decrease. A part of the fifth item is transferred to the Settlement Department.

Among the eminent personages who visited Baroda during the year under report may be mentioned:—

> The Jam Saheb of Jamnagar.
>
> The Thakore Saheb of Wadhwan.
>
> Sir H. Wedderburn and his daughter.
>
> Mr. Latham, M.P.
>
> Mr. Samuel Smith, M.P.

On the 43rd anniversary of His Highness the Maharaja's birthday a medal and the title of Tarka-Vachaspati were presented to Badrinath Shastri. On the 23rd anniversary of Yuvaraja's birthday, Mr. Kersaspji Rustomji was presented with a dress of honour as Diwan.

To various institutions and persons, His Highness gave donations amounting to Rs. 92,570. The institutions that were specially patronized by His Highness are named below:—

> Alligar Oriental College.
>
> Hindu Panchang Improvement Society.
>
> Allahabad Hindu Board Association.
>
> Ahmedabad Orphanage.
>
> Ranade Memorial Fund.
>
> Jain Conference.
>
> Ajmere College.
>
> Ootacamund Bartholomew Hospital.
>
> Poona Female High School.
>
> Mahableshwar Native Library.
>
> Industrial and Agricultural Exhibition, Bombay.

(c)—THE ARMY.

The strength of the Regular Force at the close of the year 1904-05, as compared with the fixed strength, was as follows :—

Description of Force.	FIXED STRENGTH.			ACTUAL STRENGTH.		
	Effective.	Non-effective.	Total.	Effective.	Non-effective.	Total.
ARTILLERY.						
Light Field Bat. ..	94	66	160	63	57	120
CAVALRY.						
The Moti Khas ..	455	24	479	379	18	397
The Choti Khas ..	455	24	479	384	24	408
The Fateh Singh Rao Regiment ..	455	24	479	421	25	446
The Guards ..	135	10	145	126	14	140
Total ..	1,500	82	1,582	1,310	81	1,391
INFANTRY.						
1st Regiment ..	698	29	727	870	39	909
2nd Regiment ..	698	49	747	840	38	878
3rd Regiment ..	698	29	727	711	38	749
4th Regiment ..	514	27	541	Amalgamated with the three Regiments.		
Okha Battalion. ..	461	14	475	461	14	475
Total ..	3,069	148	3,217	2,882	129	3,011
The Band ..	111	6	117	106	6	112
General and Staff Officers	6	2	8	4	0	4
Grand Total ..	4,780	304	5,084	4,365	273	4,638

NOTE.—Figures for Non-effectives in some of the Regiment have been increased according to requirements.

The cost of maintaining the above force during the year under review is shown in the following table :—

Year.	Artillery.	Cavalry.	Infantry.	Band.	General and Staff Officer.	Medical Establishment.	Veterinary Establishment.	Total.
1904-05	Rs. 36,980	Rs. 5,45,237	Rs. 4,11,313	Rs. 23,543	Rs. 24,527	Rs. 11,951	Rs. 4,685	Rs. 10,58,736

In round numbers the Regular Force cost this
State ten lacs and a half during the year under
report. The average annual cost per effective man
in the Artillery was Rs. 308, in the Cavalry Rs. 416,
in the Infantry Rs. 143, and in the Band Rs. 222,
during 1904-05. Or taking the whole force together,
the average cost per effective man was Rs. 272, or
about Rs. 23 a month.

The total fixed strength of the Irregular Force,
during the year under review was as follows:—

Horse.

Silledari.	Sibandi.	Paganihaya.	Khalsa.	Total.
908	333	182	577	2,000

Foot.

Sibandi.	Khalsa.	Total.
1139	667	1806

And the expenditure incurred on account of the
Irregular Force is shown below :—

Horse.	Foot.	Other Establishment.	Total.
Rs. 5,89,295	Rs. 5,231	Rs. 53,652	Rs. 6,48,178

It will thus be seen that the Irregular Force
cost, in round numbers, six lacs and a half. The
reduction in expenditure, as compared with the
previous year, is due to the reduction of allowances
in the case of Sirdars, Silledars, &c., at the time

of succession, and to the transfer to the Police
Department of those men who render duty in that
Department.

Taking the Regular and Irregular Force together the total cost is shown below :—

Regular.	Irregular.	Pension and Gratuity.	Total.
Rs. 10,58,735	Rs. 6,48,178	Rs. 80,818	Rs. 17,87,731

An expenditure of Rs. 3,72,460 on account of the
annual Contingent Commutation Money paid to the
British Government is also debited to the Military
Department. The GRAND TOTAL of expenditure
in the Military Department, during the year under
report, was therefore, Rs. 21,60,191.

General Nissen was acting as Senapati during the
greater part of the year under report. He retired
in the beginning of June, after enjoying three
months' privilege leave from March 1905; and
Colonel Wilcox succeeded him as General. Srimant
Sampat Rao Gaekwar, who was appointed Senapati on the 1st of March 1905, exercised the Minister's powers as regards the disposal of the work
of the Military Department.

Colonel Watson was working as Colonel of the
Infantry Brigade at the close of the period under
report.

Captain Madhava Rao Baji was appointed acting
Colonel of the Cavalry and the Artillery Brigades
in March last. He had also the charge of the
Brigade Major's Office.

(d)—RELATIONS WITH THE BRITISH GOVERNMENT.

The relations of this State with the British Government and with the neighbouring Native States were satisfactory as before.

As in previous years, no case of mail robbery occurred during the year in these territories.

Matters relating to the extradition of criminals, and co-operation in Police matters, between this State and the neighbouring British Districts and Native States, were disposed of satisfactorily.

The Postal Service in this territory is performed by the Imperial Postal Department. Every year we have permitted the multiplication of Post Offices and Letter Boxes, and the year under report has been no exception. The working of the Post Offices continued satisfactory.

In 1899, when the South African war between England and the Transvaal Republic was in progress, His Highness the Maharaja was pleased to make a general offer of State troops, and especially of cavalry horses and transport ponies. Thereupon sixty horses were selected by an officer deputed by the Government of India, and the same were sent to the Transvaal in charge of two dafadars, two farriers, two swars, and sixteen syces. During the year under review, the Government of India having forwarded for presentation to the said persons certain silver and bronze medals with clasps, fittings, and ribbon, the same were delivered to the recipients concerned. Two silver medals and one bronze medal were returned, as one of the reci-

recipients had left the service of the State, and the other was dead.

At the request of His Highness's Government, the Government of India were good enough to lend, for a period of two years, the services of Mr. C. N. Seddon, I.C.S., for work connected with Survey and Settlement operations in the State. His Highness's Government were also allowed to place Mr. Seddon on the Council of the State whenever they might consider it necessary to do so. Mr. Seddon assumed charge of his duties on the 17th November 1904, and is in receipt of a gross salary calculated to leave a net pay of Rs. 1,800 per month, plus Rs. 200 a month as travelling allowance, with exchange compensation.

Some Indian passengers having been conveyed to Beyt on the Kathiawar coast in 1903, on board the brigantine "Alice" of Nantes carrying French colours, under circumstances which at a British Indian port would have constituted an infringement of the provisions of the Native Passenger Ships Act, the Government of India, in bringing the fact to the notice of His Highness's Government, expressed a hope that they would make satisfactory arrangements at all ports in Baroda territory, to prevent the overcrowding of steamers sailing to and from Africa, by issuing rules similar to those framed by the Maritime States in Kathiawar and Cutch on the basis of the Native Passenger Ships Act of 1887. His Highness's Government co-operated in the matter with the British Government by enacting an Act on the analogy of the aforesaid

Act, and applying the provisions thereof to all ships arriving at any of their ports in the Amreli District in Kathiawar.

Certain modifications in the Act, suggested by the Government of India, are under the consideration of His Highness's Government.

The dispute relating to boundary, between the villages of Kaniel (Baroda) and Burmuada (Mahi Kantha), was decided by the Boundary Commissioner in 1904. Both the parties having preferred appeals to the Commissioner, Northern Division, against that decision, the latter officer upheld the decision of the Boundary Commissioner. The dispute comprised an area of about 2,395 Bighas, out of which Bighas 2,300 were awarded to Baroda.

To protect the customs revenue of the State from loss, which would have arisen if goods were allowed without proper restrictions to pass into the Baroda cantonment free of duty, and then sold in the surrounding villages, it was arranged in 1876, after correspondence with the Residency, that dutiable goods, required for the use of the subsidiary force and their officers, were to be allowed to pass into the cantonment free of duty, if they were covered by passes signed by the Cantonment Magistrate, and sealed with the Residency seal ; and that goods imported for the use or consumption of the civil inhabitants thereof, if taken into the cantonment, were to be subjected to the town duties leviable by His Highness's Government.

The cantonment authorities, however, desired
that His Highness's Government should not levy
any duty from the civil inhabitants of the cantonment, on goods imported by them into camp
for their use, on the ground that the levy partook
of the nature of transit duty which had long ago
been abolished by His Highness's Government. On
a representation from His Highness's Government
that the duty in question was not a new levy, but
was a customs duty which had been paid without
demur by the civil inhabitants of the cantonment
even after the abolition of transit duties in 1887,
the claim of His Highness's Government to levy the
duty on articles imported into the cantonment for
non-exempted persons was recognised.

On the occasion of the annual fair held at Unai
on the Bansda-Baroda frontier, it had been customary since a long time for the Bansda state to
obtain free certain materials from the adjoining
Baroda forests for the construction of temporary
sheds, and to supply to His Highness's Government
every year 15,000 bundles of good grass and
Rs. 35-7-0 in cash by way of *Ghasdana*. Differences having, however, arisen as to the quantity
and quality of the materials to be supplied by one
State to the other, and the Bansda Darbar having
allowed the Baroda dues to fall into arrears, the
matter formed the subject of controversy between
the two States. Both parties finally agreed, in
the year under review, to discontinue the concessions mutually allowed and to drop the claims for
arrears.

The Lighthouses at Dwarka and Sayani on the Okhamandal coast are constructed and maintained at the cost of His Highness's Government. The supervision and control over them, which formerly used to be exercised by the Assistant Resident at Okhamandal, was, on a representation from His Highness's Government, transferred to the Baroda officer stationed at Okhamandal, as a tentative measure.

Arrangements were made with certain Native States for the interchange of their Annual Administration Reports with those of His Highness's Government.

The rules enacted by His Highness's Government in 1881 for the protection of the British Salt Revenue and the prevention, detection and punishment of illicit possession of, or trade in, salt, in the Gujrat possessions of His Highness's Government, were, on a representation from the British Government, eventually revised by His Highness's Government. The modifications made mainly relate to:—

(1) Treating the possession of and traffic in salt, which has evaded the payment of British salt duty, as an offence in this territory ;

(2) Inclusion, in the definition of salt, of saline deposit other than salt efflorescence and salt earth proved to be for *bone fide* use in constructing mud walls, houses, and Bandhs, and in washing clothes, and for similar domestic and industrial purposes ;

(3) Search of suspected premises, seizure of contraband salt, and detention and arrest of suspected persons by certain State officers ;

(4) The discontinuance of the practice of surrendering to British courts, for trial, offenders against the British Salt Act captured in His Highness's territory, as a sequence of the modification referred to in clause 1 above.

Under article IX of the Definitive Treaty of 1805, His Highness's Government were precluded, among other matters, from employing in their service any Native Indian British subject, without the consent of the British Government. Though that restriction had been expressly declared to be virtually a dead letter, years ago, yet, in consequence of His Highness's Government employing in their service Mr. R. C. Dutt, C.I.E., retired, Member of the Indian Civil Service, the Government of India questioned the right of His Highness's Government to do so without their consent. After some correspondence the Government of India finally admitted that it no longer seemed necessary to enforce the provisions of Article IX of the Treaty of 1805 in so far as they related to the employment by His Highness's Government of Natives of India who were British subjects. But the Government of India reserved the right to require His Highness's Government to comply with such general orders on the subject of the employment, by Native States, of British Government servants, after they retired on pension, as it might be found advisable to issue. A general order relating to the employment, by Native States, of retired Indian Members of the Indian Civil Service, has since been issued by the Government of India, and is now under the considerations of His Highness's Government.

Formerly there was no restriction in regard to the cultivation of hemp and production of drugs therefrom in this territory. At the desire of the British Government, an arrangement has been come to with them by His Highness's Government, under which the cultivation of hemp plant in these territories is restricted to the quantity required for home consumption only. In the event of the local production of the drugs falling short of local requirements, the necessary quantity is to be imported from the Bombay Presidency, His Highness's Government receiving a refund of three-fourths of the duty levied by the British Government.

The Lloyd's system of commercial maritime signalling and collection and distribution of maritime intelligence having been extended to India, facilities were afforded by the Government of India to the Committee of Lloyds for collecting and distributing in India, maritime intelligence which is of interest and importance to the shipping and commercial community. On a motion from the Government of India, His Highness's Government issued instructions to the officers of Dwarka and Naosari Talukas to communicate

direct by telegram, to the nearest Lloyd's Agent
at Cutch, casualties that might occur to all vessels,
except Native craft with respect to which
information is to be communicated to him by
post.

Owing to the recent establishment by the British
Government of a Customs Barrier at Viramgam to
safeguard their fiscal interests, serious difficulties
were experienced in connection with the transit of
articles belonging to this State, as also of the personal kit and goods of State officers when they had
occasion to proceed on duty to and from the possessions of His Highness's Government in Kathiawar. .
A representation was therefore made by His
Highness's Government to arrive at some definite
understanding with the Government of Bombay, so
as to obviate the necessity of making constant
references to the Residency for the purpose of
obtaining refunds of the duty levied.

The jurisdiction of Native State courts over
Native officers and soldiers of the Indian Army
has been limited by the British Government to
offences committed by them while on leave in
Native State territory. An instance having occurred in which a Native soldier of the Indian Army
was tried by the courts of a Native State, for the
offence of rioting committed while on duty in the
State, the Government of India minutely defined
cases in which Native States, could exercise jurisdiction over such persons, and requested His
Highness's Government to issue instructions to the
State courts on the lines indicated. The necessary

notifications were accordingly published in the State Gazette.

In connection with the measures adopted by His Highness's Government for the drainage of the Kadi District, the Government of Bombay moved the Government of India to levy a contribution of Rs. 38,500 from His Highness's Government towards the cost of the channels constructed in British territory. The contribution was meant to cover the "cost of carrying on through British territory, the extra water due to drainage operations in the Baroda State." His Highness's Government resisted the claim, mainly on the ground that the drains completed in the eastern portion of the Kadi District had relieved several British villages, and thus saved the British Government a considerable outlay on the drains in their own territory, and that it was only equitable that the British Government should, in return, bear the cost of the improvement in their drains, necessitated by our operations in the western portion of the district. It was also pointed out by us that it was impossible to ascertain and assess our exact liability, since this State was not responsible for the cost of draining waters delivered into British limits through the natural lie of the land before the construction of our drains, and since the precise degree of interference with the natural easement, and the benefit accruing to each party, could not be determined with even approximate exactitude. To avoid these difficulties of calculation, we suggested the adoption of the principle that, in the case of works required for the common purposes of both Governments, each should bear the cost of the work in its territory. In the alternative we contended that credit should be given to us for what we had done in the Baroda District where we held the lower lands, and also in the portion of the Kadi District, to the east of the R. M. Railway. The Government of India passed final orders in the matter, and decided that the Bombay Government should drop their claim against this State. The Government of India also laid down the principle that no State or British District is entitled to construct works for drainage, intended to discharge water on to lands not owned by the State or District, without consulting the owner of the lands so affected, and without taking precautions to prevent injury. If damage is caused by such works, the party constructing them is liable.

Mr. Lakshmilal Daulatrai continued to be in charge of the Huzur English Office, i.e., of Political Correspondence work, during the year under report, and performed his duties with his usual tact, ability and care.

II.—LEGISLATIVE.

(a)—HISTORY AND PROCEDURE.

Procedure of drafting laws.—The method of legis-- lation, as it has been followed under the old and the present administrations, was briefly described in the last year's Report. There it was noted that, in 1883, a Law Committee was formed for the purposes of drafting and carrying through legislative measures. This committee was abolished in 1899. A new de- partment was however created in its place in 1904, and the Naib Diwan, with the designation of Legal Remembrancer, was appointed to be its head. Since its creation, this Department has become the central Legislative Department for the State.

The procedure followed in enacting laws is that the Legal Remembrancer, or the department con- cerned, drafts Bills according to the instructions of the Maharaja. The Bills so drafted are pub-- lished in the *Ajna Patrika*, or Government Gazette of Baroda, and a sufficient time is allowed for public criticism, and for obtaining the opinions of different officers. When these are received, a statement of the objections raised in newspapers, or in specific memorials, or in the reports of the officers consulted, is drawn up and submitted to His Highness, together with replies. The Maharaja has thus the advantage of comparing the original Bill with the comments and criticisms, official and non-official. The original Bill is often considerably modified in the light of such criticism, and is then passed into law by the Maharaja's order, and pub— lished in the *Ajna Patrika* for general information..

Important Acts of 1904.—It is interesting to note that one of the three Acts passed in 1904 is for the extention of Primary Education in the State, and another is for the Prevention of Early Marriages. People living outside the limits of this State have an inadequate conception of the degree to which public opinion influences legislation in Baroda. The utmost consideration is shown to such opinion; and His Highness the Maharaja consented to reduce the limit of age for the marriage of girls from 14 to 12 in deference to the popular wish. Other modifications were also made in the original Bill, so as to make it less obnoxious to orthodox communities.

Results of the Early Marriage Prevention Act.—It is now over a year since the Act for the Prevention of Early Marriages came into operation, and it would not be without interest to take stock of the results achieved during this first year of its operation. That freedom to contract marriages within the prohibited limits of age, with the permission of the Civil Courts, has been freely availed of, would appear from the fact that no less than 695 applications were presented for such license; and the circumstance, that such permission was accorded in 68 per cent. of such petitions, shows a liberal and sympathetic solicitude on the part of the Courts for the religious and social susceptibilities of the people. Some leniency was desirable in the first year of the execution of this law, to which the people had not been accustomed. At the same time it was necessary to enforce the new law, so.

that it might not be regarded as a dead letter; and 718 offenders were punished with fines, in sums ranging from one rupee to twenty-five rupees, during the year in the whole State. Seventy-eight per cent. of the fines inflicted under this Act fell below five rupees, and only four per cent exceeded rupees ten. No better proof can be afforded of the indulgence with which offences against this special enactment have been dealt with.

The Act has already had a wholesome educative effect on the higher classes of the Hindu society; for, we find that the percentage of convictions among the three higher castes did not exceed five. The largest number of offenders belonged to the Dhed and Bhangi classes, which had no less than 39 per cent. of convictions against them. The Kunbis or the cultivating classes had only 11 per cent, while the artisan classes had also an equal number. The percentage among Brahmins and Banias was less than two, and that among Mahomedans was about four,—a circumstance which clearly proves that it is only custom, and no religious behest or scriptural text, which supports the practice of early marriages. And when once the force of usage is broken, the progress of the desired reform is smoothed and accelerated even beyond our most sanguine expectations.

Civil Marriage &c.—The same laudable spirit of reform has led His Highness's Government to the recognition of civil marriages in the State, and a Bill, based on Act HI of 1872 (Government of India), has been on the legislative anvil. An

endeavour is also being made to codify certain
portions of the personal law and usages applicable
to the Hindus, and the Hindu Marriage Bill has
already been published as the first instalment
towards this ambitious scheme.

Local Boards and Self-governing Municipalities.
Of the important Acts passed during 1904-5, mention must be made of the Local Boards Act,
according to which the constitution of Taluka and
District Boards has been definitely fixed on workable
lines, and a system of Local Self-government has
been built up, all through the State. The principle
of Local Self-government has also received a new
impetus in the scheme of the Self-governing
Municipalities, which have been now formed in
several important towns in the State. Their
affairs were hitherto managed by Government
officials, and they had no definite sources of income
allotted to them. But the new Municipalities
Bill has been based on the Bombay Act III of
1901, makes the constitution of the advanced
Municipalities of the State partly elective, gives
them a definite income and enlarged powers, and
also adds to their responsibilities.

Religious and Charitable Endowments.—The Religious Endowments and Public Charitable Estates
Acts also formed important additions to the Legis-
lature during the year under report. There are,
in the State, numerous religious institutions dedicated to public worship, most of which are in
receipt of annual Government contributions, either
cash or in rent-free land; and there was, hitherto,

no systematic supervision over these institutions, and no means to prevent abuses, except a provision in the Civil Procedure Code which was virtually a dead letter. Similarly, in respect of charitable institutions, there was no official assignee or administrator-general in matters of public trusts, who could control the different funds and endowments, and manage them on uniform lines. The two enactments above referred to have been designed to supply these wants, and to secure an efficient management of public charitable trusts and religious endowments, in conformity with the wishes of their beneficent donors.

It is necessary to add that, in respect of religious institutions, His Highness's Government have thought it desirable to proceed very cautiously. By the Act, referred to in the preceding paragraph, the Government do not assume any powers of supervision over all religious institutions, but only over those which receive donations from the State. In the case of these institutions, the State requires accounts of property and income and expenditure to be kept, and all serious abuses disclosed are to be referred to the Civil Court for enquiry and orders. It is also provided that any of these institutions, objecting to the control of the State, can free itself from the supervision of the Government by surrendering the donation it receives. With regard to all other religious institutions, the State reserves the power of exercising some supervision only on the application of persons belonging to the community concerned, or on the disclosure of grave abuses. There was a strong expression of public feeling when it was understood that the Bill was under consideration ; but the very limited powers assumed by the State in the Act as it was finally passed, and also the very considerate manner in which the Act has been worked, have had the effect of allaying needless alarms.

Legal Remembrancer.—Mr. Manubhai Mehta, M.A. and LL.B. of the Bombay University, was Naib-Diwan and Legal Remembrancer at the close of the year under review, and is well fitted for the work by his high legal and educational qualifications. After a brilliant career in college he took service in this State, and accompanied His Highness to Europe in 1900. In 1903 he inspected the working of the various departments of the State ; and in 1904-05 he organized and supervised famine relief operations with conspicuous success. A very comprehensive and meritorious account of all the Native States of India, known as " Hind Rajasthan," is a product of his pen ; and it were much to be desired that this valuable compilation were brought down to the commencement of the present century, and the date of the Delhi Darbar. As a Member of Council, Mr. Mehta has always ably assisted in its deliberations.

(b).—LEGISLATIVE ACTS.

A list of Acts, passed by His Highness the present Maharaja, is given below :—

1 The Police Act was enacted in 1884 and amended in 1898.

2 The Registration Act was enacted in 1885 and amended in 1902.

3 The Abkari Act was enacted in 1886 and amended in 1900.

4 The Court Martial Act, 1887.

5 The Stamp Act was enacted in 1889 and amended in 1904.

6 Small Causes Act, 1890.

7 The Municipal Act 1892.

1895

8 The General Clauses Act, amended in 1904.

9 Law relating to Possession Suits, amended in 1897.

1896

10 The Court Fees Act, amended in 1904.

11 The Code of Civil Procedure, amended in 1902.

12 The Easement Act.

13 The Limitation Act, amended in 1903.

14 The Penal Code, amended in 1904.

15 The Code of Criminal Procedure, amended in 1904.

1897

16 The Maintenance Act.

1898

17 The Hackney Carriage Act.

18 The Interest Act.

19 An Act for Inspection of Boilers.

20 The Treasure Trove Act.

21 The Contract Act.

22 The Guardian and Wards Act.

1899

23 An Act relating to Lunatic Asylums.

1900

24 The Arms Act.

1901

25 The Transfer of Property Act, amended in 1902.

1902

26 The Hindu Widow Marriage Act.
27 The Freedom of Conscience Act.
28 The Opium Act.
29 The Sale of Poisons Act.
30 The Village Munsiff's Act.

1903

31 Amendments only to different enactments were passed this year.

1904

32 The Primary Education Act.
33 The Infant Marriage Prevention Act.
34 The Prisoner's Testimony Act.

The following is a list of new Acts passed and published during the year 1904—05.

(1) The Passenger Ships Act.
(2) The Local Boards Act.
(3) The Co-operative Credit Societies Act.
(4) Religious Endowment Act.
(5) An Act for the management of Public Charitable Estates.
(6) The Customs Act.

During the year the following amendments were made in the Acts already passed and published.

(1) An Act to amend the Baroda Penal Code.
(2) An Act to amend the Court Fees' Act.
(3) An Act to amend the General Clauses Act.
(4) An Act to amend the Code of Civil Procedure.

Besides these, ten sets of Rules and Regulations were made in connection with the Judicial, Revenue, Land Settlement, and other Departments, during the same year, in the Office of the Legal Remembrancer.

III.—JUDICIAL.

(a)—CONSTITUTION OF COURTS.

The Varisht Court, answering to High Courts in British Provinces, is the Supreme Judicial Tribunal in this State.

Mr. Vasudev Gopal Bhandarkar, B.A. and LL.B. of the Bombay University, was Chief Justice at the close of the year under review. He is a younger brother of the Hon'ble Dr. Bhandarkar, Member of the Governor-General's Legislative Council, and was a Pleader of the Bombay High Court, and a Professor of Law at Bombay, before he joined service at Baroda. In 1901, he was Naib Diwan of Baroda State, and subsequently performed the duties of Legal Remembrancer with ability and distinction.

Mr. Abbas S. Tyabji, of the Lincoln's Inn, Barrister-at-Law, was Second Judge. Called to the Bar in 1875, he returned to India and practised in the High Court of Bombay for four years ; and in 1879 he joined the service of His Highness the Gaekwar. He is a nephew of Mr. Justice Tyabji of the Bombay High Court, and brings to the performance of his duties a high legal training and knowledge acquired in England and at Bombay, and a valuable experience of this State obtained during a long service of twenty-five years.

The late Mr. Vinayak Mahadev Pandit, who was the Third Judge of the Varisht Court, passed the LL.B. Examination of the Bombay University in 1875, and practised at Bombay till 1884, when he joined the Baroda service. Three years after, he

was promoted to the rank of a District Judge. He
became an Acting Judge of the Varisht Court in
1892, held the important post of Naib Diwan from
1895 to 1901, and became a permanent Judge of
the Varisht Court in 1901. He was transferred to
the post of Naib Diwan and Legal Remembrancer
in the latter part of the year under review ; and in
his lamented death, which took place on the 3rd
August 1905 when he was on leave, the State has
lost a valuable and experienced officer, and an
able and conscientious Judge.

Mr. Krishanarao Vinayek Sharangpani, who also
held the post of a Judge of the Varisht Court,
passed the LL.B. Examination of the Bombay
University in 1879, and joined this State in the
following year. He, too, obtained a valuable experience in this State by serving as a Judicial
Officer in districts for fourteen years, and then
rose to the rank of Judge of the Varisht Court.

Mr. Jamshedji Dorabji Khandalawala was appointed Judge of the Varisht Court in June 1905,
after having acted in that post twice before. He
was a Pleader of the Bombay High Court, and
joined service in Baroda in 1889.

The Varisht Court has been described as the
Supreme Tribunal in the State. Nevertheless,
the Maharaja has the power of revising the decisions of the Varisht Court ; and in the exercise of
this power His Highness is advised by the Nyaya
Sabha, answering to the Privy Council.

Under the Varisht Court there is a District Judge
in each of the four Districts. Each District is

divided into some eight Talukas, (more or less,) and there is a Judicial Officer called Munsiff in each Taluka. The Munsiffs in the State possess a thorough legal training, and are generally men who have obtained the LL.B. degree of the Bombay University.

The work of the District Judges was found to be generally satisfactory during the year under review. Messrs. Damoobhai Dayabhai Mehta and Jamsedji Dorabji Khandalawala deserve special notice ; they had heavy files of cases, and kept fairly abreast of them. Mr. Hirji Pestonji Wadia at Amreli decided the important case of Pir Jada during the year. Baroda City was made into a fifth District in 1905, and Srimant Ganpat Rao Gaekwar ably performed the duties of a District Judge.

At the Baroda City Magistrate's Court, which has the heaviest file of Criminal cases of any Magisterial Court in the State, Mr. Merwanji Edulji Dadachanji acquitted himself fairly well of his heavy work.

Among the other Judicial Officers, whose work was found to be satisfactory by the District Judges, the following deserve to be specially mentioned:—

1. Mr. Sarabhai Valabhai, Assistant Judge, Baroda.

2. Mr. Ganesh Balvant Ambegaoker, Assistant Judge, Baroda.

3. Mr. Khandubhai Nagarji Desai, Munsiff, Petlad.

4. Mr. Pestonji Cursetji Thanavala, Magistrate, Naosari.
5. Mr. Ratanji Dossabhai, Munsiff, Kathor.
6. Mr. Balkrishna Bhikaji Vinze, Munsiff, Sidhpur.
7. Mr. Nanabhai Pestonji Mehta, Munsiff, Mehsana.

(b)—SEPARATION OF JUDICIAL AND EXECUTIVE FUNCTIONS.

For several years past His Highness the Gaekwar has endeavoured to bring about a separation of the Judicial and Executive duties. The Taluka Executive Officers (Vahivatdars) used to try all criminal cases in years past, while the Taluka Judicial Officers (Munsiffs) took cognizance of civil cases. This arrangement was open to many objections. In the first place, the Vahivatdars were unable to devote that degree of attention to their executive and revenue work which it needed, when much of their time was taken up in trying criminal cases. And in the second place, the exercise of criminal powers spoilt them as revenue officers, and armed them with an authority which was inconsistent with the discharge of their revenue duties.

The Maharaja did not, however, desire to introduce any sudden change. He discussed the matter with the highest officers of the State, and their recorded opinions show a thoughtful consideration of all the various aspects of the question. The literature on the subject is both instructive and interesting.

After a careful consideration of all these opinions, and with his intimate knowledge of the actual work of administration as it is carried on in Districts and Talukas, the Maharaja came to the conclusion that a separation should be effected. The officer who is virtually the prosecutor should not be the Judge. The officer who is virtually the plaintiff in the matter of revenue demands should not exercise Magisterial powers. The officer who is the head of the District or the Taluka should be free from the suspicion of doing executive work with the help of criminal powers. On these considerations His Highness resolved on a separation of functions.

The policy was cautiously and gradually carried out. It was directed that three-fourths of the criminal cases should be tried by Munsiffs, and one-fourth only should be tried by Vahivatdars. The bulk of the criminal work was thus made over to trained Judicial Officers who performed no executive or revenue work; a small portion of the work was still left in the hands of the Executive Officers; and this state of things continued till the end of 1903-04.

During the year under report an almost complete separation of judicial and executive duties has been effected. Vahivatdars or Taluka Executive Officers have been relieved of all judicial work, and devote their time to revenue and executive work; while Munsiffs are entrusted with all judicial work civil and criminal. Only in some Subordinate Talukas, and in two Talukas of Amreli District, this complete separation remains to be carried out.

(c)—OTHER JUDICIAL REFORMS.

The laws enacted between 1895 and 1900 have, to a large extent, secured uniformity and certainty in legal procedure. There is now a uniform and definite procedure followed in civil and criminal courts. Judges and the public know what the penal laws are. The people know what their rights and liabilities are with regard to contracts and the transfer of property. Fraudulent dealings have been minimised by the Registration Act. And a Code of Hindu Law for this State, now under preparation, is likely to lessen litigation, and to settle many controversial points.

In order to obtain the co-operation of the people in judicial work it was directed, in 1901, that the trials of criminal cases of certain descriptions should be held with the help of Assessors in two Districts of the State. The experiment proved successful; the order was extended to the other two Districts; and the adoption of the jury system is now under contemplation.

With the same object in view, three Village Courts were appointed in 1903-04, and some account of their work will be found later on. Village headmen have also been empowered to try cases relating to petty thefts of agricultural produce, assault, simple hurt, conservancy, etc., and to award punishments extending to a fine of Rs. 5, or imprisonment for 48 hours. The results of these experiments are watched with keen interest. And it is the desire of His Highness to extend this system of obtaining the co-operation of the villagers themselves in settling their own petty differences, and of saving the people from the trouble, the expense, and the demoralizing effects of attending Law Courts.

Lastly, with the object of keeping the administration in touch with the people, His Highness the Maharaja directed a Judicial Conference to be held in every District. The District Judge was to preside, and Munsiffs, Magistrates and Pleaders were to attend. It is a notable feature of these Conferences that they were not purely official; pleaders, who knew the requirements of the people whom they represented in Court, were invited to attend and help the discussions. And as such Conferences were held simultaneously in all the four Districts, a comparison of the suggestions made by them led to clear conclusions as to the requirements and needs of the people.

The Madras system of a careful scrutiny of all judgements passed by lower Criminal Courts led to the discovery of hasty prosecutions, instituted by the State, which ended mostly in acquittals. To remedy this evil the Maharaja has empowered the Legal Remembrancer to appoint properly qualified Prosecutors in most of the Courts. It is expected that this will lead to a more efficient conduct of cases, and save the people from ill-judged prosecutions.

(d)—JUDICIAL STATISTICS.

Number of Courts at the close of 1904-05.

Varisht Court	1
District Judges' Court	5
Assistant Judges' Courts	2
District Magistrates' Courts ...	4
Subordinate Magistrates' Courts ...	119
Taluka Courts, etc.	25
Village Courts	3
	159

The work performed during the year by the Civil Courts is shewn in the following table.

Total Civil Suits.

Year.	Filed.	Disposed of including old pending cases.
1903-04	16,819	19,099
1904-05	13,969	15,558

The number of suits pending at the close of 1903 -04 was 5,351, while the number pending at the close of 1904-05 was only 4,140 of which only 599 were more than one year old. This shows that the arrears caused previously by a large inflow of cases has now been cleared, and things are returning to their normal condition in the Judicial Department.

The total of civil suits is divisible into Ordinary Civil suits and Small Cause suits; they are dealt with separately below.

Ordinary Civil Suits.

Year.	Filed.	Valuation in Rupees.	Disposed of including old pending cases.	Average duration of contested cases.	Pending at the end of the year.
1903-04	4,718	18,13,037	7,433	301	2,697
1904-05	5,080	14,65,995	5,703	338	2,344

While the number of pending cases was greatly reduced at the close of the last year, as compared with the previous year, the average duration of contested cases was longer. This increase in duration is due to some old cases being decided in the year under report. Suits of more than one years' standing, that remained pending at the close of

1903-04, numbered 728; while the corresponding
suits, which remained pending at the close of
1904-05, was only 351. These figures shew that 377
cases of long standing were disposed of during
1904-05. Each of these 377 cases had nearly taken
3 years on the average before it was disposed of;
and the Varisht Court did well in requiring the
Courts to devote much of their time in disposing
of so many old standing cases within 1904-05. The
average duration of contested cases should be
much less in the future when old standing cases are
once disposed of.

If the 377 old standing cases be excluded from
the list, the average duration of contested cases is
reduced from 338 to 164 for 1904-05. The Varisht
Court remarks :—

> "Even the larger duration of 338 days does not
> compare unfavourably with the British aver-
> age, if it be noted that the mode of counting
> days in our State is radically different from
> that prevailing in the British Territory. We
> count the duration from the date of the in-
> stitution of the suit to the date of its final
> disposal; while in British Territory the time
> that the suit has been actually pending in a
> particular Court is alone counted. Time
> during which cases cannot be decided by
> reason of orders of the Appellate Courts is
> deducted. Similarly time spent in making
> amendments in plaints is also deducted, whilst
> the duration of suits revived is counted from
> the date of revival."

There is a great deal of force in what the Varisht Court has urged. But a reduction in the duration of contested cases is expected in the future; and when the old arrears have been cleared, *the average duration of contested cases should not exceed six months.*

Small Cause Suits.

Year.	Filed.	Valuation in Rupees.	Disposed of including old pending cases.	Average duration of contested cases.	Pending at the end of the year.
1903-04	12,101	8,24,045	11,666	121	2,654
1904-05	8,889	7,58,595	9,855	116	1,900

It is satisfactory to note that the number of cases pending at the close of 1904-05 was much smaller than the corresponding number for 1903-04; and the average duration of contested cases has also somewhat decreased. Suits of higher value are treated as Small Causes here than in British India; nevertheless *an average contested Small Cause Suit should not take more than three months.*

Civil Appeals.

Year.	Filed.	Valuation in Rupees.	Disposed of including old pending Appeals.	Pending at the end of the year.	Average duration.	
					Contested cases.	Other cases.
1903-04	1,155	2,91,375	1,274	1,174	380	374
1904-05	1,288	4,37,350	1,246	1,270	390	264

The Varisht Court explains that the increase in the duration of contested appeals was due to nearly two hundred appeals, of more than two years' standing, having been decided in the year under report. This being so, there should be a considerable reduction in the duration of contested appeals in future years.

Result of Civil Appeals.

Year.	First Appeals decided by Varisht Court.			Second Appeals decided by Varisht Court.			Appeals decided by District Courts.		
	Percentage con-firmed.	Percentage rever-sed or remanded.	Percentage modified.	Percentage con-firmed.	Percentage remanded or reversed.	Percentage modified.	Percentage con-firmed.	Percentage remanded or reversed.	Percentage modified.
1903-04	45	46	9	58	28	14	50	35	15
1904-05	62	30	8	56	35	9	56	31	13

The larger proportion of appeals in which the decrees of the lower Courts, were confirmed, both by the Varisht Court and by District Courts, seems to indicate more careful work on the part of the lower Courts.

Reference has been made before to the establishment of three Village Courts in 1903-04. The places were not selected with sufficient care, and one of the Courts, viz., that at Chanasma, had to be closed. On the other hand the Court at Bhadran has worked satisfactorily, and a new Village Court was opened at Vaso in May 1905. The Court at Ranuj has also continued, but had no work during the year under review.

The jurisdiction of these Courts is local, and they are empowered to decide suits based on money transactions. The Village Court of Bhadran decides suits up to the value of Rs. 60, and has also been invested with Small Cause powers to decide suits up to the value of Rs. 30. The Village Court of Vaso decides suits up to the value of Rs. 30. The work of these two Courts during the year under review is shewn in the following table:—

Suits decided by Village Courts 1904-05.

Number of suits.	Valuation of suits.	Averation duration of suits.
228	Rs. 5,931	14 days.

The success of these village institutions points to the possibility of establishing other Village Courts in well selected places in the future.

Criminal Cases.

Year.	Filed.	Disposed of including old pending cases.	Average duration, ordinary cases.	Average duration summary cases.
1903–04	9,045	9,647	22	13
1904–05	10,747	11,305	23	7

Although the average duration of ordinary cases was a day longer in the last year than in the previous year, yet, on the whole, there is not much reason for complaint if a criminal case takes 23 days only. Summary cases were disposed much more quickly during the last year than in 1903-04, and the average of 7 days for a case is creditable.

The number of persons whose cases were disposed of was 23,785 as against 20,253 in 1903-04. In both the years there was an average of slightly over two accused persons to each case.

Percentage of different classes of offences.

Year.	Against property.	Against person.	Against public justice.	Against tranquillity.	Against marriage.	False documents.	Against coinage.	Against public servants.	Other offences.
1903–04	29	27	1	3	2	·19	·03	·81	34
1904–05	27	28	·9	3	3	·3	·1	·7	37

In both years over one-half the offences were against property or against person. The more serious cases in 1904-05 were 49 of murder, 49 of culpable homicide, 110 cases of grievious hurt, 25 cases of rape, 33 cases of dacoity, 130 cases of robbery, 274 cases of house-breaking and theft, and 21 cases of forgery. The figures under the corresponding heads in 1903-04 were 45, 43, 75, 6, 38, 104, 237 and 13. A comparison between the two years shews some increase in offences against person, and also in robbery, house-breaking and theft. This last is probably due to the fact that the year 1904-05 was a famine year.

On the whole, the absence of crimes among the people of this State is very marked. Ten thousand offences in a year, among a population of two millions, gives an average of only three offences committed during the year in an average village of 600 presons. Four hundred cases of theft and robbery mean only one case in the year in eight such villages. And thirty or forty cases of dacoity mean less than one case in the year in a whole Taluka. In point of freedom from crimes, the people of the Baroda State will compare favourably with many advanced countries in the world.

Percentage of conviction.

Year.	Convicted.	Acquitted.
1903-04	39	61
1904-05	41	59

The total number of witnesses examined in the last year was 19,502 against 18,765 of the previous year.

Punishments.

Year.	Capital Sentence.	Fines only.	Imprisonment with or without fine.	Imprisonment with whipping	Whipping only.	Ordered to find security.
1903-04	*Nil.*	2,310	1,337	1	46	21
1904-05	*Nil.*	3,343	1,381	5	78	15

Of the persons convicted, 4,505 were males and 303 were females. Capital sentence, passed in one case by the Varisht Court in 1904-05, was commuted into a sentence of imprisonment by His Highness the Maharaja.

Appeals.

Year.	Filed and old pending appeals.	Disposed of	Percentage of persons whose sentence was confirmed.	Percentage of persons whose sentence was modified.	Percentage of re-trials, &c.
1903-04	376	313	59	14	24
1904-05	385	332	54	15	31

Income and Expenditure.

Year.	Income from Stamps, Court fees &c., in Rupees.	Expenditure.
	Rs.	Rs.
1903-04	2,94,659	3,54,262
1904-05	2,63,127	3,55,005

The decrease of income by over thirty thousand rupees is owing to fewer suits being filed, probably due to the year being a famine year.

Extradition Cases.

Year.	Surrendered to Baroda.		Surrendered by Baroda.	
	Cases.	Men.	Cases.	Men.
1903-04	103	208	70	122
1904-05	102	176	97	181

Including pending cases, 203 extradited men were tried in Baroda in 1904-05; and of these 101 were convicted, 92 were acquitted, and 10 men remained to be tried in the following year.

Pleaders and Mukhtiars.

The number of pleaders and Mukhtiars in the several Courts of the State was 331 at the close of the period under report. Special Sanads were granted in 1904-05 to 19 pleaders of British Courts to practise for specified periods in the Varisht Court and the Courts subordinate to it in the State.

REVENUE—SECTION A.

(a) SUPERVISION OF DISTRICTS.

The vast Revenue Department of the State comprised the following thirty branches at the close of the year under review :—

A.

1. Supervision of Districts.
2. Land Tax.
3. Local Cess.
4. Income Tax, etc.
5. State Boundaries.

B.

6. Garas Tenures.
7. Religious Institutions.
8. Court of Wards.
9. Attached Estates.
10. Land Acquisition.

C.

11. Customs.
12. Excise.
13. Opium.
14. Salt.
15. Agriculture.
16. Industries.
17. Registration.
18. Stamps.
19. Printing and Stationery.
20. Ports and Tolls.

D.

21. Village communities.
22. Local Boards.
23. Self-Governing Municipalities.

24. Other Municipalities.
25. Meteorological Observations.
26. Vital Statistics.
27. Sanitation.
28. Vaccination.

E.

29. Reserved Forests.
30. Unreserved Forests.

Early in the year under review His Highness the Maharaja came to the conclusion, from his supervision and personal inspection of work, that all these numerous offices could not be efficiently supervised by one single officer. Work had increased in most of the offices, and some new offices like those relating to Religious Institutions, Local Boards, and Self-Governing Municipalities were coming into existence. His Highness accordingly introduced a *scheme of decentralisation*, dividing the Revenue Department into five different Sections, as is indicated in the list given above. Changes were made from time to time in carrying out this scheme, and the list shews the division as it stood at the close of the year under report. Each Section or Sub-Department comprises a group of offices, and is under a single Officer ; and all these Officers are under the supervision and orders of the Revenue Minister who is responsible for the work of the entire Revenue Department.

Mr. Vasudeo Madhav Samarth, who is the Sar-Subah or Revenue Commissioner of the State, is in charge of the most important Section, comprising

the Land Tax and other Taxes, the supervision
of all Districts, and the maintenance of all State-
boundaries. He joined the service of the State in
1879, and was sent to Europe in 1884 in charge of
the Maharaja's brother and cousin and another
young student. Mr. Samarth afterwards accompanied His Highness to Europe in 1887 and 1892;
and his last trip to Europe in 1891 was undertaken with the laudable object of studying industries and agriculture in Scotland and Ireland. With
his natural abilities and education which are of
a high order, with his real sympathy for the
people, and with his long experience in this State
and information gathered abroad,—Mr. Samarth
makes an efficient Revenue Officer. In 1898 the
British Government bestowed on him the personal
distinction of Diwan Bahadur for his meritorious
work in combating famine and plague in this State.

As Sar-Subah or Revenue Commissioner, Mr.
Samarth is the Head of the four Subhas or District
Officers. The word Subah really means a Province
or District; but in Baroda the word is used to
mean a District Officer.

Each District is again divided into a number of
Talukas as the following table will show :—

District.	Taluka.
Baroda.	1. Baroda. 2. Petlad (with Siswa). 3. Padra. 4. Choranda. 5. Sinor. 6. Dabhoi. 7. Sankheda (with Tilakwada). 8. Vaghodia. 9. Saoli.
Naosari.	10. Naosari. 11. Gandevi. 12. Mahua. 13. Vyara. 14. Songad (with Vajpur). 15. Velachha (with Vakal). 16. Kamrej. 17. Palsana.

District.	Taluka.
Kadi.	18. Mehsana. 19. Kadi. 20. Kalol. 21. Dehgam (with Atarsumba). 22. Vijapur. 23. Visnagar, 24. Kheralu. 25. Sidhpur. 26. Patan (with Harij). 27. Vadaoli.
Amreli.	28. Amreli (with Bhimkata). 29. Damnagar (with Shrinagar). 30. Dhari (with Khamba). 31. Kodinar. 32. Okhamandal (with Beyt).

It will appear from the above list that the State of Baroda had 32 Talukas and 10 sub-Talukas at the close of the year under report.

The District Officer or Subah is assisted by one or two or three Assistants called Naeb Subahs. When the Subah has more than one Naeb Subah under him, the Talukas are so grouped that each Naeb Subah is in charge of a number of them. The Talukas grouped under a Naeb Subah comprise his Sub-Division, and the Naeb Subah or Sub-Divisional Officer is expected to make frequent tours in the Talukas under him, to inspect and supervise the work of those Talukas, and to help the District Officer with his local knowledge and information. The normal number of Naeb Subahs is three for Baroda District, three for Kadi District, two for Naosari, and two for Amreli; but the actual number of Naeb Subahs employed at the close of 1904-05 was smaller. This caused inconvenience in work, specially as, with the creation of Local Boards, Naeb Subahs were appointed Chairmen of such Boards in the Talukas under them, and thus had additional work thrown on them.

Each Taluka is under the administration of a Vahivatdar, answering to a Mamlatdar in British India. To visit the villages in his Taluka, to collect the land revenue and taxes, to inspect the boundary marks set up to demarcate field from field, to protect Government property and Government interests, and generally to maintain peace and order within his Taluka, are the main duties of the Vahivatdar. A portion of the criminal work of the Taluka also fell to his share ; but, as has been stated before, all judicial work has now been transferred to the Munsiff, except in a few places.

Each Taluka comprises fifty to a hundred villages, and the village is the basis of the Indian political organization. Self-governing villages, with their complete arrangements for civil and criminal justice, their revenue collection, and their hereditary professional services, were the foundations of old Indian society. The genius of the Indian people developed this system as suited to their wants and requirements, and through thousands of years, while dynasties came and went and empires rose and fell, the villagers were content with their primitive Self-Government within their self-contained little Republics. Much of this form of Self-Government has now unfortunately ceased to exist ; a more centralised administration has withdrawn the judicial functions of village elders ; and a new system of land revenue settlements has disturbed and demolished the old fiscal arrangements in every village. No administrative problem in Baroda, or in British India, has a higher importance than the problem of reconstructing some effective system of Self-Government, after the old Self-Governing institutions have been swept aside. This subject will be dealt with further on.

Perhaps the most important duty of the Sar-Subah or Revenue Commissioner is the supervision of the work in the different Districts and Talukas. His powers with regard to the appointment and promotion of Officers in Districts are fixed by rules; he hears all appeals from District Officers in relation to the work which is under his supervision; and in course of prolonged tours, which he is expected to make every year, he obtains an intimate knowledge of the state of the country and the people. Diwan Bahadur Samarth's tours in 1904-05 were exceptionally valuable and useful; and he helped His Highness the Maharaja in the local enquiries made in January and February 1905, with a view to the remission of the land revenue on account of the famine. He also visited Songadh and other backward tracts, settled the Jama-Bandi himself in some places, and drew up a workable scheme for the more efficient administration of those tracts which has received the sanction of His Highness. Among the other reforms, which engaged Mr. Samarth's attention during the year, may be mentioned the re-organization of the village-inspection service, and the revision of the revenue establishment in every District and Taluka. The vast body of Revenue Rules was also revised by a Committee over which the Revenue Commissioner presided. In September and October, 1905, when Mr. R. C. Dutt

went on leave, Mr. Samarth was selected by His
Highness the Maharaja to act for him as Revenue
Minister; and Mr. Vanikar was appointed to act
for Mr. Samarth as Revenue Commissioner.

What the Revenue Commissioner does with
regard to the entire State, each District Officer is
expected to do within his own District; and these
duties were efficiently done during the year under
report. The inspections of Mr. Khaserao Jadav,
District Officer of Naosari, were specially valuable
and minute; he kept note in his own hand of the
facts and figures which he compiled after patient
enquiry; and he thus obtained a complete grasp
over the state of things in Naosari. His special
enquiries and experiments in agriculture, and in
the matter of sub-soil streams, will be referred to
elsewhere. Mr. Vinayak Vanikar interested himself specially in fostering new industrial enterprises
in the Kadi District, and his endeavours have
already borne some fruit. Kazi Abdul Rahman,
the District Officer of Baroda, is a popular and
sympathetic Officer; and Mr. Yusuf Ali, the District
Officer of Amreli, has administered that District
for a number of years efficiently and well.

If the work of the District Officer is confined
to a smaller area than that of the Revenue
Commissioner, it is certainly more varied. For,
although relieved of all judicial work now, the
District Officer is still entrusted with the task of
supervising both the Judicial and Police work in his
District; he examines the judgments of Magistrates
in some cases, and refers such cases to the High

Court whenever he thinks there is a failure of justice. He has also some powers of supervision over the Customs, Excise, Opium, Stamps and Registration work in his own District; and, as Chairman of the newly created Local Boards, he has new and varied duties imposed upon him. Without combining Judicial and Executive duties as in British India, the District Officer in Baroda has ample opportunities to develop his own District, to improve tanks, wells, village roads, and village schools, to foster trades and industries, to ascertain and remove the pressing needs of the people, and generally to help them in the onward march towards progress.

During the year under report, the Revenue Commissioner spent 162 days on his tours, and visited all the four Districts. The District Officer of Baroda was on tour during 140 days only, owing to pressure of work at Head Quarters, but visited all the twelve Talukas and sub-Talukas in his District. The Subah of Kadi District and the Subah of Amreli District were on tour, each of them, for 171 days, the former visiting seven Talukas and the latter eight Talukas. It is expected that the Subah of Kadi will be able to visit all the Talukas of his District in the present year, as a tour in seven Talukas, mostly along the central lines, is not considered adequate for a large and important District like Kadi.

Among Naeb Subahs, Mr. K. G. Deshpande did good work in his sub-Division, and was selected as head of Local Boards and Municipalities in the

8

State at the close of the year under review. Mr. Prahladji Sevakram took great interest in the excavation of wells in the Kadi District during the famine, and was appointed by His Highness to be in charge of that District during the absence of Mr. Vanikar on deputation in September and October 1905. Mr. Martand Ambegaokar did excellent work in some difficult Garas cases, in settling arrears of revenue collections in Amreli and Damnagar Talukas, and in bringing the village accounts of Petlad Taluka into order. Mr. Muhammad Ibrahim and Mr. G. A. Vaidya are efficient Naeb Subahs, and Mr. Chotalal B. Patel has done exceptionally good work in connexion with the abolition of Veros and the introduction of the Income Tax, as well as in organizing Village Panchyets and Local Boards throughout the State, with a view to the introduction of Local Self-Government. Mention should also be made of Mr. B. N. Kutar, who has helped greatly in the compilation of rules, and has acted efficiently as Naeb Subah.

Among Vahivatdars and Mahalkaris, the following Officers have obtained good service badges for extending cultivation within their respective jurisdictions:—

Bhimbhai Morarji of Vaghodia.

Ranchodlal Narottamdas of Sinor.

Vishnu Balavant Gogte of Songadh.

Ramchandra Janardan Sanvat of Vyara.

Narayan Viswanath Kante of Khamba.

Mention should also be made of Mr. Shivram Raje, Mr. Manchharam Bhagwanji and Mr.

Kashinath Pradhan for prompt, efficient and very
satisfactory work done in their Talukas. In
the Revenue Commissioner's Office Mr. A. N. Datar
worked with exceptional ability and intelligence
in dealing with difficult political cases.

Cases of careless and inefficient work, done
by Vahivatdars and Mahalkaris, came to notice
within the year under report, and the Revenue
Commissioner carefully considered all these cases,
and issued prompt and adequate orders in all.

(b) LAND TAX.

The collection of the land revenue depends on
the annual rainfall and state of the crops, and
unfortunately the conditions were bad in the year
under report. The rainfall of the year is shewn
below:—

Name of District.	Average of last 5 years.	Rainfall in 1903-04.	Rainfall in 1904-05.
Baroda.......	24·77	33·67	19·37
Kadi........	17·26	21·68	10·23
Naosari	41·39	55·13	27·69
Amreli.......	16·96	24·58	16·88

Everywhere, the rainfall of the year under
report was scanty, and in many places it was
badly distributed. The result was that in most
parts of Amreli and Kadi Districts, and in large
portions of Baroda District, there was famine
during the year, and relief operations had to be
undertaken.

The average yield of the staple crops in the different Districts is shewn in the following table:—

Name of District.	Yield of crops in annas.						
	Rice.	Bajri.	Jowari.	Cotton.	Gram.	Pulses.	Wheat.
Baroda	4	4	6	8¼	4¼	8½	2
Kadi	....	3	3	3	1	1	5
Naosari	4½	5½	11	11	8	8	6¾
Amreli	8	6	2	5	....	...	5

Bajri and Jowari are the crops most extensively grown in this State, and, except in Naosari District, nowhere was more than a 6 anna crop, reaped. Cotton is also a valuable crop, and did best in Naosari last year, and failed more or less elsewhere except in Baroda where a fairly good crop was reaped. To the losses caused by scanty rainfall were added the losses caused by the unusual cold and frost of January 1905, which withered much of the winter crops. Miles of the country in Kadi and Amreli Districts, through which His Highness the Maharaja travelled in this season, and which were smiling with green crops a few weeks before, presented a scene of desolation caused by the frost.

The prices of food grains were necessarily higher than in the previous year except that of gram. They are shewn in the following table:—

Name of District.	No. of lbs. sold for the rupee.					
	Rice.	Bajri.	Jowari.	Gram.	Pulses.	Wheat.
Baroda	17½	26	29¾	25¾	18	19¾
Kadi	15¾	29¾	33½	29	17¾	26¼
Naosari	19½	27¾	32½	25¾	17	22¼
Amreli	15¾	28¼	35¼	26	14	24½

The great advantage of sinking irrigation wells is fully known in this State, and His Highness the Maharaja has, since years past, helped the cultivators by large *Tuccavi* advances on the most liberal terms, in the construction of wells in their fields. The result is, that we have a large number of wells in every District, and the severity of famines is greatly lessened in years of drought. The existing number of irrigation wells was largely added to in the last year, when Rs. 1,28,885 were advanced in Kadi District for 681 such wells, and many more such wells were constructed in other Districts. Over and above this, a large number of wells for drinking purposes were constructed at Government cost as famine relief work.

The total number of wells and tanks in the State, for irrigation and other purposes, at the close of the year under report, is shewn below:—

Year.	For irrigation.			For other purposes.		
	Wells.		Tanks.	Wells.		Tanks.
	Kuchcha.	Pucca.		Kuchcha	Pucca.	
At the end of 1903-04	19,814	39,449	1,111	2,220	10,380	5,318
Constructed in 1904-05	2,593	1,966	7	566	473	254
Total ..	21,907	41,415	1,118	2,786	10,853	5,572
Deduct those which became useless	2,940	318	197	295	238	32
Balance at the end of 1904-05 .	18,967	41,097	921	2,491	10,615	5,540

It will be seen from the above figures that a very large number of kuchcha wells and tanks went out of use last year on account of the drought. The loss in respect of wells is not much; kuchcha wells are dug by cultivators at the cost of a few days' labour; and if they dry up in a year of drought, fresh ones in favorable years can be made at little cost. It is the pucca wells, often costing Rs. 500 or Rs. 1,000 each, which really represent the agricultural assets of the State. And it is gratifying to note that there were over forty thousand such wells for irrigation, and ten thousand pucca wells for other purposes at the close of the year. It is a matter for regret, however that even in these expensive wells, the water sometimes turned brackish last year in consequence of the drought, and for want of fresh water percolating from the surface.

The question of the levy of an irrigation rate, when a well is constructed by the cultivator at his own expense, will be discussed in another part of this Report.

Larger water-works like those at Kaderpur, Anawada, and the Thol tank, have not yet proved successful for irrigation purposes, as they do not store sufficient water for irrigating the surrounding lands. The question of improving them is engaging the earnest attention of the Government in the Public Works Department.

Famine conditions became manifest early in the official year, and it became evident that the realization of the land revenue demand to its

full extent was neither possible nor equitable.
The State had suffered from famines or deficient
crops during several previous years, and the cultivators were heavily in debt to the State. All these
matters received the careful consideration of the
Maharaja; and before the close of 1904 His Highness decided, not only to suspend large portions of
the current revenue demand as is done in every
famine year, but also to order remissions of the
arrear and current revenue on an extensive and
comprehensive scale. The beneficent object which
His Highness the Maharaja had in view was to
free the large mass of cultivators from the burden
of a heavy debt, to enable them to stand on their
own legs, and to encourage them to work with
heart and hope to improve their own condition.

Extensive enquiries were made in the closing
months of 1904 and early in 1905 to carry out this
object, and in January and February 1905, His
Highness, accompanied by the Revenue Minister
Mr. R. C. Dutt, and the Revenue Commissioner
Mr. V. M. Samarth, made prolonged tours in
Amreli and Kadi Districts, to see things with his
own eyes, and to hear the complaints of the cultivators with his own ears. The state of crops
everywhere was carefully noted; the representa-
tions of leading cultivators, come from distant
villages, were received; and final orders were
passed which gave general satisfaction to the
population of the afflicted tracts.

On the 2nd February 1905, orders were issued
and proclaimed about the Amreli District :—

All past arrears from cultivators exceeding 1½ year's demand were wiped out. And one-fourth of the current year's demand was also remitted. These orders related to the whole of the District, except Okhamandal Taluka and Bhimkata village.

On the 9th and 21st February 1905, orders were issued and published about the Kadi District:—

All past arrears due from cultivators, exceeding 1½ year's demand in some places, and only 1 year's demand in some specially distressed tracts, were wiped out. And three annas in the rupee of the current year's demand was also remitted.

On the 21st March 1905 orders were issued about Baroda District, excepting Petlad Taluka and its sub-Taluka which had only recently come under settlement:—*All past arrears due from cultivators, exceeding 2 year's demand in some places, 1½ year's demand in other places, and only 1 year's demand in specially afflicted places, were wiped out. And one-fourth of the current year's demand was also remitted in the distressed portions of the District.*

The result of these orders is shown below in figures.

In Amreli District, the past arrears written off under the Maharaja's special order mentioned above, and also under the ordinary rules of remission, amounted to Rs. 3,33,151. And the remission of the current year's demand amounted to Rs. 1,95,467. Total Remission Rs. 5,28,618.

In Kadi District, the past arrears written off under His Highness's special order, and also under the operation of the ordinary rules, amounted to

`. . 12,99,965. And the remission of the current year's demand amounted to Rs. 5,06,261. Total Remission Rs. 18,06,226.

In Baroda District, the past arrears written off under the Maharaja's special order, and also under the operation of the ordinary rules, amounted to Rs. 4,20,948. And the remission of the current year's demand amounted to Rs. 85,619. Total Remission Rs. 5,06,567.

The District of Naosari was happily free from famine in 1904-05 as also in previous years. The needfulness of cultivators was therefore very little, and no special orders for remission were called for. The remission of past arrears, under ordinary rules for remission, amounted only to 44,975; and that of the current year's demand 4,047. Total Remission Rs. 49,022.

The following statement exhibits at a glance the total remissions of Land Revenue in the State for the year under review :—

Land Revenue Remitted in 1904-05.

District.	Under His Highness's special orders.		Under ordinary rules.		Total.
	Arrears.	Current.	Arrears.	Current.	
	Rs.	Rs.	Rs.	Rs.	Rs.
	3,59,908	75,528	61,040	10,091	5,06,567
	2,05,338	4,03,585	10,94,627	1,02,676	18,06,226
	Nil	Nil	44,975	4,047	49,022
	2,85,708	1,91,222	47,143	4,245	5,28,618
Total.	8,50,954	6,70,335	12,48,085	1,21,059	28,90,433

Beside this remission of nearly 29 lacs of rupees, His Highness the Maharaja ordered the suspension of the current revenue demand, on a large and comprehensive scale, in all the tracts affected by the famine. The entire revenue demand in Amreli District was suspended, except that six annas in the rupee of the demand was levied in some villages of Kodinar, where the crops had done comparatively well. In Kadi District, only six annas in the rupee of the revenue demand was collected on the average, and the rest was suspended. And in Baroda District, suspensions of the current revenue demand, varying from eight to sixteen annas in the rupee, were granted in the afflicted parts.

A special feature of these orders of suspension of revenue was, that they were published *timely*, and that they were carried out *without distinction* among the people concerned. The cultivators knew, before the first instalment of payment of revenue was due, how much of the current year's demand they would have to pay. And in the tracts where a suspension of revenue was allowed, no inquisitorial enquiries were made about the condition of the tenants, and no distinction was made between the rich and the poor. As recommended by the Famine Commission of Sir Anthony Macdonnell, the benefits of the order of suspension were granted to all without distinction, and without enquiries, in the afflicted tracts.

These liberal orders of suspension of the current revenue demand, and the remission of 29 lacs of revenue, arrears and current, had the most beneficial effect throughout the State in a year of exceptional distress and famine. All local Officers report that the orders inspired the cultivators with hope and a spirit of self-reliance. Freed from a large burden of old debts, and also freed from a large portion of their current demand, they devoted all their resources and energies to the cultivation of their fields, to the sinking of irrigation wells, and to the breaking of new land. Thousands of tenants, who would have flocked to our relief-work as helpless paupers, were enabled to stay in their own villages, and to cultivate their own fields. The numbers of those who came to our famine relief-works were remarkably small, considering the intensity of the distress, as will be shewn in another place. And, as a measure for relieving the sufferings of the distressed population, and in making them more self-reliant and hopeful and industrious in their own villages and fields, the liberal orders of remission and suspension of revenues succeeded beyond the most sanguine expectations.

The net demands and collections for the year under review, are compared in the following table with the demands and collections for the preceding year.

Land Revenue, Net demand and Collection.

District.	1903-04		1904-05	
	Demand.	Collection.	Demand.	Collection.
	Rs.	Rs.	Rs.	Rs.
Baroda	32,61,384	31,46,558	30,69,701	23,81,897
Kadi	30,30,872	27,89,668	22,01,475	11,24,109
Naosari	16,22,476	16,03,933	16,43,058	15,66,170
Amreli	8,57,188	7,95,826	6,50,744	57,058
Total	87,71,920	83,35,985	75,64,978	51,29,234

N. B.—This excludes surplus collections.

It will be seen that the collections of the last year were shorter by over 32 lacs than the collections in 1903-04,—mainly on account of the remissions and suspensions ordered.

The indebtedness of the cultivators of the Baroda State has been largely decreased by the liberal remissions ordered by His Highness during the year under review.

The decrease will be seen from the following figures:—

Arrears of Land Revenue.

District.	At the close of 1903-04.	At the close of 1904-05.	Remarks.
	Rs.	Rs.	
Baroda	36,20,180	31,99,857	The figures for 1903-04 differ somewhat from those given in the last year's report, as more correct figures have now been obtained.
Kadi	38,58,958	27,63,736	
Naosari	4,17,116	2,96,911	
Amreli......	11,29,638	8,55,989	
Total ..	90,25,892	71,16,443	

There was a great reduction in coercive measures taken in 1904-05 for the recovery of Revenue, which is a great improvement in Revenue Administration.

Coercive Measures for recovery of Revenue.

	1903-04	1904-05
Notices	1,13,628	36,246
Fines	216	591
Sale of land	6,454	399
Moveable property sold	691	33
Unmoveable property sold	1,066	33
Arrest	514	83

It is satisfactory to find that the number of notices went down to less than a third of the number for 1903-04, and the Notice Fee has also been reduced in the year under review. There was a regrettable increase in fines, but the sale of holdings went down to one-sixteenth, and the sale of other properties to one-twenty-fifth. Still more satisfactory is the fact that the number of arrests decreased from 514 to 83.

The total areas of lands relinquished by cultivators, and of new lands brought under cultivation, are shewn in the following statement.

Lands relinquished and brought under cultivation.

1903-04.		1904-05.	
Relinquished.	Brought under Cultivation.	Relinquished.	Brought under Cultivation.
Local Bigahs.	*Local Bigahs.*	*Local Bigahs.*	*Local Bigahs.*
41,817	75,291	84,513	81,382

It is satisfactory to note that in both the years more lands were taken up than were relinquished.

The number of alienated villages in the State is shewn in the following statement :—

Alienated Villages.

District.	1904-05
Baroda	88
Kadi	97
Naosari	46
Amreli	29
Total	255

The total number of inhabited and cultivated villages in the State, last year, was 3,320 ; so that the number of alienated villages represents less than one-twelfth in the State.

The following table shews the transfers of land held by cultivators.

Transfers of Lands.

How transferred.	1903-04	1904-05
	Local Bigahs.	Local Bigahs.
Partition....................	1,325	1,197
Inheritance	2,25,581	1,90,218
Gift and exchange	4,145	5,789
Mortgage	3,234	3,019
Redemption	1,096	1,210
Sale	44,386	38,632
Other reasons	20,917	24,779
Total	300,704	264,794

It is satisfactory to note that there was actually less of sale and mortgage of cultivators' holdings during the last year, which was a famine year, than 1903-04. And this favorable result is due entirely to the liberal remissions and suspensions of revenue ordered by His Highness.

It will also be noticed that comparatively very small areas are transferred by sale and mortgage, most of the transfers during both the years having taken place by inheritance. Under the old rule, a security used to be taken from the heirs who inherited the holdings, but that needless restriction has been abolished by the Maharaja.

Similarly, there are no restrictions placed on the free sale of holdings. Care however is taken, when a cultivator is sold up by his creditors, that sufficient land is left to him for the support, (*Nirvaha*) of himself and his family.

The apprehensions which are sometimes entertained, that to bestow the right of sale and transfer to the cultivators of India is to let their property pass into the hands of money-lenders, have proved groundless in Baroda, as it has proved groundless in Bengal and other Provinces. The Indian cultivator is frugal, careful, and keenly alive to his own interests ; and he sets as high a value to his property in land as the cultivator of France or any other country in the world. To recognize his free right of sale and mortgage is to enhance the marketable value of his property and improve his condition ; while to restrict that right is to take away from the value of his property, and to impoverish him. The right of sale and mortgage, freely exercised in Baroda State, has not had the effect of lands passing into the hands of non-cultivating classes. On the contrary, it has improved and assured the position of the cultivator in his own village and in the State. The Baroda *Khatedar* or tenant is a man of some status in his Taluka, because he is a man of property which has a marketable value, which he has freely inherited from his father, and which he hopes freely to transmit to his son. And through all the successive years of scarcity and famine through which the State has passed, the wise and beneficent policy of His Highness, in recognizing full rights of transfer in the cultivators, has helped them, not a little, to tide over their difficulties, because they have credit in the market. The laws of Political Economy are as true in India as elsewhere in the world;—it is possible to improve the condition of cultivators by wise legislation which adds to the marketable value of their property, not by laws which take away from its value.

(c)—LOCAL CESS, &C.

Local Cess.—No Local Cesses were imposed when the new system of Survey and Settlement was introduced in the State. But when about one-half the State had been settled, the idea of imposing a Local Cess, as is done in British India, was conceived and reduced into practice. The Cess was at first amalgamated with the Land Revenue; but as it was the Maharaja's desire to create Local Boards for the purpose of introducing Self-Government in local matters, His Highness directed in 1903-04 that the proceeds of the Local Cess should be separated from those of the Land Revenue. This order was fully carried out in the year under report. Some of the Talukas, comprising nearly one-half of the State, will come in for Revision Settlement within the next three years. With respect to these Talukas, His Highness has directed that the Local Cess should be imposed only on alienated lands, and that Khalsa or assessable lands should be exempt from Cess until the Talukas are re-settled. It thus happens that in one-half of the State the Local Cess is levied on all lands—Khalsa and alienated,—while in the other half the Cess is levied only from alienated lands. This will be clear from the following tabular statement:—

District.	Extent to which Local Cess is levied.	REMARKS.
Baroda ..	Cess levied only from alienated lands and villages.	Garassias who are under the protection of the British Government pay no Cess on the alienated lands which they hold.
Kadi	In Sidhpur, the Cess is levied from alienated lands and villages only. In other Talukas it is levied from all lands.	
Naosari ..	In Vyara the Cess is levied from alienated lands and villages only. In the other Talukas it is levied from all lands.	
Amreli ..	It is levied from all lands in Okhamandal. In other Talukas it is imposed on alienated lands and villages only.	

The demand and collection of the Local Cess during the last two years is shewn in the following Statement:—

Local Cess.

1903-04.		1904-05.	
Demand.	Collection.	Demand.	Collection.
Rs.	Rs.	Rs.	Rs.
2,47,069	1,79,131	3,88,480	2,09,803

The Local Boards Act has come into operation from the commencement of the present official year 1905-06. Under Section 48 of that Act one-fourth of the total Local Cess Demand has been reserved for special expenditure in famine years, and a small deduction has also been made for collection charges.

10

The remaining sum of Rs. 2,84,000 has been distributed among the different Local Boards of the State for the performance of those duties which the law imposes on them. To this sum has been added a sum of Rs. 87,000 for Revenue Public Works, which used to be executed by the Revenue Department, and are now transferred to Local Boards. A grant for Vaccination, amounting to Rs. 14,000, and a grant for Gramyashalas or Village Schools amounting to Rs. 60,000, have also been handed over to Local Boards. In all, therefore, the Local Boards start with an income of Rs. 4,45,000 from 1905-06, as will be shewn further on.

There is a great scope for the increase of the Local Cess in future with the re-settlement of all the Talukas in the State. And at the rate of an anna in the rupee of land revenue, the total proceeds of the Local Cess is estimated to rise to over five lacs. The future development of the State in the way of village roads, tanks, drinking water wells, village schools, and sanitary improvements, will therefore largely depend on the wisdom and foresight with which the Local Boards will exercise those administrative powers which His Highness has reposed in them.

(d)—INCOME TAX.

A great reform has been introduced by His Highness the Maharaja by the levy of the Income Tax on one uniform scale throughout the State, in place of numerous and vexatious Profession and Caste taxes, called Veros, which used to be levied previously. As stated in the last Annual Report, the Income Tax was gradually introduced in different places in different years, and in 1903-04 two different scales were suggested, one for towns and the other for villages. The inequality of the two scales was so obvious that a further revision was inevitable, and a uniform scale was proposed by the Revenue Minister in September 1904, and adopted from the commencement of 1904-05. The scale is given below:—

Annual Income.		Annual Tax.	
Under Rs. 300		No. Tax.	
Rs.	300 to under Rs. 500..........	Rs.	3
,,	500 ,, ,, ,, 750..........	,,	6
,,	750 ,, ,, ,, 1,000..........	,,	10
,,	1,000 ,, ,, ,, 2,500..........	,,	15
,,	2,500 ,, ,, ,, 5,000..........	,,	30
,,	5,000 ,, ,, ,, 10,000..........	,,	50
,,	10,000 ,, ,, ,, 15,000..........	,,	75
,,	15,000 and above......................	,,	100

The advantages of this new system are:—

(1) It makes a clean sweep of all the numerous and oppressive Veros which used to be levied before, mostly from the poorest classes of the people.

(2) It exempts the poor from taxation.

(3) It imposes on the richer classes, a proportionate burden which they had evaded before.

(4) It imposes on the official classes a fair share of taxation which they had escaped before.

(5) It makes no distinction between towns and villages, or between different classes of His Highness's subjects.

(6) It is a moderate tax, approximating to one per cent of the income, or about 2½d. in the pound as it would be described in England, which all subjects of the Maharaja, down to those who earn Rs. 300 a year, are able to pay.

The Veros which have been abolished on the introduction of the Income Tax were an inheritance from the past. They were taxes on various castes and professions, and often on various local customs, added on from time to time, and retained because they were once imposed. A list has been made, shewing no less than 214 kinds of Veros which have recently been abolished. I have counted no less then seventy of them which did not bring as much revenue to the State as Rs. 10 a year each; and the only Veros which brought any appreciable income,—over Rs. 1,000 a year,— were the following:—

Veros.	Annual proceeds.
	Rs.
Rabari, (tax on shepherds)	3,943
Tafarik, (tax on travellers)	4,589
Kohad, (tax on blacksmiths)	4,252
Ghanchi (tax on oil-manufacturers)	1,926
Darji (tax on tailors)	1,430
Bham (tax on special sites)	10,592
Vania (tax on shopkeepers)....	9,939
Sal (tax on weavers)	4,675
Soni (tax on goldsmiths)	1,153

Veros.	Annual Proceeds.
	Rs.
Mahajan (tax on caste-guilds)	8,024
Vanta (tax on certain alienated lands)....	1,219
Umra (tax on door steps)	1,461
Dhed (tax on the Dhed caste)	1,363
Koli (tax on the Koli caste)	4,476
Kasab (tax on embroiderers)............	1,433
Chamadias (tax on skinners)	1,178
Ubhad (tax for certain sites)	2,210
Mukan Maparu (tax on weighers and measurers)	1,107

These eighteen Veros brought in a revenue of over sixty thousand rupees a year, and all the other Veros, put together, brought in a little over twenty thousand; the total income from the 214 Veros being estimated at Rs. 84,862.

When an Income Tax on a uniform scale on all non-agricultural incomes was first proposed in place of these Veros, it was apprehended that the net result would be a loss to the State. The Veros were then supposed to bring a revenue of about a lac of rupees, and the proposed Incom Tax was estimated to bring in Rs. 90,000. His Highness the Maharaja, however, was anxious to abolish the harassing old Veros at all cost; and he insisted on the immediate introduction of the reform, both by written orders, and by wire from Darjeeling where His Highness had proceeded for a short change in October 1904. And the reform was accordingly introduced with effect from the commencement of the official year 1904-05.

Incomes were assessed with the utmost moderation. The Assessing Officer was, in every instance, accompanied by two leading and representative men of the town or village in which assessments were made, and acted in consultation with them. This wise provision made the assessments generally fair. There have been remarkably few appeals against assessments, and the introduction of a new tax on the rich and well-to-do people has not been attended with any such complaints or expressions of public feeling as are usual on such occasions.

At the same time the result has agreeably surprised us. Early in 1905 it was perceived that the proceeds of the new tax would be about a lac of rupees, and this was the estimate given in the last Annual Administration Report. The anticipation has been verified, and the Income Tax Demand, according to the latest figures available, is Rs. 99,080.

The net gain to the State from the levy of the Income Tax, as compared with the old Veros, is over Rs. 14,000 a year. But it is a greater gain that the new tax is levied from the richer classes and exempts the poor. A fresh revision of the Income Tax, calculated to raise the minimum of taxable incomes, and to impose a higher percentage on large incomes, is under consideration in the current year.

A small revenue is obtained from the rent of homestead lands in villages, levied from non-agriculturists; and some revenue is also derived at Dwarka from licenses to collect valuable shells and from certain rates on pilgrims. The proceeds of these sources of income, were less than one lac.

A revenue is also obtained from ferries, and interest on advances, and other sources of income, which are grouped together as Miscellaneous Revenue. The total proceeds in 1904-05 were Rs. 4,29,546.

(e)—STATE BOUNDARIES.

The territories of His Highness the Gaekwar are so scattered and interlaced with British territories and those of other Native States, that the work of keeping the boundaries fixed is exceptionally heavy and arduous. In 1884, when the Revenue Survey and Settlement of the State had just been undertaken, His Highness made some proposals on this subject which were approved of by the British Government, and instructions were issued to Political Officers to the effect that other Native States should be represented by competent and trustworthy agents for the purpose of the delimitation of boundaries.

Mr. F. A. H. Elliot, C. I. E., then in charge of the Survey and Settlement of certain Talukas, issued orders for the demarcation of their boundaries at the same time. The two descriptions of work, however, could not be satisfactorily performed by the same staff, and a Boundaries Settlement Office was organized in 1891. Ten years after, this office was amalgamated with the Revenue Office, which was doing much the same work; and the delimitation and maintenance of State

Boundaries thus form a part of the varied duties of the Revenue Commissioner.

Mr. R. R. Kothawala has been in special charge of the Boundaries Office under the general supervision of the Revenue Commissioner; and the zeal, ability and technical knowledge of details, with which he has performed his duties has received deserved commendation year after year.

When boundary cases arise, he conducts cases on behalf of this State before the Boundary Commissioner. His further work consists of inspections of boundaries, which requires him to be out during 8 months in the year. During this inspection, he examines the state of the boundary pillars, and takes note of all encroachments made either by foreign subjects, or by the Railway Department.

The magnitude of the work of the office will be understood from the fact that the State has about 3,800 "boundaries," measuring about 3,150 miles. Of these 1,500 "boundaries" are in relation to other Native States, and the rest are in relation to British territory. With regard to the former we should have a map for each ; but, so far, only four hundred are ready and some eleven hundred more have yet to be prepared. Each map has to be prepared after survey and measurement in presence of an agent of this State and an agent of the other State concerned ; it is clear therefore that we have a work of several years before us.

The work done in this office during the last two years is shown in the following statement :—

Nature of work.	1903-04.	1904-05.
Foreign boundaries examined....	228	188
Taluka Boundary records inspected	24	8
Boundaries surveyed	80	131
Boundaries verified	36	64
Boundaries settled	21	48
Boundaries demarcated by the Boundary Commissioner.	9	1
Boundary cases prepared or conducted before the Boundary Commissioner.	3	1
Mileage of railway surveyed for demarcation or demarcated.	64	60
Copies of boundary maps supplied to other offices.	173	137
Copies of boundary field books supplied to other offices.	153	102

It will be seen from these figures that in respect of boundaries *surveyed, verified*, and *settled*, the work done in the year under report was considerably more than in 1903-04 or in any previous year. The most important work falling under these heads during 1904-05 was the settlement of the Sarthan-Varacha boundary, the case having originated in 1895, and being finally disposed of in favour of the State.

The most important case of *demarcation* of boundary disposed of in the year under report was that of the Kaniel-Barmuwada boundary. This demarcation has virtually restored to the State nearly 1,500 Bigahs of land, which to all intents and purposes had been lost for more than three-quarters of a century.

11

It should be noted that a piece of alluvial land in the Mahi river, measuring 1,366 Bigahs, and which had not been measured by the Survey Department at the time of the original Survey, was discovered by Mr. Kothawala in the year under report. And a large forest tract of about 5,500 Bigahs, which had not been included by the Survey Department in any village, was discovered by Mr. Gokhale of the Boundaries Office.

Good work was also done by the Boundaries Office in settling the Umri-Deliatla boundary dispute. Mr. Kothawala personally explained the case to the Resident at Baroda, who, thereupon expressed his opinion in favour of this State to the Bombay Government. A long standing dispute was thus settled, and the boundary line was demarcated by iron rail posts, which placed us in possession of about 175 acres of land forming the river bed.

V.—REVENUE.—SECTION B.

(a)—GARAS TENURES.

Mr. Gunaji Rao Rajba Nimbalkar, B. A., of the Bombay University, was in charge of the B. Section of the Revenue Department. He joined the service of the State in 1888, and has passed nearly the whole period of his service in the Survey Settlement Department. His ability and zeal have been recognized by successive officers, and in 1893 he was specially rewarded by His. Highness the Maharaja for good work. In 1903 he was confirmed in the post of Settlement Commissioner and, on the decentralisation of the Revenue Department in the year under report, he was placed in charge of one important Section.

This Section comprised five distinct offices at the close of 1904-5 as shewn below :—

1. Garas Office.
2. Religious Institutions.
3. Court of Wards.
4. Attached Estates.
5. Land Acquisition.

The Garas Office deals with the tenures of Garasias, who either held lands under the rule of the Moghals, or rose into power in subsequent times, and often levied black mail from the peaceful population. With the return of peaceful times, the claims of the Garasias generally took the form of grants of land, money or grain. And some of the Garasias obtained a guarantee from the British Government that their rights and grants would not be interfered with. It is the tenures of these

Guaranteed Garasias only which are dealt with by the Garas Office.

The total number of Guaranteed Garasias is shewn in the following table :—

Name of the District.	Those holding land and getting cash payment.	Those getting cash payment only.	Those holding land only.	Total guranteed holders.
Kadi	94	126	565	785
Baroda	254	308	397	959
Naosari	5	1	1	7
Huzur Treasury..	3	1	0	4
Total ..	356	436	963	1,755

Lists of Garasias who receive cash have been re-written within the last two or three years, and copies of them have been sent to the different Talukas for information and guidance, and also to the Accountant-General. Corrections made are also communicated regularly, so that their copies of the registers are upto date. But the lists of the Garasias who hold lands are very defective, and are now being re-written with full particulars. When this is done, copies of them will be sent to the different Talukas.

The work done by the Garas Office may be divided into two classes, *viz.*, (1) enquiries into and decisions on applications made by the Garasias to the office, and (2) correspondence with the Residency and the conduct of cases before the Residency, when the Garasias appeal to the British Government.

The work coming under the first head, done in the year under report, is shewn in the following table :—

Office Cases.

Nature of Case.	Balance from previous year.	Cases filed in 1904-05.	Total.	Disposed of within the year.	Pending at the end of the year.
New claims to land	4	39	43	19	24
Succession cases....	29	80	109	91	18
Claims by co-sharers	*nil*	32	32	24	8
Miscellaneous cases....	7	188	195	124	71
Total	40	839	379	258	121

The number of succession cases disposed of within the year was satisfactory ; but the number of new claims to land, and of miscellaneous cases which remained undisposed of, at the end of the year, was very heavy.

The work coming under the second head, *viz.*, references to the Residency, done in the year under report, is shewn in the following table :—

Residency References.

Balance from previous year.	Fresh References in 1904-05.	Total.	Disposed of within the year.	Pending at the end of the year.
24	327	351	330	21

The work disposed of was satisfactory.

In the Garas Office, the original cases were done by the Assistant, and appeals from him were heard by Mr. Nimbalkar. The result of these appeals is shewn below :—

Office Appeals.

Pending at the end of the previous year.	Received during the year.	Total.	Decision confirmed.	Decision reversed or modified.	Case remanded.	Summarily rejected.	Pending at the end of the year.
32	47	79	19	8	4	3	45

With respect to appeals preferred to the Residency against our orders, 78 decisions were received,—as shewn below :—

Residency Appeals.

Amicably settled.	Decision confirmed.	Reversed or modified.	Slight alterations made,	Remanded.	Total.
1	17	49	3	8	78

The result of appeals, both in the cases disposed of in the Office and in the Residency cases, was unsatisfactory.

The Garas Assistant continued his inspection of the Garas work done in the Taluka offices during the year under report, and visited six Talukas, including the headquarters of Kadi and Naosari Districts. These inspections have a salutary effect, in as much as they ensure a uniform method of work, and expedite the disposal of pending references which always give rise to complaints. A still closer scrutiny into Taluka work, undertaken in the future, will, it is hoped, minimise many petty differences between the local officers and the Garasias as regards their rights and claims.

Mr. Vinayak Anant, Garas Assistant, did good work in the year under review. He came to the service of the State from the British service two years ago, and his large experience in Garas work makes him very useful in this office.

Since the conclusion of the year under report, the Garas Office has been transferred from the Revenue Department to the Settlement Department, and Mr. Seddon of the Bombay Civil Service, whose services have been lent to the State as Settlement Commissioner, is now also in charge of Garas work, under the special sanction of the Government of India.

(*b*)—RELIGIOUS INSTITUTIONS.

It has been stated in the *Legislative* Chapter of this Report that, by a recent Act, the State has been empowered to assume some powers of supervision over Religious Institutions of three classes, *viz* :—

(1). Those aided by the State.
(2). Those in respect of which the community concerned ask for Government supervision.
(3). Those institutions the mismanagement of which becomes notorious.

No institution of the second or third class has yet come under Government supervision. It is hoped that the passing of the Act will of itself

ensure the good management of all unaided institutions, and that the interference of the State with
respect to them will rarely be needed.

The Religious Institutions, aided by the State,
comprise 28 which are directly managed by the
Government, and about seventeen hundred more
which receive aid from the Government in money
or in land. The list given below shews the Institutions under Government management.

Religious Institutions under State Management.

Serial number.	Name.	Annual grant.	Saving effected in 1904-05 out of the annual grant.
		Rs.	Rs.
1	Kedareswar Khichri	22,963	9,264
2	Gyarmi	17,568	862
3	Becharji	12,032	4,693
4	Vithal Mandir	5,268	493
5	Kailas Vasini	4,757	995
6	Tarakeswar	4,432	595
7	Khanderao (two)	3,195	46
8	Kedareswar Mahadeva ..	2,686	183
9	Bhimnath Mahadeva	2,382	369
10	Kasi Viswanath	2,235	31
11	Sarveswar Mahadeva	1,747	381
12	Dameswar (Benares)	1,672	4
13	Radha Ballabh	987	223
14	Nil Kantheswar	962	65
15	Javateswar	300	6
16	Bhairaveswar	300	*Nil*
17	Kuberji Samadi	247	20
18	Kalikamata (Dabhoi)......	788	32
19	Krishneswar (Sinor)	755	185
20	Arjun Shah (Petlad)	565	167
21	Anusuya Mata (Sinor)	10	5
22	Becharji Mata (Vadauli) ..	18,109	2,445
23	Javateswar (Kadi)	2,554	*Nil*
24	Siddheswar (Sidhpur)......	1,798	244
25	Pimpleswar (Mehsana)....	1,663	*Nil*
26	Koteswar (Kalol)	987	176
27	Jaleswar (Pattan)	850	*Nil*
28	Maheswar (Vijapur)	239	42
	Total Rs. ..	1,11,951	21,317

It should be noted that out of these institutions the first seventeen were originally managed by the Palace Department, and were then transferred to the Settlement Department, and have now been transferred to the Revenue Department. The remaining eleven are not a complete list yet, a few more institutions are managed by the Government. But full information about them has not yet been obtained, and so they have been excluded from the present list.

The total expenditure on the institutions managed by the State exceed a lac of rupees, as shewn in the preceding list. The total savings of these institutions, including those of previous years, amount to Rs. 1,37,443, most of which is invested. They have also jewellery and gold ornaments, temples and houses, silver and brass articles, etc., valued at Rs. 13,82,796, besides landed property which has not yet been valued.

Some details about a few of these 28 State Institutions will be interesting.

The first two,—the Khichri and Gyarmi institutions,—are mainly for the distribution of food to Hindus and Mahomedans respectively. The recipients of the food hold passes which are not transferable. These passes in the case of Hindus have lately been revised by a Committee, and reduced to 1,090. The passes held by Mahomedans, about 1,200 in number, have not yet been revised.

The institution No. 3 in the above list, i. e., Becharji, is perhaps the most famous in Baroda. It was originally established by a blacksmith, and dedicated to goddess Behachar, over a hundred years ago. The late Maharaja Sayaji Rao appointed five Brahmans for the performance of the daily worship to the goddess. At the end of each Varni, which comes about once a quarter, large sums and various articles are distributed to the poor.

The institution No. 7 in the list is dedicated to the presiding deity of the ruling house of Baroda, and is held in high esteem by the Mahratta community.

We next turn to the large number of institutions which are under private management, but which receive aid from the State in land or in money, and have therefore come under State supervision by the new Act which came into force on January 12, 1905. The total number of these institutions is not yet known, but definite information regarding 1,693 of them has been obtained, and they may be classified thus :—

State-aided Institutions.

Deity to whom the institutions are dedicated.	Number.	Annual Cost.
	Rs.	Rs.
Siva	549	38,656
Vishnu	605	79,448
Sakti	208	19,428
Ganapati	27	6,287
Maruti	99	4,062
Others	205	30,163
Total ..	1,693	1,78,044

The above list includes about 175 temples situated outside the State, in holy places like Benares, Brindavan, Nasik, &c.

Simple rules have been framed for the guidance of these State-aided institutions, and distributed among them. Only 75 of them receive aid from the State exceeding Rs. 200 a year, and these only have been called upon to submit annual budgets and lists of property belonging to them. Mr. Nimbalkar has received definite instructions to carry out his delicate duties with the least amount of friction, and without offending the feelings of the communities concerned. The object of the State in passing the new Act is not to interfere in the private management of religious institutions, but simply to prevent gross abuses.

Mention has been made of the clause in the new Act which empowers any State-aided institution to withdraw completely from State-supervision by surrendering the aid received. No such surrender has yet been made ; but the managers of two Vaishnava temples have claimed exemption from Government supervision on other grounds, and the applications are under enquiry. The managers of other institutions are watching the proceedings with some interest.

The supervision of something near two thousand institutions, and the keeping of regular accounts with regard to the more important among them, impose a very heavy work on this newly created office. Mr. Nimbalkar, the head 'of the office, is ably assisted in these duties by his Assistant Mr. Sindhe, who has had long experience in the management of the State-managed institutions, and whose work in organizing this new office has come to my very favorable notice.

(c)—COURT OF WARDS.

The *Palya Palak Nibandh*, or Wards and Guardians Act, was passed in 1898, but it was only during the year under review that steps were taken to bring the administration of the Wards' Estates into order by placing them all under the supervision of one responsible officer. No less than 42 Wards' estates are now under Mr. Nimbalkar's supervision and control. Twelve of these belong to minors who are mostly relations of the ruling family, or Sardars or Darakdars of the State; and their estates were formerly managed by the Settlement, the Palace, or the Military Department. The remaining thirty estates were under the management of the Officers of the Districts in which they were situated. With regard to the first twelve estates, His Highness the Maharaja sanctioned certain rules for management as far back as 1899. These rules have now been extended to the other thirty estates.

The work of the Court of Wards embraces (1) the management of the minors' estates, and (2) the education and proper training of the minors themselves.

For the proper management of the estates, Mr. Nimbalkar has prescribed a form showing the assets and the annual income and expenditure of each estate. The statement shews at a glance the pecuniary position of each minor, and is the basis on which the annual budgets are framed. A notification has also been issued to stop the unlimited borrowing which used to be practised by the minors, and calling upon creditors to bring forward their

claims for scrutiny. Applications have poured in
from creditors who had lent money to the minors,
their mothers, wives, and relations; and it appears
from an examination of these claims that some of
the Sardars habitually lived beyond their means,
and continued to borrow as long as the creditors
would lend. It is needless to state that this has
now been checked.

One or two instances will indicate the steps which
it has been thought necessary to adopt, to liquidate
debts already incurred. The Shirke brothers had
a debt of Rs. 65,412, which, with the consent of the
creditors, was compounded for Rs. 62,827. About
three-fourths of this, *i.e.* Rs. 46,909 have already
been paid off from the proceeds of the sale of the
jewellery already pawned. The Dhaebar brothers
were also deeply in debt, and had pawned virtually
all their jewellery. With great difficulty the mort-
gagees were made to produce these; and 92 articles
which had been valued in the Sardar Court at
Rs. 21,170, and pawned for about the same amount,
were sold by auction for more than double that
value, *i.e.*, for Rs. 46,690; and the debt of the
family has been reduced to this extent. The re-
mainder will shortly be liquidated by the sale of
the remaining articles.

Proper agents have been appointed for the
management of the estates, and they have been
warned to limit the expenditure to the budget
framed for each estate. A monthly statement has
also been called for from each estate to help the
office to control expenditure. Lastly, new Rules of

Management, incorporating those already in force, have been framed; and they will be applied to all estates under the management of the Court of Wards as soon as they are passed. All these improvements have been introduced since the Decentralization of the Revenue Department.

It is unnecessary to exhibit in this Report the accounts of all the 42 estates under our management, but the following statement concerning ten of the most important estates will convey some idea of their income and expenditure, and also of their former indebtedness.

Accounts of Wards' Estates, 1904-05.

Serial Number.	Name of Ward.	Annual Income.	Annual Expenditure sanctioned.	Amount of debt.
		Rs.	Rs.	Rs.
1.	Madhav Rao Anand Rao Dhaeber	11,511	8,140	90,860
2.	Vasant Rao Anand Rao Dhaeber	9,746	6,914	62,368
3.	Sansthan Bolai	8,343	7,033	.....
4.	Ramchandra Rao Madhav Rao Phadnis	7,776	5,706	15,020
5.	SankarRao Sadasiv Puranik	7,317	4,425	7,226
6.	Krishna Rao Bhawan Rao Kadam	5,033	1,892	62,713
7.	Ganpat Rao Khaserao Sirke	4,413	2,061	6,561
8.	Barhanji Santaji Bhonsle	3,362	2,556	8,953
9.	Sankar Rao AnandRao Kamatekar	3,178	2,553	....
10.	Bapusingji Jaswant Singji.	12,153	10,877	6,469

The education and proper training of the minors is as onerous a task as the management of their estates. The idea is to bring most of them to central places like Baroda, Amreli or Pattan, and to keep them under the personal supervision of Head Masters of High schools or other responsible Officers. Mr. Nimbalkar has not yet been able to arrange this, and contents himself with monthly certificates from school masters and private tutors regarding the general proficiency and conduct of the minors. Those who are in Baroda attend on Mr. Nimbalkar once a month.

One Ward has been placed in the New English High School at Poona under His Highness's special orders; and it is proposed to place another in some school outside Baroda.

Great difficulty is experienced in some cases to extricate the boys from the bad company in which they are found, and opposition is offered by intriguing agents, and even sometimes by the mothers of the boys, to any proposals of reform. It has been found necessary to dismiss some of the agents to carry out the reforms. Steps are also being taken for proper medical attendance on the minors.

The work of framing some general rules for the amelioration of the condition of Sardars, Darakdars, and other notable men in the State, was entrusted to Mr. Nimbalkar by His Highness the Maharaja. The rules have been framed, and have been modified and approved by the Council.

(d)—ATTACHED ESTATES.

The number of estates now under attachment, under orders issued by the Judicial, the

Revenue, or the Settlement Department, and the causes which led to their attachment, are exhibited in the following table :—

Attached Estates.

Attached under the Wards and Guardians Act.	Mortgaged to Govt. for loans.	Attached for arrears of Revenue.	Attached owing to disputes among holders.	Attached for mis-management of temples &c.	Attached pending mutation of names.	Attached for protection of Govt. shares.	Attached as properties of temples under Govt. management.	Attached for other causes.	Total.
50	50	31	19	53	63	16	13	62	357

A glance at these figures raises the suspicion that estates are sometimes attached on inadequate grounds, that they are sometimes kept under attachment after the reasons which lead to it have ceased to exist, and that altogether the private estates under attachment are too numerous for proper management and supervision by one Central Office. By an order, dated 1878, Attached Estates are managed as Government property, and 2 per cent. on the assets are charged for the cost of management. A glance at the figures given in the table below shews that the 357 estates under attachment were not well managed under the old system, *i.e.*, before the Decentralization of the Revenue Department.

Arrears in Attached Estates.

Number of attached estates.	Annual Assets.	Arrears at the end of 1903-04
357	Rs. 4,06,224	Rs. 6,23,418

In other words more than 18 months' demand from these estates is in arrear. The reasons assigned by Mr. Nimbalkar for this state of things are :—

(1) that the rules for the collection of revenue in Khalsa villages have not been enforced in attached private villages,

(2) that officers are frequently transferred,

(3) that the supervision of District and Taluka officers over so many attached estate has not been sufficiently close.

It may however be urged in extenuation of the unsatisfactory collection in these villages that harvests have been bad during several years past, and that the arrears of land revenue all over the Raj were heavy at the end of 1903-04, though not proportionately so heavy as in the Attached Estates. The arrears in the Raj were about a year's demand at the close of 1903-04, while those in the Attached Estates exceeded 18 months' demand, as stated before.

"It will be my sole duty, next year, "—writes Mr. Nimbalkar,—"to see that the *Jamabandi* of every (attached) estate is done by the officers concerned, and that the management is put on a sound basis." But it is hoped that Mr. Nimbalkar will also carefully look into the reasons which led to the attachment of these 357 estates, and will obtain orders for their release from attachment where those reasons have ceased to exist, or where such release is desirable. Over one-half of them, *i. e.* 185 estates have been under our management for over four or five years.

Most of these 357 estates are very petty, with very small incomes. Only a hundred of them have an annual income exceeding Rs. 500. Is it not possible to free from attachment all the estates, 257 in number, with smaller incomes than Rs. 500 a year, after making adequate arrangements for the safety of Government dues?

(e)—LAND ACQUISITION.

In no branch of the Revenue Department was the attention of a special officer more needed than in dealing with the acquisition of lands and houses; and in none is the *Decentralization Scheme*, introduced by orders of His Highness, likely to prove more beneficial. Until the vast work of the Revenue Department was divided into separate Sections, the Land Acquisition cases were almost lost sight of, and delay was made in paying compensation which was not creditable.

Various Revenue Officers have various powers in acquiring property for the Government. The Taluka Officer has powers up to the value of Rs. 200; the Naib Subah up to Rs. 500; the Subah or District Officer up to Rs. 1,000 in Gamthan cases, and up to Rs. 5,000 in other cases. For acquiring property of higher value, the orders of superior officers are required. A party dissatisfied with the award has the right of appeal.

It is laid down in the Compensation Rules that payment should be made within a year's time after acquisition of the land. But it was found in course of an inspection of the office held by the Revenue Minister in June 1905, that this rule was hardly

ever attended to. There were cases in the Talukas
of Dabhoi, Petlad, Pattan, Kalol, Vyara, and
Gandevi in which the compensation due had not
been paid for ten to fifteen years; while many
other Talukas had cases over five or six years old.
Orders were passed to dispose of, at once, all old
cases dating from before 1900,—and also to dispose
of, by the end of December 1905, all cases over a
year old. · Some progress has been made in pursu-
ance of these orders; but the exceptionally heavy
work which was imposed on all Revenue Officers
druing the year under report prevented them from
fully carrying them out.

There are still, therefore, over a hundred cases
pending over a year, in which compensation
has not yet been paid, as the following table will
shew :—

Old Compensation Cases.

District.	Dating from before 1900.	Dating from 1900 to 1904.	Total of old cases.
Baroda	36	20	56
Kadi	7	14	21
Naosari	25	1	26
Amreli	*nil*	4	4
Total	68	39	107

It is confidently hoped that *all* old cases will be
disposed of within the current official year; and
that the rule of paying compensation within a
year of the acquisition of land or houses will be
strictly adhered to in the future.

The actual work done within the year under report is shewn in the following table :—

Compensation paid in 1904-05.

District.	Number of cases in which compensation was given.	Area of land for which compensation was given.		Amount paid in cash.	Area of land given in exchange.
		Bigahs.	Sq. ft.	Rs.	Bigahs.
Baroda	45	322	nil	18,264	nil
Kadi	205	573	nil	4,635	12
Naosari	13	189	nil	549	61
Amreli	3	13	10,851	2,613	1
Head office.	1	71	nil	613	nil
Total	267	1,168	10,851	26,674	74

N.B.—Cultivable fields are measured in Bigahs, while lands inside towns and villages are measured in square feet.

The account given above relates to lands &c., acquired by the District and Taluka officers and the Head Office. Certain other officers, viz., the Settlement Commissioner, the Customs and Excise officer, and officers of the Public Works Department, have also the power to acquire lands. Mr. Nimbalkar has lately been empowered to place himself in communication with those officers, with a view to ensure the speedy disposal of the cases before them.

REVENUE—SECTION C.

(a)—CUSTOMS.

A large and important group of revenue offices, shewn in the list given below, is placed under Mr. Raojibhai Patel.

1. Customs.
2. Excise.
3. Opium.
4. Salt.
5. Agriculture.
6. Industries.
7. Registration.
8. Stamps.
9. Printing and Stationery.
10. Ports and Tolls.

Like many other promising young men, Mr. Patel was sent to Europe by His Highness the Maharaja at State expense; and he learned agriculture at Cirencester and sugar manufacture in Germany. On his return to India in 1892, with the titles of Member of the Royal Agricultural College of Cirencester and Member of the Royal Agricultural Society of England, he took service under the State. When the decentralisation of the Revenue Department was carried out, Mr. Raojibhai Patel was placed in charge of an important Section, directly under the Revenue Minister.

Mr. Patel's various duties took him out into the different districts every month from October to June last; and in July he was sent to Kashmir to examine and report on the silk industry of that State.

Among the different offices of which **Mr. Raoji-bhai** was in charge, that of Customs comes first. A great and important reform was proposed by the Revenue Minister, and sanctioned by His Highness the Maharaja, in the levy of Customs, in September 1904.

The principles followed in carrying out this Tariff Reform were these :—(a) A large number of harassing duties on petty articles were abolished. (b) All export duty was abolished except on Cotton and Mahua. (c) Import duties on the frontiers of the State were retained on a few articles generally used in villages, and these articles were not subjected to any fresh duty on entering towns. (d) Octroi duties were retained on a few other articles generally used by townspeople; (e) *Ad valorum* duty was abolished altogether, and all duties were levied on articles by the weight without unpacking goods. (f) The vast body of Nakadars or Customs Officers was reduced by over a hundred, and the pay of those retained was improved. (g) Instructions were issued forbidding the search and harassment of travellers, while protecting the revenues of the State.

The revision of tariffs was carried out, with effect from 1st November 1904, in the two compact Districts of Baroda and Kadi, and is shewn below in a tabular form.

Tariff Reform introduced in Baroda and Kadi from 1st November 1904.

Old System.	New System.	Remarks.
Frontier Duties on 36 articles imported.	Frontier Duties specific on 8 articles only, viz— (1) Jaggery and Sugar. (2) Groceries and Spices. (3) Kerosine. (4) Salt. (5) Beer, Wines, Spirits. (6) Apparel. (7) Metal and Metalware. (8) Timber.	In Chandod, which is under the joint juris-diction of this State and another State, the tariff remained unchanged. In Pet-lad an export duty on tobacco was abo-lished and a small rate per Bigah was imposed on tobacco actually grown. Im-port duty on oil seeds was abolished in Kadi District. Export duty on Cot-ton and Mahua was levied only in Ba-roda District. Du-ty on white sugar was removed from towns and placed on frontiers from 1st August 1905.
Additional Octroi Du-ties on the same 36 articles imported.	Octroi Duties on 8 different articles, viz— (1) White sugar Candy. (2) Butter and Ghee. (3) Edible Oils. (4) Oil Seeds. (5) Tobacco. (6) Paper. (7) Furniture. (8) Grass and Firewood.	
Export Duty on Cot-ton, bones, hides, horns, &c.	Export duty on Cotton and Mahua only.	

When this Tariff Reform was carried out, it was expected that the removal of harassing duties from a large number of petty articles would natural-ly give facilities to trade and business, and that, on the whole, the State would suffer no loss of revenue. The result more than justified these expectations. The cotton crop in Baroda District happened to be a good one; and this, coupled with a large expan-sion in trade incident to the removal of harassing imposts, not only saved the State from a loss, but gave us an increase in revenue of *a lac of rupees* in six months, as compared with the previous years.

Financial Results of the Tariff Reform of November 1st 1904.

	1902-03	1903-04	1904-05
Income from 1st November to 30th April.	Rs. 3,27,407	Rs. 3,33,421	Rs. 4,28,877

These results, so favorable and unexpected, paved the way to a second Tariff Reform within the year under report. The Districts of Naosari and Amreli, interlaced with British territory and the territory of other States, were excluded from the benefits of the first revision, and the second revision was undertaken to benefit these two Districts. The principles on which this second reform was carried out were much the same as characterized the first reform, and may be thus enumerated :—
(a) Octroi duties in petty towns were abolished.
(b) Octroi duties in large towns were limited to a few important articles. (c) Frontier duties at Kodinar were limited to a few important articles.
(d) Duty on timber at Okha Mandal, which was a tax on ship-building, was abolished. (e) All *ad valorem* duty was abolished, and customs were levied on articles by weight, without unpacking goods. (f) The system of letting duties in farm was abolished, and State Officials were appointed to realize the same.

The second Tariff Reform was proposed by the Revenue Minister in May 1905, and was sanctioned by His Highness the Maharaja from London in June 1905; and it came into operation from 1st August 1905, *i.e.*, from the commencement of the current financial year. The changes made are shewn below in a tabular form.

Tariff Reform introduced in Naosari and Amreli from 1st August 1905.

Places.	Old System.	New System.	Remarks.
Naosari town	Toll on carts and Octroi on numerous articles.	Toll on carts and Octroi on Butter, Ghee and Kerosine only.	The duties imposed in Okha Mandal Taluka were retained except the duty on timber which was abolished. In Kadi District the Octroi duties levied in the small towns of Dehgaon and Atarsamba were also abolished on this occasion.
Kathor town in Naosari District.	Octroi on numurous articles.	Toll on carts and Octroi on Butter, Ghee and Timber only.	
Songadh and Vyara towns in Naosari District.	Octroi on numerous articles.	All abolished.	
Billimora and Gandevi towns in Naosari District.	Toll on carts and Octroi on numerous articles.	Toll on carts. All Octroi duties abolished.	
Amreli town......	Octroi duties on numerous articles.	Octroi duties on 7 articles only *viz*. (1) Ghee and Butter. (2) Sugar. (3) Edible oils. (4) Oilseeds. (5) Kerosine. (6) Groceries and Spices. (7) Cloth.	
Dhari and Damnagar towns in Amreli District.	Octroi duties on numerous articles.	All abolished.	
Kodinar Taluka in Amreli District.	Octroi duties in Kodinar town. Frontier duties on numerous articles.	Octroi duties abolished. Frontier duties limited to import duties on cloth, sugar, groceries, and kerosine, and export duties on cotton and fish.	

The financial results of this second Tariff Reform will be known in the course of the current year. It is necessary to mention that Mr. Raojibhai Patel rendered valuable assistance, both in sug-

14

gesting changes introduced by both these reforms, and also in promptly carrying out all the administrative changes which were necessary for introducing them. Both on the 1st November 1904, and on the 1st August 1905, administrative changes were made in time, and the arrangements made were found perfect in their operation.

It may also be added here that a third Tariff Reform of a sweeping nature, intended to give still further relief to the trades and industries of the State, is now under the consideration of His Highness's Government.

The following figures shew the Customs Revenue during the past three years.

Customs Revenue.

1902-03	1903-04	1904-05
Rs. 5,99,247	Rs. 6,24,275	Rs. 6,96,090

There has been an increase of very nearly a lac of rupees in the revenue within the last two years.

The expenditure incurred for the Customs offices and establishments in the State was Rs. 80,757 in 1904-05, against Rs. 79,189 in the previous year. It comes to less than 12 per cent. on the income, and is less than half the sanctioned rate of 25 per cent.

(b)—EXCISE.

A notable reform in excise administration was effected in the separation of the toddy and liquor farms in Naosari District, which came into force from the 1st August 1905 ; and a similar separation will be effected in Baroda District from the 1st August 1906, when the period of the present farm expires. Under the new system, the liquor arrangement remains the same, it is the Central Distillery system. But with regard to toddy, instead of one farmer having the monopoly for the whole District conjointly with the liquor monopoly, shops are given to licensed vendors singly, or in small convenient groups, and the toddy revenue is made up of the tree-tax and license fees. A healthy competition is thus created among the toddy shopkeepers, and also between the toddy and liquor shops, and a decided improvement in the quality of the drinks supplied is expected to be the result. At first it was feared that the liquor revenue would suffer from this arrangement ; but the separated liquor farm in Naosari has already been sold for 1905-06 to 1907-08 for Rs. 4,12,250 a year, against Rs. 3,73,080 under the old system ; and the toddy shops have been licensed for Rs. 70,568. This, with the annual tree-tax of about Rs. 70,000, gives a toddy revenue of Rs. 1,40,568, against Rs. 91,920 under the old system. The total increase of Excise Revenue in Naosari District is thus nearly *ninety thousand rupees* in 1905-06.

It may be noted here that the ownership of all toddy trees in occupied lands has been generously bestowed by His Highness on the cultivators. On the other hand, the tree-tax has been doubled to prevent toddy being sold unduly cheap.

The following table gives the Excise Revenue during the last two years.

No.	Item.	1903-04.	1904-05.
		Rs.	Rs.
1	Manufacture and sale of liquor..	5,78,248	5,80,494
2	Extraction of sale and toddy....	92,978	92,977
3	Fees for licenses to sell foreign liquor.	1,325	1,050
4	Miscellaneous	11,115	3,209
	Total...	6,84,062	6,77,729

The rates of the still head duty remain unchanged. The slight decrease in 1904-05 is explained by the famine conditions of the year.

The following table gives the total Demand and Collection in the year under review.

No.	Divisions.	Demand 1904-05.	Collection 1904-05.	Arrears.
		Rs.	Rs.	Rs.
1	Baroda	1,49,709	1,49,549	160
2	Naosari	4,67,579	4,67,509	70
3	Kadi................	52,290	45,413	6,877
4	Amreli	8,151	7,969	182
	Total..	6,77,729	6,70,441	7,288

It will be seen that in Kadi District the collection was unsatisfactory. No good explanation for this has been given.

The following statement gives the number of

shops of liquor and toddy during the year under review :—

District.	Liquor Shops.	Liquor and toddy.	Toddy Shops.	Foreign liquor Shops.	Total.
Baroda....	266	7	....	4	277
Naosari ..	123	200	43	7	373
Kadi	206	....	....	*nil*	206
Total..	595	207	43	11	856

The above statement does not include liquor shops in Amreli District, where the Outstill System still prevails.

The expenditure of the Excise Department during 1904-05 was Rs. 28,120 against Rs. 25,915 of the previous year. The expenditure is about 4 per cent. of the revenue. 166 offences against the excise law were reported in 1904-05 against 161 in the previous year, and conviction was obtained in 111 cases.

(c)—OPIUM.

The sources of Opium Revenue are these :—

(a) Profits on the sale of Opium in the Bombay market for exportation to China.

(b) Profits on Opium issued to the farmers and licensed vendors for consumption in the State.

(c) Fees for licenses for retail vend and miscellaneous receipts.

The manufacture of Opium is a State monopoly, and is conducted under a system similar to the Bengal system ; while the retail sale for consumption within the State is managed under the system in vogue in the Bombay districts.

The cultivation and manufacture of Opium were carried on in the Kadi District during the year under report. Opium poppy was cultivated under licenses in the Sidhpore Kheralu, Visnagar, Vadaoli, Pattan, Vijapur and Mehsana Talukas of that District.

The following comparative statement shews the area under poppy cultivation and its yield.

Year.	Area under cultivation in acres,	Total yield of juice lbs.	Average yield in lbs.
1903-4.	18,553	3,71,388	20
1904-5.	12,272	2,78,080	22

The decrease in the area under cultivation in 1904-05 was due to the year being less favourable than the previous year. The yield per acre was, however, better.

Licensed cultivators are bound to sell all the juice to the State at a rate fixed previous to issuing the licenses. The rate for the year under report was Rs. 3 per Seer of 40 tolas. The juice, brought by cultivators, is taken to the Opium Warehouse at Sidhpur, where it is manufactured into Opium. From this warehouse, the Opium is sent to the State Depots in the different districts to be issued to the licensed vendors, or is conveyed by rail to Bombay for export to the China market. The following statement shews the quantity of Opium sent to the Government Depots, and to

Bombay, during the year under report and the previous year.

Year.	Opium sent to Government Depots for local sale in Seers.	Opium sold at Bombay for export in Seers.	Remarks.
1903–04	24,290	1,12,124	
1904–05	23,170	1,09,044	

The system which prevailed during the year under report for the retail sale of Opium by licensed vendors is described below.

   (1). In Naosari and Amreli Districts, the license for retail sale was given to one farmer for the whole District by auction.

   (2). In Kadi District the license was given to a selected man on payment of a lump sum.

   (3). In Baroda District licenses were given for individual shops by auction.

The financial results of the sale of Opium within the State are shewn in the following table.

Year.	Cost of production.	Realised from licensed vendors.	Profit to State.
1903-04	90,135	3,22,959	2,32,823
1904-05	95,774	3,47,550	2,51,776

Eight hundred chests were sent to Bombay and sold through Messrs. David Sassoon & Co. in the

year under report. The following table will shew
the financial results of the sales at Bombay.

Year.	Cost price including interest, Railway freight, Agency &c.	Transit duty paid at Ahmedabad.	Total cost at Bombay.	Sale proceeds.	Profit to the State.
1903-4	4,97,900	4,32,200	9,30,100	11,59,836	2,29,735
1904-5	4,94,629	4,80,000	9,74,629	12,98,250	3,28,621

On account of a short crop in Malwa, due to
frost, the prices were much higher during 1904-05
than in the year previous.

Mr. Mohamed Ali the Opium Superintendent is an
Oxford Graduate, and performed his duties during
the year with his usual zeal and energy. In order
to ensure a better control over the cultivation and
manufacture of Opium, he was relieved of all district administrative work relating to the Customs,
Excise and Opium, and was in sole charge of the
manufacture and sale of Opium. With his Assistant, Mr. Rana, he was deputed in the month of April
1905 to Benares, Patna and Gazipur Opium factories
to study the process of manufacture in those
places. Suggestions made by the Superintendent since his return are now under consideration.

His Highness the Maharaja visited Sidhpur in
the month of November 1904, and the construction
of a new Warehouse at a cost of over half a lac was
sanctioned. The building is under construction.

(d) — SALT.

Our policy with regard to salt, in the three
Districts of Baroda, Kadi, and Naosari, consists in

preventing the production of salt locally, and thus guarding the interests of the British Indian Salt Revenue. The Baroda State has undertaken not to manufacture salt, not to permit the collection of earth salt, and not to allow the smuggling of British salt, in the three Districts named above. There is a special establishment for this purpose, posted at Dabka and neighbouring places on the Mahi, to prevent any salt collection or manufacture. The cost of maintaining this staff was Rs. 864 in 1904-05. In other Talukas the Vahivatdars do the needful. The entire population of the three Districts, therefore, contribute to the British Indian Revenue. The question was decided in this way in the letter of the Governor-General's Agent, No. 3682, dated 7th May, 1881; and the rules which were accordingly framed by Raja Sir T. Madhava Rao, and operate to this day with some alterations, form an enclosure to Sir T. Madhava Rao's letter No. 5585, dated 14th June 1881.

The Peninsula of Kathiawar is outside the British Indian salt line, and the manufacture of salt in Amreli District, situated in that Peninsula, is permitted under Articles of Agreement which form an enclosure to letter, dated 5th May 1887, from the Assistant Agent to the Governor-General. By these Articles, the manufacture of salt in Amreli District is limited to salt made from sea water or brine; and its importation to British India or any other Indian State, or even to Baroda, Kadi, and Naosari Districts, is prohibited. As German and other foreign salt is now imported to British India on payment of duty, it is possible that Amreli salt may be allowed at some future time to be imported into British India on payment of the same duty. At present the merchants of Okha Mandal in Amreli District export salt to Zanzibar and other places outside India, but not to the Indian Continent. Salt locally produced sells at Okha Mandal at over 260 lbs. per Rupee. British Indian salt sells at Baroda at 28 lbs. per rupee. In other words the people of Baroda pay nearly ten times as much for salt as the people of Okha Mandal pay for their local salt.

At Okha Mandal there is no restriction on the manufacture and consumption of local salt, but a royalty is paid to this State on export. At Kodinar the State has a sort of monopoly; the people who manufacture salt have to sell it to the State; and the State sells it at a higher price to the traders for local consumption. The royalty on about 23,700 local maunds of salt exported from Okha Mandal was Rs. 573 in the year under report. The income from the monopoly at Kodinar in the same year was Rs. 348, against an expenditure of Rs. 230 on the establishment,—shewing that the monopoly brings little to the State.

(e)—Agriculture.

A brief account of the principal crops of this State is given below.

Bajri (Millet) is consumed by all classes of people in the State. It is sown in June or July, requires the monsoon rain, and is reaped in October. Sometimes it is sown with pulses, and as these require a longer time to ripen, they remain in the field after the Bajri has been reaped. The refuse of the Bajri stalk is used as fodder for cattle.

Jowar (Millet) is the food of the common people. It is sown in October and reaped in January or February. Like Bajri the grain is ground and turned into bread, but sometimes it is parched or roasted. Cultivators and their wives and children, sitting in their fields day and night to protect the crops, often take a 'supply of parched Jowar with them. The stalk is used as fodder.

Wheat is consumed by the rich only, and is quite a luxury for the poor. It is sown in October and November, and reaped in March. Fields for wheat are prepared and irrigated with great care, specially in Kadi District, where wells are numerous.

Rice is sown in black soil in the month of June, and is generally reaped in September or October. It is a staple produce only in some Talukas, and depends largely on the monsoon rains.

Cotton is grown largely in Naosari and Baroda Districts. It is sometimes sown with rice, and after the rice has been reaped it grows rapidly. It flowers in October and is gathered in February or March. When full grown its height is three or four feet. It is a valuable crop for the cultivators, and is extending in Kadi and Amreli Districts. The Naosari cotton is considered the best in India.

Tobacco is a valuable crop, which grows mainly in Petlad Taluka in Baroda District, the soil of which is specially suited to the plant. The seed is sown in June, and the fields are then covered to protect them from the sun and excessive rain. The seedlings take about two months to grow to a height of about 4½ inches. In the meantime other fields have been prepared, and the seedlings are then taken away from the nursery to be transplanted in rows, in the places prepared for them. When the crop has grown to a height of a foot and a half, it begins to flower, and the cutting of the crop begins when the leaves turn yellow. The skill of the Petlad tobacco grower was greatly appreciated by Dr. Voelcker, when he visited India fifteen years ago. But the process of curing and dressing the leaf is susceptible of improvement.

Sugarcane is a valuable crop and requires good soil, much care, and a great deal of water. It is cut in the month of November or December, and the juice is turned into molasses, while the stalks are used as fuel or fodder for cattle.

Pulses.—Chana and Mug and Adhad and other pulses are grown in the winter. They are generally sown with some other kind of grain, and reaped after that grain has been harvested.

Different Crops.—The following table gives the area under the principal corps.

Area under different Crops.

No.	Name of Crops.	1903-04.		1904-05.	
		Area under Crops.	Percentage.	Area under Crops.	Percentage.
1	2	3	4	5	6
		Bigahs.		*Bigahs.*	
1	Rice......	2,96,350	6·10	2,12,449	4·47
2	Bajri	10,28,536	21·27	8,72,787	18·39
3	Jowar....	9,97,610	20·63	8,62,405	18·18
4	Wheat ..	1,49,512	3·09	1,68,104	3·54
5	Other Cereals.	3,28,182	6·78	3,28,062	6·91
6	Pulses....	4,71,799	9·69	2,82,122	5·92
7	Cotton ..	8,41,768	17·41	10,38,029	21·88
8	Opium....	29,405	·60	16,255	·34
9	Tobacco ..	33,730	·69	23,787	·66
10	Sugarcane.	2,137	·04	4,718	·09
11	Oilseeds...	5,53,464	11·42	2,53,124	5·33
12	Garden Crops.	30,729	·63	4,491	·09
13	Others....	72,002	1·49	7,77,795	16·39
14	Total	48,34,224	....	47,44,128	....

In years of scanty rainfall, cotton often yields some harvest when other crops fail. This, coupled with the good prices, has maintained a continued rise in the cultivation of cotton, which attained the first place in area during the year under report.

Agricultural Banks. — The two banks at Songadh and Harij continued to work during the year. The following table shews the business done:—

No.	Item.	Songadh Bank. 1903-04	Songadh Bank. 1904-05	Harij Bank. 1903-04	Harij Bank. 1904-05
1	Nominal capital	25,000	25,000	50,000	50,000
2	Paid up capital—				
	[a] State	12,500	12,500	12,500	12,500
	[b] Private ...	360	360	200	200
3	Deposits during the year.	2,034	12,537	....	....
4	Deposits at the end of the year.	5,378	13,768	....	......
5	Advances during the year for seeds and bullocks, marriage and funeral expenses, paying revenue and debts, etc.	13,561	15,713	7,444	1,842
6	Total outstanding ..	38,481	39,461	11,744	14,861
7	Net profit ..	563	828	674	518

The rainfall in Harij was only 5˙10 inches, and there being little cultivation, the business done by the Harij bank was insignificant. The deposits in the bank are *nil*, while the amount outstanding is nearly fifteen thousand rupees. The Songadh bank did more business, the deposits there are nearly fourteen thousand rupees, and the amount outstanding nearly forty thousand. It is satisfactory to find that both banks shew a nett profit. An Act on the lines of the Co-operative Credit Societies Act was passed during the year, and

Rules under the Act are under consideration of the Legal Remembrancer.

Seed Depots.—Of the four seed depots working before the one at Kheralu in the Kadi District was closed during the year. An Agricultural Bank is shortly to be opened in Visnagar, which will meet the local necessities better than the seed depot. A new depot was opened at Dwarka to advance good seed out of Famine Takavi advances. Seed to the value of Rs. 7,740 was sold from the depots to agriculturists during the year under report.

Baroda Agricultural School.—The School attached to the Model Farm at Baroda was placed under the charge of this department during the year under report; and the subject of Agricultural Entomology was added to the curriculum. Arrangements are also being made to train selected Circle-Officers from the different districts in this important subject at the School. The School will thus have three classes of students, viz, eight teachers from vernacular schools to be trained as agricultural teachers in village schools, eight circle-officers to be trained in entomology, and lastly the ordinary students. During the year under report, there were 31 students, 7 in the senior, and 24 in the junior class.

Baroda Model Farm.— The Baroda Farm continued to work with the same aims as in the previous year, viz.—

1. Instruction to students.
2. Experiments.
3. Production of good Seed.

Several foreign varieties of tobacco were grown side by side with local varieties under similar conditions. The local varieties gave the best yield.

Ground nut is a new crop in Gujarat, and the object of the experiment is to introduce it as a dry rotation crop in the Baroda District, and as an irrigated crop in other Districts. The big Japanese ground nut proved the most successful, but the experiment was affected by want of rain last year, the total fall amounting only to 12 inches against an average of 22 inches. The crop had to be irrigated once, and although the result is fair, further experiment will be necessary before it can be introduced.

The Kajli cane of Burdwan, which was reported by Dr. Leather to be one of the best of the hardy varieties, was tried with a view to its introduction if successful. It proved a practical failure last year, and the experiment will have to be given up.

Varieties of Cotton, Tapioca and Rami were continued, but there is no satisfactory result so far.

As mentioned in last year's report, the number of dairy cattle was reduced, and a small pure bred Gir herd of 20 cows with necessary young stock and bulls was kept up, the strength being reduced from 103 to 57.

Songadh School.—The arrangements for a seri-culture class being completed, the subject was added to the curriculum of this School, and rearing began in March 1904. 106 boys attended the School during the year. 78 appeared at the annual practical examinations in agriculture, and 60 passed. Three out of seven boys passed the Talati-examination.

Songadh Farm.—The farm continued to do very good work. As all the labour was done by the school boys and girls, the total income Rs. 2,311, left a profit of Rs. 1,189 after an expenditure of Rs. 1,122. As most of the boys on leaving the school go home and work their fields, a gradual bettering of agricultural practices in the district is expected. The Director of Agriculture visited the Farm thrice during the year, and Mr. K. B. Jadhav, District Officer of Naosari, took a great interest in the work of the farm, and made several practical and useful suggestions. The Revenue Minister visited the Songadh Farm and School and mulberry plantation there in June 1905, and was greatly interested in the institutions.

Travelling Instructors.—A further move for the introduction of improvements was made during the year, and a travelling Agricultural Instructor was appointed in Amreli in October 1904. The duties of a travelling instructor are :—

1. To induce cultivators to try plots of such crops and methods as may be approved by the Director for introduction.

2. To induce cultivators to try plot experiments of crops and methods which are likely to suceed.

3. To give lectures to cultivators on agricultural subjects.

4. To show the use of impliments approved for introduction, and to induce cultivators to use them.

Plots of Muzfurnagar wheat and Mahableshwer potato were tried in seven villages. The potato is a new crop in the district, but the people were so pleased with the results that there has been a demand for seed, and arrangements will be made to supply it this season. The wheat was not satisfactory, and a suitable variety will be selected for further trials after the next Pusa conference, where wheat is one of the subjects for consideration.

Experimental plots of eleven varieties of cotton and several good vegetables were tried in eight villages, but without any appreciable result, on account of the scarcity of rainfall.

For the Kharif season of 1905-06, ground nut and Bhaonagar Bajra have been tried for introduction in eight villages. No regular lectures were given during the year, but a large number of informal meetings were held with the cultivators.

The results in Amreli being encouraging, Travelling Instructors have been appointed in Kadi and Okhamandal from July and October 1905 respectively. The seed depot clerks are also being utilised as Travelling Instructors, and good results are expected.

Naosari Experiments.—Mr. Khaserao B. Jadhav, M.R.A.C., District Officer of Naosari, takes a very great interest in the improvement of agriculture in his district. He tried side-irrigation in Naosari and Palsana, and reports very favorably

on the results. Trials of side-irrigation have been
commenced in the Baroda and Songadh farms, and
the results will be reported next year. He is also
trying experiments in growing cotton by keeping
up a crop of Naosari cotton continuously for four
years on the same land with constant tillage between the rows, and reports satisfactorily on the
results.

Kodinar Cocoanut plantation.—The cocoanut
plantation at Sarkhadi in Kodinar was maintained
in good condition, and some of the plants are expected to fruit next year. On account of short rainfall
two·new wells had to be constructed. About 500
plants have been raised in the nursery for distribution to the people. The total cost during the year
was Rs. 718, and the income from interculture was
Rs. 20.

Bombay Exhibition.—Two cultivators from each
district were sent to the Bombay Industrial and
Agricultural Exhibition in charge of the Superintendent of the Baroda Farm, and above thirty others,
who came at their own expense, were provided with
quarters and shown the Exhibition. They seemed
most interested in the impliments and their
trials.

Entomology.—Mr. Chhotabhai Umedbhai, trained
under Mr. Lefroy, Entomologist to the Government of India, was appointed Entomologist on the
1st April 1905. Most of his time during the year
under report was passed in setting up a proper
laboratory, and attention was given to the two
diseases of the season viz., the sugarcane moth

borer and the *katra*. A trap crop of maize, sown with the sugarcane, attracts most of the moths to lay their eggs, and by destroying the maize crop the cane is saved. The trial being successful, a leaflet was prepared and printed. This will be issued to the cultivators at the next cane planting season, in order to be in their hands just at the time at which it would be most useful. *Katra* moths are being reared in the laboratory, and their life history studied, in order to find the most valuable stage when they can be destroyed. So far, the new Entomologists' work has been fairly good; but now that his laboratory is started, I expect to see greater activity in him in affording practical help to agriculturists.

Arboriculture.—The work of planting Babul seed in waste lands was continued in Baroda, and extended to the Kadi district, where 90,676 bighas of waste land were planted during the year with 16,000 lbs. of seed. The expenses during the year were Rs. 3,232 and the income Rs. 8,838. During the fourteen years this work has continued, the income has been Rs. 80,685 against an expenditure of 16,475. It must, however, be noted that the income includes the proceeds from the sale of old Babul trees on waste lands, not planted by the Department. The exact pecuniary value of the work done by the Department cannot be ascertained. A sample consignment of half a ton of Babul bark has been sent to Europe for valuation and report as to the best method of extracting tannin. The bark has very little value as fuel, and if a method of extracting tannin can be found, a new industry will be introduced.

Veterinary Surgeons.—The two Veterinary Surgeons at Baroda and Mehsana continued to do good work. 2,049 animals were treated during the year, against 1,750 in the previous year. The principal disease in the districts was foot and mouth disease. The Baroda and Kadi Veterinary Surgeons visited 117 and 61 villages respectively. The total expense was Rs. 2,493, or about one rupee per head of cattle treated.

(f)—INDUSTRIES.

Weaving.—The weaving industry of Naosari District is of ancient repute. Fine *Dhoti*, *Sari*, *Basta*, and *Bafta*, made at Naosari and Gandevi, were in great demand at the Portuguese Dutch, and English factories in Surat, in the seventeenth and eighteenth centuries, for export to Europe. The industry practically died out early in the nineteenth century, but Parsee women still manufacture quantities of *Kasti* worn by men and women, and are skilful in making ornamental borders.

In Baroda District, there is a considerable weaving industry still at Dabhoi, were fine turbans are prepared. And cloth, superior to the common coarse cloth of the lower classes, is produced at Petlad and Vaso and some other places.

In Kadi District, Pattan the old capital of Gujrat, was famous for its weaving industry. A great part of the trade was transplanted to Ahmedabad when that place was chosen as the capital, but the weaving community of Pattan still turn out a superior quality of cloth which has a fair sale. Silks, however, are the speciality of Pattan, the silk *Potala* of this town is largely in demand in all parts of Gujrat, and forms the bridal trousseau of high caste Hindu women all over the Province. The rise of Ahmedabad diverted a part of the silk as well as the cotton weaving from Pattan; but in the 18th century heavy duties were imposed on the Ahmedabad weavers by the Peshwa and the Gaekwar, and weavers in large numbers returned to their old home at Pattan. In 1818, Ahmedabad became British, cesses on manufacture were abolished, and the export duty of 15 per cent. was reduced to $2\frac{1}{2}$ per cent. The weavers of Pattan, therefore, once more migrated to Ahmedabad, and Pattan has never flourished since. The history of the weaving trade of Pattan and Ahmedabad is a lesson which fiscal reformers and administrators should remember in Baroda.

Embroidery.—Some embroidery with gold and silver and silk thread is done in Baroda, and the work, both in pattern and execution, is of a superior description. But the industry, which is largely carried on by women, is not considerable.

Dyeing.—In Padra, Sankheda, Petlad, Dabhoi, and other places in the Baroda District, dyeing and calico printing are old industries, and the colors employed are generally red, indigo and black. In the Kadi District, there is a large community of dyers at Visnagar, which is a flourishing town.

Metal work.—Dabhoi and Petlad in the Baroda District, and Kadi, Visnagar and Pattan in the

Kadi District, are known for their brass and copper ware. European copper and brass sheets are used in the manufacture, and the articles made are those in ordinary use among the people. Gold and silver ornaments of a superior description are prepared at Baroda, Pattan and Amreli. Excellent silver articles known for their fine polish are made in the last named place. The ornamental silver, copper and brass work of Raghunath Tribhuvan of Visnagar received high commendation at the Delhi Darbar Art Collection in 1903.

Pottery.—This, of course, is an extensive industry in a country were the mass of the people use earthenware for storing drinking water and other purposes. Pattan is known for its ornamental pottery.

Carpentry.—This, too, is an extensive industry, but wood engraving of a superior quality is done at Baroda, Pattan, Kadi, Visnagar, Vadnagar, and Naosari. Articles prepared in these places, of sandalwood and mahogany and other kinds of wood, have a sale in Europe.

Sculpture.—The industry has almost died out, though specimens of fine Hindu sculpture, dating from the time when Pattan was the capital of Gujrat, are to be met with everywhere. The sculptured gates of Dabhoi, and the equally fine remains of temples and structures at Sidhpur and Pattan, are among the best specimens of the Hindu sculpture of the twelfth and thirteenth centuries. Stonemasons of this State have still a good repute, and have not quite lost their ancestral skill.

Dyeing Factory.—Mention should now be made of industries carried on under modern methods, and the dyeing factory of Petlad deserves an honorable place. It was established by Parekh Narainlal Keshavlal some ten years ago, and he suffered some losses in the beginning. But he persevered, and made the concern profitable in the end, and the factory turns out about 15,000 lbs. of dyed yarn every day. The yarn is in demand in many parts of India and outside India.

Ginning Factories.—There were 49 ginning factories and 4 cotton presses in different parts of the State, in the year under report. The number of ginning factories is on the increase, and a large one with weaving apparatus has been started at Kadi in the current year, through the help and encouragement of the District Officer, Mr. Vanikar.

Chocolate and Rice Factories.—The rice factory at Billimora ought to be successful as Billimora commands a good market for rice. A chocolate factory has been started at Billimora by Mr. Godbole, who learned industries in England and Germany, and the requisite machinery has been imported from Europe. The concern is managed by a limited Company, and the Baroda Government has taken 70 shares of Rs. 100 each to encourage the promoters. Mr. Godbole, who is a Government servant, has taken a year's leave to devote himself entirely to the work of this factory.

Rectified Spirit Factory.—There is one at Naosari, the promoter being Mr. Bana. Another has been started at Baroda by Mr. Kotibhaskar.

Matches and Cigarettes.—Mr. Gokhale has started a match factory at Vyara which is still in its infancy, but promises to be' a success. Mr. Khaserao Jadhav, District Officer of Naosari, is also something of an inventor, and has produced matches and cigarettes, but the business has not yet been placed on a commercial footing.

State Cotton Mill.—In 1883–84 His Highness the Maharaja established a Cotton Spinning and Weaving Mill at Baroda at a capital expenditure of Rs. 6,35,000, with a view to encourage local manufacture. State undertakings of this kind are seldom financially successful, but the Maharaja's object was more to educate the people than to create a source of gain to the State. The Mill worked for 21 years and paid a poor interest on the capital at about 3 per cent. As the people of Baroda have now become aware of the importance of mill-industry, and as signs of private enterprise are apparent, His Highness decided to sell the State Mill with a view to encourage private capitalists and private undertakings. The State Mill was accordingly sold for Rs. 5,00,000, and was handed over to Messrs. Javerchand Laksmichand of Ahmedabad and Baroda on the 10th February 1905. The buyers have floated a Company, and their shares are selling at a high premium.

His Highness the Maharaja has not been disappointed in his expectations as to the effect of the sale on private enterprise. The successful management of one cotton mill at Baroda by private owners has encouraged others. A second Spinning and Weaving Mill Company has been successfully floated by Mr. Samal Bechar of Baroda ; the building, is approaching completion, and the requisite machinery has been ordered from Europe. A third Company has been formed by Rao Bahadur Har Govind Das, and the foundation stone of the Mill building has been laid by Yuvaraj Fateh Singh. A fourth Weaving and Spinning Company is being organized by Mr. Cowasji Thanawala, and a fifth by Mr. Hari Bhakti. Baroda will soon take its proper place as a centre of Mill-industry in Western India.

State Sugar Factory.—A factory for manufacturing sugar was started at Gandevi, some twenty years ago, by a Joint Stock Company, the State taking half the shares. The Company failed to make it a success, and the concern was bought up by the State. But it succeeded no better under State management, and the working of the factory was closed in 1894. The factory has now been sold to Messrs. K. A. Ghaswala & Co. of Poona for Rs. 60,000, and it is hoped that the concern will prosper under private management.

Private factories.—The following table shews the private factories using steam, during the year under report.

Year.	Ginning.	Cotton Presses.	Flour Mill.	Dyeing Mill.	Rice Mill.	Oil Mill.	Rope Machine.	Sawing Machine.	Weaving Mill.
1903-04	48	4	0	1	1	1	1	1	0
1904-05	49	4	1	1	1	1	1	1	1

A perceptable increase in the number is expected in the current year.

Boiler Inspection.—The Boiler Inspector inspected all the boilers in the factories mentioned above. There were two prosecutions under the Boiler Act, one for using a higher than the allowed pressure, and the other for working without a certificate. The cases were pending at the close of the year. The expenses of boiler inspection were Rs. 1,257 and the income from fees, &c., was Rs. 1,305.

Hand-looms.—With a view to introducing improved hand-looms among our weavers, a Weaving School was opened during the year under report, and Serampore, Ahmadnagar and Japanese looms were obtained for trial. The Serampore loom is cheap and useful for both fine and coarse counts, but it works only 60 picks per minute. The other two give better outturn by working from 100 to 120 picks, but they are too costly for the poor weavers. An effort was therefore made to construct a loom that would be cheap and easy of repair, and at the same time would give a large outturn. Such a loom, we believe, has been constructed, and is named *Saya-ji Loom* after His Highness the Maharaja. It was greatly admired at the Industrial Exhibition at Benares ; and, in consequence of frequent orders received for this loom from all parts of India, arrangements have been made for its construction by a private firm according to demand. Along with the construction and trial of looms a certain number of boys have been admitted into the School, and they are taught the making of healds and reeds in addition to practical weaving on the fly shuttle and improved looms. And it is intended to introduce the use of the improved hand looms in the different weaving centres of the State through the boys educated in this Weaving School.

Sericulture.—Two men were sent during the year to Bangalore to learn the Japanese system of rearing silkworms and reeling silk, and one of them has been employed at the Songadh Sericultural School on return. About 100,000 cuttings of white mulberry were obtained from Bangalore and placed in the Songadh plantation. The rearing was begun in March 1905, and three crops of Nistari worms were taken by the end of July. There were no deaths among the worms notwithstanding the excessive heat of last summer, and this points to the suitability of the climate for the multivoltine Indian worm. The services of Mr. N. G. Mukerjee, the silk expert of the Bengal Government, were borrowed by this State for three months in the current year, and arrangements have been made, with his advice, to largely extend sericulture operations in the Naosari district, under the immediate supervision of the District Officer, Mr. Khaserao B. Jadav.

Pearl Fishery.—The services of an expert Mr. Hornell were borrowed from the Ceylon Government to make enquiries as to the possibilities of pearl fishery in the Dwarka coast. The result of his investigations is not yet known.

(g) REGISTRATION.

The subjoined table gives the number of documents received for registration, their aggregate values, the gross receipts from them, and the expenses incurred on them, for the years 1903-04 and 1904-05.

Year.	No. of documents.	Their Aggregate values.	Gross receipts.	Expenditure incurred.
1903-04	25,249	81,74,604-0-0	79,899-7-6	39,791-9-3
1904-05	20,641	70,31,130-0-0	65,488-10-1	34,535-3-7

The decrease in the year 1904-05 is probably due to the famine conditions of the year.

The following is a detailed classification of documents received for registration under different heads for the year under report and for the preceding year.

Classes of documents.	1903-04.	1904-05.
Immoveable Property — I. Compulsory,		
Gifts	160	198
Sales	4,545	5,575
Mortgage with possession.	13,165	10,648
Do. without do. ...	4,679	2,055
Instruments of partition ..	234	242
Leases (above 3 years)....	507	371
Others	378	406
Total ..	23,668	19,490
II. Optional		
Leases for a term within 3 years	306	347
Total ..	306	347
III. Wills and authorities to adopt..................	337	356
Total ..	337	356

Classes of documents.	1903-04.	1904-05.
I. Compulsory, Money bonds above Rs. 1,000.	162	140
Total ..	162	140
II. Optional, Instruments of pledges with possession	14	17
Instruments of pledges without position	31	24
Divorce	20	22
Others	279	247
Total ..	344	310
Grand Total ..	24,817	20,643

Moveable Property.

The following table gives the number of the documents registered in 1904-05 and classified according to their nature.

Nature of Documents.	Number of documents registered in 1904-05
Mortgage with Possession................	10,852
Mortgage without Possession	2,666
Sales	4,842
Partition	250
Leases	759
Wills and Authorities to adopt	356
Money bonds	141
Others	834
Total ..	20,643

It will be seen that over eighteen thousand registered documents were of mortgages and sales, and all other kinds of documents aggregate to somewhat over two thousand. The small number of money bonds is remarkable in a famine year, and is partly due to liberal advances, and remissions and suspensions of revenue, ordered by the State.

Besides the Head Registrar and the four District Registrars, there were 44 Sub-Registrars or Nondhi Kamdars as they are called; and the offices of all of them except two were inspected in the year under report. These Sub-Registrars were paid by fees on income according to certain rules. But, in order to promote the efficiency of the service, and to attract a better class of men, His Highness the Maharaja has sanctioned the payment of regular monthly stipends from the 1st August 1905. The Sub-Registrars have accordingly been classified into five classes according to their seniority and past services, and the salaries fixed for the different classes are Rs. 20, 30, 40, 50, and 60 a month. A number of posts have been left open for men who have passed the Bombay University Matriculation examination, as well as the Baroda Sub-Registrar's test. It is proposed to gradually improve the tone and efficiency of the service by the introduction of such men.

Both the Inspectors of Registration, Mr. Manirai and Mr. Nadkarni performed their duties efficiently and well during the year.

(h)—STAMPS.

As before, the Accountant-General was in charge of the supply and sale of Stamps, while the supervision of the arrangements and the general working of the Stamp Act rested with this office.

The revenue derived from the sale of Stamps during the year under report, as well as during the preceding year, is shown in the following table:—

Year.	Court Fee.	Documentary.	Special Levies.	Miscellaneous receipts.	Total.
	Rs.	Rs.	Rs.	Rs.	Rs.
1903-04	3,00,182-13-6	1,15,633-3-0	11,085-12-5	14,621- 6-1	4,41,473-3-0
1904-05	2,78,437- 2-6	1,13,632-1-6	8,087- 1-5	11,691-11-5	4,11,898-0-5

The decrease during the year under report is due to the scarcity and famine which prevailed during the year.

The following statement will show the expenditure incurred under the head " Stamps " in course of the last two years:—

Year.	Expenditure.
	Rs.
1903-04	23,563- 5-1
1904-05	18,576-10-6

The decrease in expenditure is chiefly due to a smaller stock of Stamps having been ordered out from London during the last year.

No amendments were made in the Stamp Act during the year. Some changes in the law, proposed by this office, are under the consideration of the Legal Remembrancer.

The two Inspectors of Registration visited 19 Stamp Depots and 77 public offices during the year, besides the Registration offices. The breaches of the Stamp Act, reported by them, received attention. Thirty-two cases were referred for the decision of the Varisht Court, out of which the latter agreed with the office in fifteen and dissented in three. The remaining fourteen cases are pending decision.

(i)—PRINTING AND STATIONERY.

Printing.—The printing for the State is done by a contractor in the State Press at Baroda. The following are the various kinds of printing work done:—

1. The *Ajna Patrika* (Government Gazette) issued every week.
2. Forms common to all the Departments as well as special forms for each Department.
3. Books, comprising laws, rules, orders, civil lists, and works published by the Educational Department, &c.
4. Annual Reports of all Departments.
5. Inspection Reports.
6. Other miscellaneous printing work.

The period of the existing contract expires in November 1906. Some reforms are in contemplation before a fresh contract is given. The present mode of calculation for paying the printers is needlessly complex, and creates work for the establishment. And the contract itself requires to be much simplified in its conditions and details.

The total cost of all the printing work during the year under report was Rs. 93,432 as compared with Rs. 85,344 during the year preceding it.

18

Stationery.—All offices, spending more than Rs. five per month on contingencies, have to buy their stationery from the State Stationery Contractors. The following table gives the cost of principal articles during the year under report.

Writing Paper.	Note Paper and envelopes.	Leather Covers.	Candles.	Inks.	Writing Materials.	Mis.	Total.
Rs.	Rs.	Rs.	Rs.	Rs.	Rs.	Rs.	Rs.
22,536	2,926	4,350	4,253	3,686	4,133	6,187	48,071

Notice has been taken of the excessive consumption of candles and leather-covers.

The Stationery Contractors are the same firm who have the contract for printing, and it is proposed to introduce some reforms when the contract expires next November. As paper and stationery articles of a serviceable kind are now produced in India, it will be possible to arrange for the supply and use of such articles, in preference to those imported from Europe.

(j)—PORTS AND TOLLS.

Ports.—The important ports of the State are :—

1. Dwarka including Rupan.
2. Beyt.
3. Mool Dwarka.
4. Velan.
5. Billimora.
6. Naosari.

All these are Customs Ports. At the first four ports goods arriving from *Foreign Ports* pay duties not less than those prescribed by the British

Indian tariff. Goods arriving from *Indian Ports*, pay duty according to the Baroda tariff. At the last two ports, Billimora and Naosari, the customs levied belong to the British Indian Government according to an agreement with the State, and the customs levied there are therefore the same as in British Indian ports.

Improvement of Ports.—The first four ports in the list given above are in Amreli District in the Peninsula of Kathiawar. Dwarka is a famous place of pilgrimage, and attracts crowds of pilgrims from all parts of India. It is also a port of considerable importance and sends out salt, cloth and other merchandize to Zanzibar, South Africa, and elsewhere. An improvement of this port and of Beyt has long been contemplated; but no real improvement can be effected till these places are connected by rail. Negotiations for making such a connexion are on foot.

It has been stated elsewhere that some encouragement has been given to ship building in these two ports by remitting the customs duty on timber in the whole of Okhamandal Taluka. The levy of port dues has also been regulated, and small boats are exempted from such duty.

It has also been mentioned before that the trade of the ports of Mool Dwarka and Velan has been facilitated by simplifying the tariff of Kodinar Taluka. A similar simplification of the Okhamandal tariff is under contemplation.

The last two ports given in the above list are in Naosari District, and Mr. Khaserao B. Jadav,

District Officer of Naosari, takes great interest in their improvement. A tax which used to be levied on ship builders at Billimora has been abolished with other Veros. The complex port dues which used to be raised both at Billimora and at Naosari have been much simplified. And provision has been made in the current year's budget for the improvement of both the ports.

Tolls.—Outside towns, there were no tolls on roads in Baroda State, a few years ago. But after the construction of some pucca roads, certain tolls were levied in Amreli District for the maintenance of the roads. These tolls were let in farm, and caused a degree of harassment to the people and to trade out of proportion to the small income derived, especially as the last year was a year of famine. The levy of the tolls has accordingly been suspended by order of the Council till November 1906, and it is hoped their re-imposition after that date will not be found necessary.

Tolls on carts levied in towns are considered a portion of the Municipal income, and are credited to the Municipal funds. A toll is levied on the road from Bahadurpur to Sankeda for the upkeep of a causeway in the road. But as those two places now form one town, the road connecting them falls within the limits of the town, and the toll levied is a part of the Municipal income.

REVENUE—SECTION D.

(a)—Village Communities.

The Village Community, as was stated in the last Annual Report, is the basis of Indian Society and of Indian Polity; and extracts were given in that Report shewing that this ancient institution was still in a flourishing condition in the latter half of the eighteenth and the earlier portion of the nineteenth century. In his celebrated Minute of 1830, Sir Charles Metcalfe, afterwards Acting Governor-General of India, recorded the following significant remarks :—

"The union of Village Communities, each one forming a separate little State in itself, has, I conceive, contributed more than any other cause to the preservation of the people of India through all revolutions and changes which they have suffered; and it is in a high degree conducive to their happiness and to the enjoyment of a great portion of freedom and independence. I wish, therefore, that the village constitutions may never be disturbed, and I dread everything that has a tendency to break them up. I am fearful that a Revenue Settlement with each individual cultivator, as is the practice in the Ryotwari Settlement, instead of one with the Village Community through their representatives the headmen, might have this tendency."

What was foreseen by Sir Charles Metcalfe has happened in Madras and in Bombay. With the introduction of the Ryotwari Settlement, the village as a political organization has ceased to exist ; the powers and privileges of Self-Government have terminated. Common rights, common sharing of burdens, common petitions against fiscal demands, common action in emergencies, are at an end. Each individual tiller is isolated from his co-villagers, and is a separate unit in the eyes of Government. Each stands ignorant and feeble before a powerful Government, and pays the revenue which the Settlement Officer demands, or silently surrenders his land. Among the many undoubted improvements in the modern methods of administration, the ignoring of Village Communities in India will not be classed as one.

It was remarked in the last Annual Report, that in the Hindu State of Baroda, endeavours were made from the commencement of the Settlement operations to preserve as much of the old forms of Self-Government in villages as was possible. It was due to his Highness the Maharaja's personal exertions that all the old land-marks were not swept away. In a report, dated 1893, Mr. F. A. H. Elliot, then Settlement Officer, speaks of the scheme of maintaining the old village services as a scheme which " His Highness the Maharaja has personally fostered and made his own. His generous wish is that the village should once again be self-ruling." And provision was made in every village to appoint a Panchayet, and to maintain the services which it enjoyed before the introduction of the Survey and Settlement. A deduction was made from the revenue demand of every village for the maintenance of these village services.

A good beginning was thus made from the commencement of the present system of Settlement. The entire cost to the State was estimated to be 12½ lacs (Rs. 12,58,957). But the service lands held previously and the old cash payments were estimated at Rs. 9½ lacs a year, (Rs. 9,50,946). The additional annual expense which His Highness's Government undertook was, therefore, 3 lacs (Rs. 3,08,011). At this cost the State was able to maintain a village service in all the villages in the 32 Talukas of the State.

Mr. Elliot speaks with justifiable pride of this village service as a service which "cannot be paralleled on this side of India." Hereditary claims were recognised in filling up the service. The names of the servants with particulars about their services and remuneration were registered. And they were allowed the option to hold land on service tenure, or to receive their remuneration in cash. Most of them preferred the latter system. The Patel got Rs. 12 in backward villages, but in well-to-do villages Rs. 30 a year or more. The school-master got Rs. 36. It was His Highness's own idea that a school-master should be added to the body of village servants, and that one should be provided in every village which had no regular school and could produce 16 scholars of either sex. Under this rule 632 new schools were established in the State, i.e., about twenty in each Taluka, between 1891 and 1893. How this beneficent provision has contributed to the extension of primary education in Baroda will be noticed in a subsequent chapter.

But the good work was only half done yet. The unity of village was preserved to some extent under Patels and Panchayets; common services were provided; and a schoolmaster was set to work in every village. The time has now arrived for making a further advance, and this brings us to the transactions of the year under report.

Recently, the Maharaja decided to introduce the elective system in the village Panchyets, and to bestow on them ampler powers of village administration. And His Highness also conceived the idea of building up a complete system of representation from the Villages to the Taluka, and from the Talukas to the District.

The new rules for the organization of Village Panchayets were passed on December 27, 1902, and provide that every village with a population of one thousand or more should have a Panchayet of its own. When the population is less, villages should be grouped together and have a common Panchayet. The members of the Panchayet should not be less than five or more than nine in number; one-half of them should be appointed by the District Officer or the Naib Subah, and the other half should be elected by the cultivators themselves. The Patel is to be the President of the Village Panchayet, and the Accountant and the Schoolmaster are to be *ex-officio* members. The supervision of village roads, wells, tanks, and schools, of Dharamshalas, Chowras and

Devasthans, of model farms and all Government or common property, vests in the Panchyets. They help in the work of medical relief and of famine relief in times of emergency. They co-operate with village Munsiffs in settling civil disputes, and with Sub-Registrars in their official work. They see that the boundary marks in the fields are kept in order, and that the village cattle pound is properly managed. They hold monthly meetings; and each group of villages returns one member to the Local Board of the Taluka in which the villages are situated.

Panchayets were formed on these principles, and with these powers, throughout the four Districts in the year under report, and the mumber of Panchayets thus constituted in each District is shewn in the following table.

District.	Number of Panchyets.
Baroda	627
Kadi	788
Naosari	444
Amreli	212
Total ..	2,071

In this way the old system of Village Self-Government has to some extent been perpetuated, and has also been connected with the new scheme of District Self-Government.

(b)—LOCAL BOARDS.

The Local Self-Government measure, passed on September 12, 1904, provides for the creation of a Taluka Board for each Taluka, and a District Board in each District. The failure of the last monsoon, and the scarcity which had already begun to be felt in many parts of the State, were at one time thought to be unfavorable to the development of this scheme. But His Highness the Maharaja felt that Local Boards would be a help to our famine relief operations, and therefore pressed for the early organization of these Boards, so that they might be in working order when the famine was at its worst.

As regards the constitution of the Taluka Boards, it may be stated that all the villages in a Taluka are divided into a number of groups, and each group of villages returns a member to the Taluka Board. Similarly, each separate Municipality in the Taluka returns a member. And lastly, all the alienated villages in the Taluka have the privilege of choosing a member. The persons thus elected form not less than one-half of the total number of members, the other half being nominated by Government. Of the nominated members not more than half are Government servants; and the Naib Subah is the chairman of the Taluka Board.

As regards the constitution of the District Boards, it may be observed that each Taluka Board within the District elects one or more members of the District Board, and each Municipality with a population of over ten thousand, situated within the District, also sends up a member. These, with one member elected by alienated villages, are the elected members of the District Board, and their total number is not less than one-half of the total number of members. The other half are nominated by Government; and among nominated members not more than one-half are Government servants. The District Officer is the chairman of the District Board.

The total number of members fixed for the District Boards of the four Districts of the State are shown below :—

District.	No. of elected members.	No. of members nominated. (Not including the President.)
Baroda	16	16
Kadi	20	20
Naosari........	10	10
Amreli	7	7

The number fixed for each Taluka Board is shown in the statement given below, District by District.

Baroda District.

Name of Taluka.	Number of elected members.	Number of nominated members. (Not including the President).
Choranda....................	10	10
Dabhoi	10	10
Tilakwada	4	4
Padra	10	10
Petlad	18	18
Siswa	7	7
Baroda	9	9
Vaghodia	7	7
Saoli	8	8
Sinor....................	8	8
Sankheda....................	7	7

Naosari District.

Name of Taluka.	Number of elected members.	Number of nominated members. (Not including the President).
Kamrej	9	9
Gandevi	6	
Naosari	9	
Palsana	7	7
Mahua	7	7
Velachha	8	
Vyara	8	
Songadh	8	8
Vakal	3	3
Vajpur	3	3

Kadi District.

Name of Taluka.	Number of elected members.	Number of nominated members. (Not including the President).
Kadi	10	10
Kalol	10	10
Kheralu	10	10
Dehgam	9	9
Pattan	12	12
Mehsana	10	10
Vadaoli	10	10
Visnagar	9	9
Vijapur	9	9
Sidhpur	10	10
Harij	6	6
Atarsumba	6	6

Amreli District.

Name of Taluka.	Number of elected members.	Number of nominated members. (Not including the President).
Amreli	9	
Okhamandal	7	
Kodinar	8	
Damnagar	6	
Dhari.................................	8	8
Khamba	5	5

District and Taluka Boards having thus been constituted, it was necessary to provide funds, and to lay down rules, so that the Boards might commence work with the commencement of the current financial year,—1st August 1905. At a meeting of the Council on the 15th May 1905, twelve fundamental rules were laid down which may thus be summarised :—

(1) Local Boards shall have charge of village roads.

(2) May open village and temporary dispensaries and village markets, and shall manage Dharamsalas.

(3) Shall construct village tanks and wells for public use.

(4) Shall be in charge of village schools or Gramyashalas.

(5) Shall be in charge of vaccination and sanitary improvements in villages.

(6) Shall plant trees by the side of village roads where necessary.

(7) Shall maintain property vested in them.

(8) Shall maintain wharves and harbours vested in them.

(9) Shall perform the above eight classes of duties, vested in them by the law, out of the proceeds of the Local Cess, and specific grants made by the Government under the Act, as shewn below.

(10) A Government contribution of Rs. 87,000 for what were called Revenue Public Works is distributed among the Local Boards of the four Districts.

(11) The estimated proceeds of the Local Cess, after deductions provided in the law and of collection charges, amount to Rs. 2,84,000. This is distributed among the Local Boards of the four Districts. The annual Vaccination Grant of Rs. 14,000 and Primary Education Grant of Rs. 60,000 are also similarly distributed.

(12) Allotments according to the above rules, and amounting in all to Rs. 4,45,000, are made to the four Districts.

In addition to these fundamental rules laid down by the Council, some general rules were also framed by the Revenue Minister for the guidance of the newly created institutions. These rules relate to the conduct of business, the keeping of accounts, the entertainment of adequate establishments, the distribution of the District allotments among the Talukas comprised in each District and among the village Panchyets in each Taluka, the proper supervision of village schools, the construction of village works, and generally the performance of all the duties imposed on the Local Boards by the law. In the conclusion of his rules the Revenue Minister pointed out to the District Officers the added responsibilities thrown on them in the following words :—

"Every District Officer must now feel that the future development of his District in the matter of water supply, primary education, and general improvement of villages, is largely in his hands. If the District shows satisfactory progress in these matters, it will be largely due to his energy, his industry, his consciencious work. If the District shows slow and unsatisfactory progress, it will be due to his want of zeal, his lack of interest in his duties. Thus a new field of usefulness, a new scope for his industry, is opened out to every District Officer ; and I know of no part of his work which is intrinsically more important, or to which I shall attach greater importance, than the steady and gradual improvement of his District, and the development of Self-Government in the State."

It is satisfactory to note that all the District Officers have zealously responded to this call. And it is still more satisfactory to observe that the elected members of the Local Boards and of Village Panchyets have shewn a keenness and aptitude for work, and a capacity for intelligent and combined

action, which betoken happy results. His Highness
the Maharaja has evinced every desire to take
these elected members into confidence, and has
sent out orders from Europe that the Administration Report of each Taluka and of each District
should be submitted to Taluka and District Boards
for their criticism and remarks, for the consideration of the Government.

The work of the Local Boards commenced on the
1st August 1905, and will therefore form the subject
of the next Annual Report. But it may be noted here,
that, before the Boards came into legal existence,
the elected members rendered valuable service in
an informal manner in famine relief-work, in
making payments to labourers, in the distribution
of doles, and in the construction of village wells.
District Officers gladly availed themselves of these
services, and have written very favorably of the
work done. Both in Kadi and in Naosari, nearly
all the wells sanctioned as famine relief-works, for
the supply of drinking water to villagers, were done
by the villagers themselves, and done economically
and well. The following remarks of the District
Officer of Naosari deserve to be quoted :—

"No better example is required to shew that the
people are capable of working together for common
good, under intelligent guidance, than the work the
Village Panchyets did this year, all over the District,
in the repair of old wells and the construction of
new ones, to the extent of half a lac of rupees.
There are not instances wanting in which more
work was done, when found necessary, than the

estimated amount; and there are no instances in which a single work was badly done by them. This speaks volumes in their favour. These very men,—in the absence of encouragement and timely help,—would have sat with folded hands, and complained, after the work was done by contractors, that the work was badly done, and that their wants remained unsatisfied."

(c) SELF-GOVERNING MUNICIPALITIES.

About the same time that the Local Boards Act was passed, His Highness the Maharaja also issued orders for investing the more important municipalities of the State with powers of Self-Government. An Act based on the Bombay District Municipal Act of 1891 was directed to be drafted, but in the meantime His Highness ordered that the advanced municipalities should start work in the spirit of the British Indian Act, till ours was passed.

Besides the town of Baroda, eight other towns were named for the introduction of Self-Government. It has not yet been found possible, however, to make Petlad into a self-governing town ;—the other towns, in which the new system has been introduced, are these :—

> Baroda, Dabhoi, Pattan, Sidhpur, Visnagar, Naosari, Gandevi and Amreli.

The accounts of these eight towns were accordingly separated from the commencement of the year under review. Elections were held in all of them, except in Baroda, in July 1905, and the new members, partly elected and partly nominated, began their work from 1st August 1905. In this way the work of the Self-Governing Municipalities in the State commenced on the same date with that of the Local Boards.

In Baroda, the elections were delayed till October 1905, and the newly constituted Municipality of Baroda began to work from the 1st February 1906. The Municipal Act, shaped on the Bombay Act referred to above, came into operation from the same date.

There is no house tax in any of the Municipalities. But the receipts from Customs Duties and the Local Cess, and a percentage on the Excise Revenue derived in the towns, were assigned to them. Special Grants were made by the Government also, in some cases, to bring up the income of the towns to their estimated annual expenditure.

The Special Grants thus made to some towns, together with the fixed sums allotted to them for Customs, Excise, and Tolls, are shewn in the following statement.

Town.	Number of Elected Members.	Number of nominated Members including the President.	Special Grant.	Allotment from Customs, Excise, and Tolls.
			Rs.	Rs.
Amreli	12	12	3,000	7,000
Pattan	12	12	5,000	10,000
Sidhpur	10	10	Nil.	6,500
Visnagar	10	10	2,000	5,000
Dabhoi	10	10	Nil.	6,000
Naosari	12	12	5,500	8,500
Gandevi	8	8	Nil.	3,500

The above figures do not represent the total incomes of the towns, as they do not include the proceeds of the Local Cess granted to towns, nor incomes from local taxes and sources of income. In Baroda City, a Special Grant of Rs. 1,30,000 a year has been made, and the actual receipts from Octroi Daties are handed over to the Municipality. deducting the cost of collection ; but no grant is made from Excise Revenues and there are no Tolls. All towns are expected to develop their local taxes and sources of income, but no new tax can be imposed by them without the sanction of Government, and such new taxes can be only of the kinds specified in section 59 of the new Municipa Act.

Full instructions relating to the appointment of Managing Committees, the preparation of budgets, the collection of taxes, the improvement of thoroughfares, the removal of sewage, and the appointment of Municipal officers and clerks, were conveyed in the Revenue Minister's Memorandum, published in July 1905. From the accounts received from District Officers, it appears that the members of the newly created Self-Governing towns understand and appreciate their duties, and have entered on them with energy and zeal.

It will be seen from what has been stated before that Baroda town has been classed with the other Self-Governing towns for administrative purposes, and will be subject to the same Municipal Law. Nevertheless, the special importance of Baroda is recognized. It is the capital town of the State, and the seat of the Ruling Family. Its population is more than three times the population of any other town in the State ; and its income, including the Government Grant, is more than twenty times that of any other Self-Governing town. Special works to improve the sanitation and the appearance of a town so large and crowded are required from year to year ; and it is for this purpose that a special grant of Rs. 1,30,000 has been made by the Government, in addition to its other income of about two lacs.

The improvement on which His Highness the Maharaja has rightly insisted, during some years past, is a thorough drainage of this crowded town ; and it is ordered that a sum of Rs. 20,000 should be spent annually towards the completion of the great drainage scheme which has been undertaken, and partly executed. In the year 1904-05, the Municipality spent little on this drainage scheme, and a sum of Rs. 47,477, out of the Government Grant of Rs. 1,30,000, remained unexpended. The question arose if this saving had not lapsed to Government. The Council, however, with a view to push on the drainage work, decided that the saving of Rs. 46,477 would be available for the current year 1905-06, provided the Municipality added to it another sum of Rs. 40,000 from the current year's income,—the total sum of Rs. 86,477 to be spent in executing the drainage work during the current year. To this proposal ;the Municipality has consented, and measures have been taken to effect this great sanitary improvement in the present year, under the superintendence of the Chief Engineer.

The supply of drinking water for Baroda is obtained from the Ajwa lake, which is filtered and brought into the town by pipes. The water rate is still collected by the Engineering establishment, but it is proposed to hand over the collection work to the Municipality.

The system of latrine tax, which was in vogue, caused much complaint among the poorer people, and was therefore revised by the Council; and all grounds of complaint have been removed. Considerable improvements in roads and thoroughfares in the crowded localities have also been effected in the year under review, and are going on in the current year.

The principal items of expenditure in Baroda town, during the last two years, are shewn in the following statement. Making allowance for large drainage works and other improvements, a total income of 2½ lacs ought to suffice for the town in future years.

Heads of Expenditure.	1903-04.	1904-05.
	Rs.	Rs.
General Establishment	30,383	31,868
Roads	67,309	90,504
Other Public Works	9,740	10,919
Conservancy	64,008	61,483
Road Watering	14,608	14,020
Lighting	18,007	17,716
Other charges	23,071	12,470
Total	2,27,126	2,38,930

Mr. Maneklal Sakerlal Desai, M. A., of the Bombay University, was entrusted by His Highness the Maharaja with the management of the Municipality, so long as it was under Government management. He has performed his somewhat difficult duties with ability and vigour, and with much zeal for the interests of the Government. As the administration of the town passes into the hands of the elected and nominated members under the new Act, Mr. Maniklal will continue to be their Chief Officer, and will help them with his long and valuable experience in the administration of the town. Dr. Cooper, the Health Officer of the town, has also worked well. It is hoped that, under its new constitution, the Municipality will shew more rapid progress in sanitary improvements than has been done in the past, and that the by-lanes and of "poles" of this crowded city will be more thoroughly looked after.

(d)—OTHER MUNICIPALITIES.

Municipalities which are not yet sufficiently advanced for Self-Government are managed by the Vahivatdars of the Talukas in which they are situated. An annual grant is made by the Government to these towns for carrying on Municipal work, roughly in accordance with the importance and population of the towns. The 27 Municipalities of this class are shewn in the tables below, with figures shewing the population and the Government Grant in each case.

Baroda District.

Towns.	Population.	Government grant for expenditure in Rupees.
Petlad	15,282	3,144
Padra	8,289	1,705
Sinor	5,186	1,067
Sojitra	10,578	2,176
Vaso	8,765	1,802
Saoli	4,686	956
Bhadran	4,761	979
Sankheda	4,296	843
Makarpura	1,156	2,110

Kadi District.

Towns.	Population.	Government grant for expenditure in Rupees.
Kadi	18,070	2,689
Kalol	6,465	1,330
Mehsana	9,898	4,690
Kheralu	7,617	1,567
Vadnagar	13,716	2,822
Unjha	9,800	2,016
Chanasma	8,183	1,663
Vijapur	8,510	1,730
Dehgaon	4,884	2,010

Naosari District.

Towns.	Population.	Government grant for expenditure in Rupees.
Billimora	4,693	1,256
Kathor	4,467	907
Vyara	6,117	1,061
Songadh	2,533	823

Amreli District.

Towns.	Population.	Government grant for Expenditure in Rupees.
Damnagar	3,651	751
Dhari.........................	4,262	877
Kodinar......................	6,664	1,371
Dwarka.......................	7,535	1,885
Beyt	4,615	927

The Government Grants shown in the above tables virtually represent the whole Municipal incomes in respect of all the towns; and Octroi Duties levied in the towns are credited to Government. The other sources of income, like sale of manure, &c., do not bring a hundred rupees in the case of any of those towns; and there is no house tax or general assessment of property. The people are in the happy condition of paying no Municipal taxes, and having no Municipal constitutions. The Government pays virtually all their expenses, and Government Officers manage their affairs.

The Sanitary Commissioner inspects these towns in course of his tours, and suggests improvements which are carried out by local officers. Prickly pear and manure heaps were removed under his directions from many of the towns, and pits were filled up and roads repaired in Sojitra, Saoli, Sankheda, Kalol, Kheralu, Unjha and Kathor. Suggestions for the prevention of fever, &c., were printed in the form of a pamphlet, and promulgated during the year under review.

(e)—METEOROLOGICAL OBSERVATIONS.

Since the passing of the Local Boards Act in September 1904, there is no clear line of distinction between the duties of the Sanitary Commissioner and some of the duties imposed on Local Boards. The work of sanitation in villages has been imposed by the law on Local Boards. The work of vaccination, too, which the Sanitary Commissioner has hitherto supervised under the control of the Medical Department, is to some extent imposed on Local Boards by the Act. It is no longer possible, therefore, to clearly demarcate the work of the Sanitary Commissioner from that of the Local Boards Officer who is at the head of all Local Boards and Municipalities. His Highness the Maharaja has, therefore, directed that the Sanitary Commissioner should act as a colleague and help-mate to the Local Boards Officer,—both of them presiding over Revenue Section D., and supervising the same group of offices.

The Local Boards Officer, Mr. K. G. Deshpande, attended to administrative matters, and the Sanitary Commissioner, Dr. Dhurandhar, supervised the sanitation and the health of towns and villages. The duties which specially devolved on the Sanitary Commissioner are the following :—

> Meteorological Observations.
> Sanitation.
> Vital Statistics.
> Vaccination.

Dr. Krishnarao Viswanath Dhurandhar joined the service of the State in 1888, and was made

Sanitary Commissioner in 1892. He is a Fellow of the Royal Sanitary Institute of Great Britain ; and the personal distinction of Rao Bahadur was conferred on him by the British Government for his organization of Plague Relief operations in 1898, in co-operation with British Officers.

There is a second class Meteorological Station in the Central Jail in Baroda town. The results of the readings taken in this Observatory during the year 1904-05 may be summarized thus :—Barometer average monthly records,—lowest in July, 29˙488, and highest in January, 29˙926. The lowest average temperature during the same year was reached on January 30th, when the thermometer fell to 36˙6 degrees, while the highest point was reached on May 21st, when it rose to 113˙1. The average temperature in 1904-05 was 78˙5 degrees. "The mean increase in heat," says Dr. Dhurandhar, "synchronized with the less number of plague cases and deaths in the city."

The prevailing winds during most part of the year have a decided westerly component, and this west wind is from the sea. The direction of the wind points to the direction in which the main streets in Baroda and other towns ought to run. The average daily velocity varied from 92 miles in October to 314 miles in June ; and the mean daily velocity during the year under report was 178 miles.

(f)—SANITATION.

The Sanitary Commissioner's winter tour commenced on the 21st November 1904, and, with few intermissions, lasted till 19th June 1905.

At each place visited, the general cleanliness of the town and its adjacent places was observed and recorded. Some of the local nuisances were at once removed, and suggestions were made to the District Officers to remove the rest. Attention was principally directed towards the purity of wells, tanks and rivers, and the prompt removal of human and animal ordure and their safe deposition in places set apart by Government for the purpose. Some progress has been made in this direction.

The work of setting apart lands outside all places having a population of two thousand and upwards, for the storage of manure and for natural purposes, is very nearly completed. This measure, unique in this part of the country, has contributed largely to the surface and subsoil purification of inhabited areas.

In the absence of drainage, the removal of dirty water from houses is causing some anxiety. In a few places sullage water carts are provided, but their number is very small. Arrangements are being made for experimental Septic Tank installations in Baroda City and in the Districts.

The Municipalities of Kathor, Sojitra and Vaso had no resident officers. This difficulty is now overcome, and the sanitary condition of these places is expected to show marked improvement in future. The twin towns of Sankheda and Bahadurpur have been put under one Municipality.

Markets and Slaughter Houses were inspected, and recommendations were made for their improvement.

Model wells for providing potable water were built at Chanasma and Harij, and more will be shortly constructed in other parts of the territory.

At some of the places visited by the Sanitary Commissioner, popular lectures were delivered on sanitary subjects, such as personal care of health, cleanliness, purity of water, air and soil, mosquitoes and malaria, &c. Similarly, by command of His Highness the Maharaja, small tracts on sanitary subjects are being published in the Vernacular, and distributed broadcast. Two of this kind, *viz.*, Principles of Sanitation, and Benefits from Good Water, have been issued. Other leaflets are in course of preparation.

A circular was issued during the year under report, containing suggestions for the sanitary improvement of villages.

(g)—VITAL STATISTICS.

Births and deaths during the last 3 years are shown in the following table :—

Year.	Births.	Deaths.	Births per mille.	Deaths per mille.
1902–03	36,095	61,718	17·4	31·6
1903–04	39,730	64,892	20·3	33·2
1904–05	43,584	48,227	22·3	24·7

Making every allowance for imperfect registration, the increase in the number of births, and the decrease in the number of deaths, in 1904-05 as compared with the two previous years, are satisfactory. They are due firstly to the decrease of plague, and secondly to the disappearance of famine in 1903-04.

More than one-half of the total deaths was due to "fever," a name in which are ignorantly included many diseases, the prominent symptom of which is a rise in the temperature of the skin. The beginning and the end of the cold weather, December 1904 and March 1905, were the worst months for fever in the last year, as they are in most years. The month of July 1905 was, curiously enough, the month most free from fevers.

Deaths from cholera were not many—141 in 1904-05 against 151 in 1903-04. Small-pox carried away 1002 in the last year as against 601 in the previous year. No explanation has been given for this increase. The deaths from dysentery and diarrhœa were 958 in 1904-05 against 1,050 in 1903-04.

The largest mortality, next after fever, was from plague, the figures for which are given below for the last eight years :—

Years.	Attack.	Deaths.	Remarks.
1896–97	} 3,289	2,637	From October 1896 to June 1898.
1897–98			
1898–99	4,289	3,086	
1899–1900	501	365	
1900–01	583	350	
1901–02	4,838	8,308	
1902–03	14,207	10,196	
1903–04	19,982	14,949	
1904–05	13,030	9,360	

These great variations in deaths from plague during the last nine years lead one to the conclusion

that plague follows on the heels of famine.
The years 1897 and 1898 were famine years, and
deaths from plague were high in the 1897-98 and
1898-99. Then there was a sudden drop in the
figures in years of comparative prosperity. There
were famines and scarcity again from the latter
end of 1900 to the latter end of 1903, and deaths
from plague mounted higher than before in
1901-02, 1902-03, and 1903-04. The harvests of
1903-04 were comparatively good, and plague cases
went down in the year under report.

(h)—VACCINATION.

The strength of the Vaccination Department
remained the same as in the previous year, except
that the posts of the General Duty Vaccinator and
his peon were abolished from the 1st of June 1905.

The subjoined table gives the number of persons
vaccinated during the year under report as compared with the preceding year :—

Persons.	1904-05	1905-04
Males.................	30,520	28,016
Females	27,955	24,786

The total expenditure for vaccination during the
year under report was Rs. 13,732.

By an order of the Council, dated 17th October
1905, the Sanitary Commissioner has been invested
with the powers of the Chief Medical Officer in
respect appointments relating to Sanitation and
Vaccination. And the four Sanitation and Vaccina-

tion Inspectors have been graded as shewn in the following list :—

> 1 Place of Rs. 70.
> 1 ,,   ,, Rs. 60.
> 1. ,,   ,, Rs. 50.
> 1 ,,   ,, Rs. 45.

It was also ordered by the Council on the same date that men with the qualifications of Hospital Assistants should be appointed Sanitation and Vaccination Inspectors.

The Sanitary Commissioner exercises control over all Vaccination operations. It is the duty of Local Boards to look after the needs and requirements of the people in the localities within their jurisdiction.

REVENUE–SECTION E.

(a)—RESERVED FORESTS.

Before 1873, Land Revenue was often realised by men to whom the revenues were farmed; and the farmer was free to do anything he liked with the forests of the Taluka for which he got a lease. He fixed his rates for forest produce, and made as much money as he could during his tenure. On the abolition of this farm system, the State directly realised the forest revenue by locating Nakas or forest depots at several places. At these Nakas passes were issued for all sorts of forest produce, green or dry, at fixed rates. This system obtained till 1877, when a separate Department was established to look after the State's forest interests. From 1877 to 1884 the Department was under two junior Officers of the Bombay forest service, Messrs. Ukadvei & Oke. The former succumbed to the malaria of the forest, and the latter did not give satisfaction, and reverted to the British service.

From 1884 to 1890 the forests remained in charge of several Naib Subhas of the Revenue Department. These Officers unfortunately continued the system introduced by Mr. Oke, *viz.*, selling green timber from one end of the forest to the other at the option of the contractors, who undertook to pay certain fee per khandi (about 12½ cubic ft.) of timber removed. This completed the work of denuding the forests of all timber of large dimensions.

In 1891 the services of Mr. E. E. Fernandez of British India Service were obtained, and he gradually put a stop to the old system. He got sanction to a Forest Act which gave a legal basis to State Forests, but reverted to British service in 1894. The chief work of defining the State Forests, reserving the promising portions, fixing their boundaries, and preparing Working Plans, still remained to be done. This work was undertaken, and has been accomplished, by the present Conservator, Mr. Gustadji Mediwala, who received his education in Europe, and was appointed head of the Forest Department in 1894.

It was found necessary to give the Forest Reserves a long rest. With this object in view the forest revenue from 1894 to 1903 was confined to the area left out of the Reserves, *i.e.*, the area which is open to extension of cultivation. None of the Reserves during the period was called on to contribute to forest revenue except dead fallen wood and bamboo.

The forests which are to be permanently maintained as such are called Reserved Forests, while the rest of the area is called Unreserved Forests. The intermediate class of Protected Forests is not recognised, so that the whole of the non-reserved area is left open to extension of cultivation. The area of Reserved Forests remained unchanged during the year under report, except for an addition of 1950 bighas in Songadh Taluka, the notification for which came into force on the 1st August 1905. The

total area of Reserves on the 31st of July 1905 was
7,39,220 bighas.

Name of Range.	Name of Taluka.	Area in Bighas	Total area of each range in Bighas.
1. Mahua	Mahua	11,457	13,273
	Naosari......	1,816	
2. Vyara.	Vyara	91,803	91,803
3. Sadadvel ..	Songhad	73,631	73,631
4. Tapti......	Vyara	1,943	288,994
	Songhad	11,091	
	Vajpur	275,955	
5. Vakal	Vellachha	1,168	127,314
	Vakal........	19,296	
	Vajpur	106,850	
6. Gir.........	Dhari........	78,848	87,077
	Kodinar......	8,229	
7. Sankheda..	Sankheda	13,514	57,131
	Saoli	24,651	
	Vaghodia	18,966	
	Total		739,223 or 680 sq. miles.

Settlement and Demarcation.—The Settlement
work is practically completed. No alterations in
the limits of the Reserves, or in the concessions
made to the Ryots therein, were made during the
year. Marking out the external boundary by
proper marks is done by a cleared line and special
stone cairns or earthen bands. During the year, 7¼
miles of boundary were cleared. The eight coupes
of Mahua and Vyara Ranges, worked during the
year, were marked out by some 2,000 earthen bands.

Working Plans.—Having completed the work of
demarcating all the Reserves, Mr. Mediwala
took in hand the work of prescribing regular
Working Plans for each Reserve.

Plans for Mahua and Vyara Ranges came into
force during the year under report, 1904-05. Eight
coupes were worked, bringing Rs. 9,726 to the

State. In these eight coupes, everything under a certain girth, and trees marked as Standards, were left uncut and allowed to stand over for 20 years more. The object of the plan is to build up forest capital, and not to draw on it. The Standards left over, and a detailed description of the crop and ground, with a stock map of each coupe, are carefully recorded in a register kept in the Conservator's office, and changes are noted therein from time to time.

Eight other coupes in Mahua and Vyara, to be worked during the current year 1905-06, were marked out on the ground, their boundaries defined, and the Standards therein marked, counted, and duly registered. As a result of the working of the coupes in accordance with plans, villagers have profited greatly by the steady supply of small material, and the working has given labour and occupation to all who required it. Local trade has developed, and the revenue realised has been fair.

Working Plans were also submitted during the year for Sadadvel and Sankheda Ranges. They were sanctioned towards the close of the working season.

Working Plans have still to be prepared for the remaining three Ranges, *viz.*, Tapti, Vakal, and Gir. The Assistant Conservator and the Working Plan-Officer toured for a considerable time in parts of Tapti and Vakal, and made preliminary and valuation surveys and estimates, and also collected other information for the preparation of Working Plans for those forests.

Protection from fire.—In spite of the fact that this is only the third year for work of this nature, the work done has proved encouraging. Many areas, specially in Sankheda, Gir and Mahua Ranges, were self-protected, owing to the grass having been either grazed or cut off. In Vyara, the Reserves being interlocated with the villages that have to be maintained within its body, nearly sixty per cent. of the area was overrun by fire.

As only Rs. 1,000 was sanctioned for an area of 680 square miles, all that could be done for protection was to clear the important boundary lines. It was not possible employ fire-guards within the allotment sanctioned; and all our endeavours at present are confined to a general protection against fire, and furthering the work of cutting and clearing foreign boundary lines. During the year about 7½ miles of foreign boundary were cut, and 37 miles of roads were cleared.

Protection from Cattle.—Out of the total area of 7,39,223 bighas of Reserve, 42,752 bighas only were closed against grazing. In the open area cattle were allowed to graze on payment of fixed fees, preference being given to local cattle. No grass was removed from this open area except in Gir.

The closed area was as follows :—

Sankheda Range	...	21,610	bighas
Gir	,,	... 18,225	,,
Mahua	,,	... 2,582	,,
Vyara	,,	... 335	,,

Total... 42,752

Grass was extracted from these closed areas, the revenue being realised by auction sales, except in Gir where departmental agency was employed.

Grazing offences committed consisted of (1) grazing in closed forests, (2) grazing in open forest without pass, (3) trespass of sheep and goats which were not allowed except in certain portions of Gir, Tapti and Vyara Ranges. Such offences were generally punished by impounding the cattle which had committed the offence, but in cases where such impounding would cause great harassment, due to the distance of the cattle-pound, sums were taken in compensation, and the offences compounded by the order of the Conservator himself. No prosecution under this head was instituted during the year. The number of cattle impounded was only 165.

Protection against Injuries.—Creeper cutting was carried out in the coupes worked according to the Working Plans in portions of Mahua and Sankheda Ranges. An attack of locusts, which did some damage in 1903-04, was feared this year as well ; but natural causes seem to have checked their development rather than the efforts made to destroy them in their hopper state.

Sylviculture.—The rainfall, though defective in parts, was on the whole good, and natural regeneration has made fair progress in localities that have been immune from fires. Teak and Sadad have seeded freely. Particular attention was paid by the Conservator during his tour to the subject of natural reproduction of teak. He found it generally good in Mahua and Songadh, and excellent in Vyara. Teak seedlings were abundant in the valley of the Tapti. In the coupes that were closed in Mahua and Vyara Ranges, the coppice growth from the stools of teak was very vigorous. The "coppice with standard" system adopted for these Reserves offers sufficient shelter to seedlings without unduly exposing the ground covering.

The process of artificial reproduction, being a costly concern, is adhered to only in those localities where natural reproduction is considered insufficient. During his tour, the Conservator, after inspecting the work of last season, gave instructions on the subject, pointing out the areas to be treated, and the species to be tried. The table below shows the work done during the year.

Kinds of seeds.	Weight in lbs.							
	Tapi.	Sadadvel.	Vyara.	Vakal.	Mahua.	Sankheda.	Gfr.	Total.
Teak	35	10	24	180	110	65	12	436
Khair ..	...	10	5	37	110	....	....	162
Biya	....	15	2		....	....	....	17
Sadad ..	33	15	30	110	...	25	18	231
Sisam ..	....	15	1	....	....	—	....	16
Babul ..	....	0	....	....	....	156	10	166
Tanach..	....	15	....	1	....	....	...	16
Nim	....	....	....	....	....	....	11	11
Tibru ..	....	....	....	...	....	....	16	16
Behda ...	....	....	....	....	....	....	2	2
Aritha ..	....	....	....	....	....	....	1	1
Sabda ..	....	....	....	....	....	....	6	6
Kagar ..	....	....	....	13	....	....	....	13
Kati	....	....	....	15	....	....	....	15
Befri....	½	....	....	....	....	....	....	½
Total Wts..	68½	80	62	356	220	246	76	1,108½
Number.								
Bamboo..	25	—	—	—	—	1,500	—	1,525
Aloe	—	—	—	—	—	4,000	—	4,000
Mango ..	—	—	2,751	—	—	—	263	3,014

Befri, a wild plant growing in wooded parts of the country, yields seeds which are found nutritious enough to sustain health, as was pointed out by the Chief Medical Officer Dr. Shamsuddin. They were freely made use of during the last famine. Seeds were sown broadcast, year before last. The plants grew up well and yielded seeds. These are now being scattered over different parts of the forest.

Wherever the Working Plan is brought into force, this work of artificial regeneration is confined to the coupes cut over. The seeds are mostly dibbled in, grass is removed from about the plants, and sometimes the area is closed in with a temporary fence of babul branches.

The Sankheda and Gir Ranges are badly in want of such reproduction, or more correctly speaking of more vegetation. The Conservator supervised the efforts made in this direction by both the Rangers, who have succeeded in starting and establishing special spots in their Ranges. The work of bringing in and establishing bamboo in Sankheda was well attended to. At three places in this Range, bamboo was introduced during the year ; and as a result some 1,500 rootstocks are established.

Khambhalia Mango Plantation.—At Kambhalia, in Vyara, a great annual fair is held in honour of Unai Mata on the 15th day of Chaitra. The fair lasts five or six days, and thousands of people collect there. There is not enough shelter for the pilgrims. Along the net-work of roads laid out there, a few mango trees exist of the former plantation, and 200 seedlings were transplanted in August 1904, of which 169 have survived and attained a height of 3 to 4 feet. During July and August 1905, 82 more of the best variety of Gandevi mangoes, and a dozen seedlings of Fans (Artocarpus Integrifolia) and Jamboo (Euginia Jambolana) were put in on a plot adjoining the famous hot water springs. The nursery there has 2,500 plants of mango in stock for use next year. The cost of the undertaking upto date is Rs. 200 only. The results achieved have proved satisfactory in every respect. It is proposed to extend the work, and to bring some 40 bighas in all under mango plantation.

Umrat Reboisement work.—Between the Midhola on the north, and Purna on the south, extended a stretch of about 10 miles of low sandy coast afflicted with the invasion of fine sand brought up by the tides. Owing to this invasion, the inhabitants of Dipla were obliged to remove their village site several hundred yards inland. The sand advanced inland and threatened to cover that site as well. Large mounds of sand also accumulated before the huts of Danti village. And the sand plague affected the palace grounds of Umrat as well.

It was in 1894 that the work of fixing the flowing sand was undertaken. Every kind of cattle was kept out. Efforts were directed to secure grass on the dunes. Extensive planting of the creeper called Mariad-vael was undertaken year after year.

All sorts of trees in cluding palms, casuarina, agavas, date, babul &c., were tried on the area, and a permanent nursery was maintained besides two temporary ones. During the course of the first nearly a lac of palm seeds were sown, and more than three-fourths germinated. The results of these operations are apparent. The new site of Dipla is secured, the inflow at Danti is stopped, and the palace and the grounds of Umrat are free from sand invasions. The frontage is covered with all sorts of bushes, the babul and the casuarina showing up prominently. For the last three years no seeds from outside are indented for, as the established plants are now capable of supplying the quantity of seeds required. Among the results of this reboisement it may be noted, that, whereas formerly no water was to be had in this tract, good water supply is now available. Two big wells are sunk, and these are the only reliable sources of water in the neighbourhood.

Improvement Fellings.—Owing to great mortality among several species, these were more extensive in 1904-05 than in the year before. Dead wood, if not removed in time, is money lost; besides it helps to add to the annual fires. The area exploited was about 100 square miles. Dead teak, tanach, and khair fetched Rs. 6, and Biya Rs. 3 a cartload. In all, 886 cartloads were removed, realising Rs. 4,528. This came from the reserved as well as the unreserved area.

Coppice Fellings.—These spread over an area of 3,584 bighas in the Mahua and Vyara Ranges in accordance with the Working Plans. Every thing under 12 inches girth, and 33,535 promising sound trees marked as Standards, were left on the ground untouched, to stand over for the next rotation, 20 years hence; the rest was cut and removed. The realisation came to Rs. 9,726. The realisation from the coupes of the current year is Rs. 20,927.

Minor Forest Produce.—The minor forest produce was taken from the forests on permits principally for bamboo, dead fuel, fodder, and grazing and thatching material. Articles like honey, wax, dying-material, gum, several oil seeds, oil grass, katechu, and cigar leaves, were taken under contract. Grass was sold from certain reserved areas and from closed forests.

To encourage local industry, special concessions were given to Mr. Bana of Naosari to experiment on trees in the Reserves for lac, by artificially ingrafting Khakar and Kosham trees with the impregnated seeds of the lac insect. Unfortunately the experiment could not be prolonged, owing to Mr. Bana's continued absence from Naosari. It is proposed to try and take up this matter departmentally next season.

Very liberal concessions have been made by His Highness to the firm of Gokhle and Tambat for match manufacture. The factory is established at Vyara, the wood required for the business is given practically free, a nominal charge of ½ anna per cartload removed from forest being made. Though this system is working for the last four years, very little progress has been made by the firm, and only 51 cartloads were taken during the last year.

Exploitation by the Department.—Fellings of this nature consisted of trees cut in clearing boundary lines, and of trees cut for Working Plan purposes. The produce thus extracted realised Rs. 161. The operation of removing big timber from Kherwada and Amkuti forests comes under this head.

Exploitation by Lessees.—The articles extracted and their net realizations in 1904-05, compared to those for the previous year, are given below :—

	1903-04.	1904-05.
Minor produce—	Rs.	Rs.
Grass	7,179	9,518
Asitra and Temru Leaves..	1,045	1,942
Rosa oil	72	38
Mahua fruit, flower	1,256	775
Gum etc.	105	493
Hides	44	199
	9,700	12,964
Major produce—		
Tapi Range	13,646	8,648
Sadadvel Range	424	1,908
Vyara ,, ...	6,211	12,972
Vakal ,, ...	787	229
Mahua ,, ...	834	3,075
Sankheda ,, ...	901	....
	22,754	26,852

Exploitation by Purchasers.—Under the permit system forest depots are established at the chief outlets, and a special establishment is entertained to issue permits and check the material trough out from the forests by permit holders.   The quantity thus removed is given below :—

Items.	1903-04.	1904-05.
Dry timber—		
Cartload..................	996	917
Number	33,303	617
Fuel.—		
Cartload..................	15,584	9,086
Number	877	496
Bamboo.—		
Cartload..................	346	130
Number	11,49,233	15,05,288
Grass.—		
Cartload..................	364	12,140
Headload	158	9,842
Grazing.—		
Heads of cattle	34,597	37,351

Exploitation by Free Grants.—The table below shows the classes of produce given away free and their value in money. This grant is regulated by a special regulation which allows Rs. 5 worth of forest produce to each household of the area named. The total value of such free grant came to Rs. 8,484 during the year. The statement does not include the hundreds of thousands of headloads of firewood and thatching material removed for *bona fide* home consumption:—

Produce given free.	1903-04.	1904-05.
	Rs.	Rs.
Sadad	97	200
Kagar	24	22
Rafters	13	14
Axle for carts	74	122
Poles ,, ,, ...	30	140
Plough pieces	378	234
Fuel	2,677	2,537
Bamboo	3,408	3,694
Fencing material	885	860
Thatching ,, ...	690	429
Poles for hut...............	507	68
Miscellaneous	345	246

By a further concession His Highness the Maharaja has bestowed on cultivators the ownership of trees standing in their holdings. This will save them from much harassment from the subordinates of the Forest Department.

Summary of Produce removed.—The statement below shows at a glance the figures for the whole State :—

Produce.	1903-04.		1904-05.	
	Quantity.	Rs.	Quantity.	Rs.
Produce of clear and improvement cuttings.	...	25,983	...	33,448
Dry timber.—				
Cartloads	996	2,532	917	4,539
Number	3,197	878	617	153
Card axles and poles	30,124	2,460	28,031	2,198
Fuel.—				
Cartloads	15,584	5,822	9,086	3,942
Number	877	27	498	13
By auction sales..	...	1,921	...	8,959
Bamboo.—				
Cartloads	346	173	130	86
Number	11,49,233	24,520	15,05,288	32,141
By sales..........	...	4,200	...	4,465
Miscellaneous.—				
Produce sold at depots	...	9,693	...	9,940
Miscellaneous.—				
By passes and sales	...	10,323	...	21,082
Fines, refund &c.,	...	46	...	73
		89,778		121,039

Grass Operations.—During the year under report crops failed in the greater portion of Kathiawar; and Amreli, Damnagar and Okha Talukas were badly in need of fodder as early as September 1905. Speedy means were taken to preserve all the grass produced in the forest of Gir Range. The two large plots in Dhari and the whole of Kodinar Reserve were kept for departmental work. Grazing was supplied to the cattle, preference being given to the Baroda State cattle. In addition to the three pacca wells sunk during the famine of 1900, three more, costing Rs. 600 each, were undertaken by way of affording relief to those who accompanied cattle from distant parts, and some 20 kacha wells were cleaned and deepened from time to time. Head loads of grass were allowed at a nominal charge of 2 pice. 9,842 headloads were taken to Dhari for sale. Export of grass outside Baroda limits was prohibited. From the Dhari plots, 8366 cartloads of grass were supplied to the cultivators of Amreli and Damnagar Talukas—the cultivators being required to come to Gir with permits from local Revenue Authorities. The price charged for grass by private persons ranged from 1-12 to 2-8 per cartload; however these cultivators were charged the usual rate 0-12 only by the State. The work of cutting and stacking grass procured about Rs. 9,000 to the labourers residing on the borders of the forest.

Departmental agency was employed in cutting and transporting grass from Kodinar forests to Okhamandal. 5,46,227 lbs. of grass were cut at a cost of Rs. 614, and sent via Kodinar bunder to Dwarka by sea. 2,134 cattle grazed free in the Reserve, and 4,192 headloads of grass were given free.

(b)—UNRESERVED FORESTS.

In unreserved forests all produce except grass was under the jurisdiction of the Forest Department. The grass was auctioned by Officers of the Revenue

Department. This dual jurisdiction caused endless trouble to the State, and much harassment to the people. After a great deal of discussion and controversy it has at last been decided, that unreserved forests,—which are mere waste-lands and not real forests,—should be managed by the Revenue Department alone, the sale-produce of certain valuable trees being credited to the Forest Department.

Another improvement introduced during the year was in the matter of duties levied on timber taken to Vyara or Songadh. The duty levied was Rs. 1 and anna 1 per cartload of timber and fuel respectively. This duty was abolished. The result is that there is already a rush of forest contractors for obtaining suitable sites for establishing timber depots. Several plots of ground near and adjoining to the Railway Station have already been secured by forest contractors. Thus there is every possibility of timber trade being established at Vyara in course of a year or two.

Financial Results.—The arrears out-standing from previous years were reduced from Rs. 14,603 to Rs. 12,098. The realizations of the last four years are shown in the following table :—

Year.	Demand.	Actual Realisation.
	Rs.	Rs.
1901–02	91,152	88,364
1902–03	58,582	54,828
1903–04	89,177	88,552
1904–05	1,21,089	1,18,303

Adding Rs. 2,253 collected out of the arrears, the total realization during 1904-05 was 1,20,556, including the income from reserved and unreserved forests.

The total expenditure during these four years is shown in the following table :—

Year.	Expenditure.
	Rs.
1901–02	53,812
1902–03	52,451
1903–04	54,607
1904–05	63,939

Great credit is due to the Conservator Mr. Medhi-wala for the zeal and constant care with which he has supervised forest operations, and has succeeded, after years of toil, to make the forests of Baroda a substantial source of revenue to the State, and of undoubted benefit to the people.

IX. LAND SETTLEMENT.

(a)—History of Past Years.

His Highness the present Maharaja assumed the reigns of administration in 1881-82, and in the following year the new Survey Settlement operations were introduced. A proclamation was issued in 1883, forbidding the alienation of lands. Steps were taken to redeem lands which had been previously alienated. And it was declared that future alienations would not be valid, and lands so alienated would be considered and treated as *Khalsa*, without the payment of any compensation to the vendee or the mortgagee. The new Survey Settlement was entrusted to Mr. F. A. H. Elliot, a Bombay Civilian, who had been tutor to His Highness, and who had acquired an extensive and minute knowledge of Baroda by his long residence in the State. The varied and valuable information acquired by him has been carefully arranged and published in the *Baroda Gazetteer* published in 1883, and forming Vol. VII of the *Gazetteer* of the Bombay Presidency.

The system introduced in 1882-83 is virtually the Bombay system, and has all the merits and demerits of the Bombay system. It introduced fixity and order where there was uncertainty. It equalized the Land Tax to a large extent, basing it on the capabilities of the soil. And it imposed rates which were somewhat lower than the previous demands. On the other hand, it finally took away from Village Communities that function which Village Communities had performed in India since

times immemorial, and thereby weakened a
useful organization indigenous to the land. It
made the revenue payable by tenants dependant
on the will and judgment of one Officer, without
any consultation with the tenants themselves, either
individually, or collectively through their headmen
and representatives. And lastly it swept away that
Bhagbatai system, or payment in kind, which was
still prevailing in some Talukas of Amreli, and
fixed one unvarying money demand which, to the
cultivator, means a larger demand on the produce
of his field than the current prices of crops would
indicate. The lowering of the revenue demand
brought no relief, when that demand had to be
met by cash payments.

It reflects high credit on the discernment and
the sound judgment of Mr. Elliot that, although
he introduced the fixed cash *Bighoti* system in
imitation of the Bombay rules, he did not altogether desire to surrender the old *Bhagbatai* system.
Before leaving the service of this State, he strong-
ly recommended that, in the District of Amreli,
where seasons are so variable and uncertain, a
Varying Bighoti system should be introduced.
His idea was, that the assessment should vary from
year to year, according to the character of the
harvests obtained, so that, taking good years with
bad years, the Government demand would average
what is now the fixed annual demand. In years of
bumper harvests the Government should take more
than the present demand, and in bad years they
should take less. The scheme prepared by Mr.

Elliot on this principle, which corresponds with the principle of the old *Bhagbatai* system, is still under the consideration of His Highness the Maharaja. And the recent orders passed by the Government of India, for granting remissions when corps fail, follow to some extent the principle of the old *Bhagbatai* system.

The Settlements made by Mr. Elliot and his successors were generally for fifteen years, and a large number of Veros, or special taxes on agriculturists, were abolished as the new Settlement was introduced. A tabular statement showing the dates on which the new Settlement was introduced in the different Talukas is given below :—

Serial Number.	Name of Taluka.	In what year the new Settlement introduced.	Period of Settlement.
1	2	3	4
	Kadi District.		
1	Sidhpur	1891-92	15 years.
2	Pattan	1893-94	,,
3	Dehgaon and Atarsumba	1894-95	,,
4	Harij	1895-96	,,
5	Kheralu	Do.	,,
6	Visnagar	1896-97	.,
7	Kadi....	Do.	,,
8	Mehsana	Do.	,,
9	Vadaoli	1897-98	,,
10	Kalol	1898-99	,,
11	Vijapur ... ... —	1899-1900	,,
	Baroda District.		
1	Padra	1888-89	15 years.
2	Dabhoi	Do.	,,
3	Sinor	1889-90	,,
4	Jarod	1890-91	,,
5	Choranda	1891-92	,,
6	Baroda	Do.	,,
7	Sankheda	Do.	,,
8	Tilakwada	1892-93	,,
9	Petlad and Siswa	Under consideration.	

Serial Number.	Name of Taluka.	In what year the new Settlement introduced.	Period of Settlement.
1	2	3	4
	Naosari District.		
1	Gandevi	1896–92	,,
2	Naosari	Do.	,,
3	Palsana	Do.	,,
4	Kamrej	Do.	,,
5	Velachha..............	Do.	,,
6	Mahua	1896–97	,,
7	Songadh	1902–03	2 years.
8	Vyara	Under Set-tlement.	
9	Vajpur..............	Not introduc-ed as yet.	
	Armeli District.		
1	Damnagar	1884–85	15 years.
2	Amreli, except Bhim-katta.	1885–86	,,
3	Kodinar	1886–87	,,
4	Dhari	Do.	,,
5	Okhamandal	1902–03	2 years.

It will be seen that, except at Songadh and Okha Mandal, where the Settlements made were of a tentative nature, all other Settlements were made for 15 years. It is proposed now to make revised Settlements for 30 years, and in the case of Songadh, a Settlement for 30 years has already been made.

(b).—WORK DONE IN 1904-05.

Mr. C. N. Seddon of the Bombay Civil Service, whose services have been lent to the Baroda Government, joined his duties here on November 17, 1904, and has been in charge of the Settlement Department since. Mr. Seddon's thorough knowledge of the Persian and Gujrati languages, his sympathy with the people, and his experience in revenue and administrative work, eminently befit him for the duties now entrusted to him as Settlement Commissioner of Baroda.

The principal work done during the year under report is noted below :—

Vyara Taluka.—The original measurement and classification work of this Taluka was completed within the year under review ; and it is expected that the new *Jamabandi* will be proclaimed in the current year, and the new Settlement introduced from the next year.

Padra Taluka.—The revision measurement and classification work of this Taluka was completed within the year under review ; and it is expected that the new *Jamabandi* will be proclaimed in the current year, and the revision Settlement introduced from the next year.

Songadh Taluka.—This Taluka was tentatively settled for two years in 1902-03. In some villages, called *Holbandi*, lands were formerly assessed according to the number of ploughs used in cultivation. This primitive system has been changed, and lands have been assessed according to their areas. The Revenue Commissioner, after visiting the Taluka, recommended that the rates fixed in these *Holbandi* villages should be reduced. As it is necessary to proceed with extreme caution in introducing a new system of assessment among an aboriginal and ignorant population, the suggestion made by the Revenue Commissioner was accepted. The rates fixed in these *Holbandi* villages were somewhat reduced by the Settlement Commissioner; and with this modification the Settlement made in 1902-03 was confirmed for thirty years, including the two years which have already elapsed. It is expected that, under this long term of settlement, and under the liberal orders passed by the Maharaja with regard to trees standing on the holdings of cultivators, there will be a steady extention of cultivation in this Jungle Taluka.

Petlad Taluka.—Petlad is one of the richest Talukas in the State, and is famed for its tobacco, of which some account has been given elsewhere. But the difficulty in settling this Taluka arose from a peculiar tenure called the Narva tenure, prevailing here from centuries. Each village is owned by families who are called Narvadars, and are no doubt descended from a common ancestor who established and populated the village. The Narvadars had their respective shares in the village lands, and paid the Government revenue according to their shares. But in times of disorder, or under pressure from State Officials, portions of the Narva lands were alienated by sale or mortgage, and it was difficult to realise from the remaining Narva lands the total assessment which was due from the village. Threatened with the full assessment, the Narvadars of many villages offered to relinquish their Narva rights. If these relinquishments had been accepted, the Narvadars would have sunk to the position of ordinary tenants in Ryotwari villages, and an old institution of the land would have been swept away.

Mr. Seddon acted with a great deal of moderation and foresight. He introduced the Ryotwari system where the old Narva tenure had virtually ceased to exist; while in a large number of villages, where the Narva tenure was still a living institution, he took care to recognize and preserve it in the new Settlement. His Highness the Maharaja, also, largely reduced the old revenue demand of this Taluka in view of its present distressed condition, and sanctioned equitable rules about alienated lands. All difficulties were thus removed; and the new *Jamabandi* will be proclaimed, and the Settlement will come into operation, from the current year.

Mewasi villages in Kadi District.—Mr. Seddon also shewed great tact and judgment in introducing Settlement rates in 36 Mewasi villages in the Kadi District during the year under report. These villages are situated in the Talukas of Kadi, Kalol and Mehsana; and from olden times the turbulent population of these villages were permitted to cultivate what lands they liked, and to pay revenue only for such lands as they chose to cultivate. This primitive system has now been changed; lands have been assessed according to their areas; and a reduction of 20 per cent. has been allowed, in consideration of the peculiar nature of the former system, and the poverty of the people.

Okha Mandal Taluka.—A Settlement was made tentatively for two years in 1903-04; and the

Settlement Commissioner has now recommended that the Settlement may be confirmed and continued for 15 years, including the two years which have already elapsed.

City Survey.—The survey of the city of Baroda has been proceeding very slowly. The work was unfortunately commenced under a very dilatory system, and the enquiries made were needlessly minute and detailed. It almost seems that, in the want of proper supervision, the subordinate officers devised a method calculated to prolong the work indefinitely, and the cost already incurred is excessive. Mr. Seddon has now revised the method of work so as to make it more expeditious, and has also settled equitable principles for the levy of fees for *Sanads* to be given to the owners. During the year under report the measurement of 13,141 houses was completed, enquiries were made into 2,185 cases, and 492 *Sanads* were prepared.

Irrigation rates.—Rates are levied from cultivators for irrigating their fields from wells, excavated by themselves, under different systems in different Talukas and Districts, as will be explained further on. The *Bagayat* system, prevailing in Naosari and Gandevi Talukas, received special attention during the year under report, and valuable suggestions were made by the Settlement Commissioner and the District Officer of Naosari to remove the more glaring faults of the system.

Barkheli lands.—Alienated lands, which do not pay any Land Revenue to the State except perhaps a small fixed *Salami*, are called Barkheli lands. Two temporary establishments were employed in the year, one for enquiries in alienated villages, and the other for arranging records. The enquiry work in Kadi and Naosari Districts is almost finished, and that in Baroda District is in progress. The Main Committee records for Kadi District and for Baroda Taluka have been arranged.

In the Cash Branch, 225 claims were disposed of within the year under report. The amount claimed was Rs. 31,839, of which Rs. 12,328 were continued. Allowances of the annual value of Rs. 1,838 were purchased on payment of Rs. 15,836

In the Watan Branch, 28 claims were disposed of. The total amount claimed was Rs. 10,730, of which Rs. 8,938 were allowed with the usual conditions of service. Watans to the annual value of Rs. 447 were purchased on payment of Rs. 4,836.

1,074 Barkheli land succession cases were disposed of. Nazarana to the amount for Rs. 13,350 was charged in 445 cases. Land measuring 126 Bighas was purchased for Rs. 2,586.

Fifty-two Sanads were issued, out of which 41 were of the first class given in exchange for those of second class, according to the *Zahernam* issued by the Minister.

Ninety-five non-guaranteed Garas cases were dealt with. Out of Rs. 7,956 claimed, Rs. 113-8 were discontinued. Garas of the annual value of Rs. 169 was purchased for Rs. 2,970.

2,279 Bighas of Barkheli land were resumed for failure of heirs, non-payment of dues, non-performance of duties, and other reasons.

Six hundred claims from Petlad Taluka to have *Gharania* and *Vechania* land treated as *Barkehi* wre inquired into.

There were 77 appeals to His Highness, of which 58 were rejected, 14 allowed, and 4 remanded. 2,895 petitions were received during the year under review.

Expenditure.—The accounts of the Settlement and Barkheli branches are kept together. The total expenditure during the year under review was Rs. 2,00,236 against Rs. 1,59,083 of the previous year.

Cost of Measurement and Classification—The average cost of measurement and of classification per Bigah during the last two years is shown below :—

Measurement.		Classification.	
1903-04.	1904-05.	1903-04.	1904-05.
Rs. a. p.	Rs. a. p.	Rs. a. p.	Rs. a. p.
0 2 3	0 1 9	0 1 0	0 1 0

On the whole there was a fair outturn of work during the year, and the reduction in the average cost of measurement is satisfactory.

(c)—IRRIGATION CESS.

Water is found in wells at different depths in different parts of the State, and a Cess is added to the Land Assessment for the water used for irrigation, where such water is easily available. There are three different methods in which this Cess is realised in different Districts and Talukas.

According to one system, known as the *Subsoil system*, fields are charged according to the depth at which water is available, and where no water is available within a depth of about 40 feet, nothing is charged. This system is followed in the neighbouring British Districts, and the disadvantage of the system is that it taxes cultivators for a benefit which many of them are too poor to derive. In many parts of the State, where water is available at a depth of 30 or 40 feet, a well costs a thousand rupees or more, and cultivators cannot, as a rule, sink a well, even with the help of advances, without ruining themselves. Thus the *Subsoil* system imposes a general tax for improvements which cultivators may or may not be able to make.

The second system is known as the *Bagait system*, which is universally condemned by all officers who have worked it. It taxes lands all round a well as soon as a well is sunk. It is, thus, not only a tax on improvements made by the cultivators, but it often is a tax where the improvements are of no avail. Lands around the new well may or may not be benefited by the well, but the tax remains.

The third or *Kasar system* is somewhat better. It taxes, not the lands, but the well itself, so long as the water is used. Its disadvantages are that it is a tax on improvements effected by cultivators, and has the tendency of deterring them from using water for fear of paying the tax.

It will be seen from the foregoing account that the Water Cess, in whatever form it is levied, is open to some objections. It is either a tax on *possible improvements* which the cultivator may not be able to make, or a tax on *actual improvements* which the cultivator makes at his own cost. In some parts of the State, as in Naosari District, the careful observations made by the District Officer, Mr. Khaserao, seem to shew that wells are successful only along certain routes,—beds of dried up rivers, where a stream still runs underground. If this be a fact, then an imposition of the water tax for wells seems to be premature before a complete survey of such tracts has been made.

The nominal demand on account of the Irrigation Cess throughout the State is about Rs. 2,70,000 in round numbers, but scarcely one half of this is realizable if the tax is levied for water actually obtained by cultivators. On the other hand the tax on wells has a deterrent effect on the extension of cultivation, and it is likely that the Water Rate has, in the long run, brought more loss than profit to the State.

X.—FINANCE.

WORK OF THE DEPARTMENT.

Mr. Dayabhai Harjivandas Nanavati, B.A., of the Bombay University, held the post of Accountant-General in Baroda during the year under report, and performed his duties with his usual care, ability and zeal. He joined the Baroda service in 1878, and served for 17 years in the Garas Department, and was then, for one year, Secretary to His Highness the Maharaja. With the varied experience thus acquired he was appointed Accountant-General in 1896.

A great reform in the Accounts Department was introduced in 1892 by the late Mr. Rajani Nath Ray, whose services were lent to this State by the Indian Government. The great change which he introduced was to bring the Accountant-General in direct touch with every Taluka Treasury. The Taluka Treasuries were made the smallest units both of Revenue and of Financial Accounts. The Taluka Treasuries were the place where the two accounts were compared and checked. And the Taluka Treasuries sent Monthly Statements direct to the Accountant-General, so as to keep him posted in the receipts and expenditure of the entire State.

Another great principle which Mr. Ray insisted upon, and introduced in this State, was the absolute independence and the supreme authority of the Audit Department. Other reforms introduced by Mr. Ray concerned the working of the Treasury Department. Some modifications have been made in his rules within the fourteen years which have elapsed since, but the principles he laid down are still adhered to.

In 1900, the British Indian currency was introduced in Baroda, 130 Babashai rupees being considered equivalent to 100 British Indian rupees. And it is worth recording that all revenue demands were proportionately reduced when made payable in the rupee of higher value.

The function of the Finance Department is three-fold, *viz.*, audit, accounts, and finance.

As an Audit Department it has to examine all vouchers of expenditure. If they appear on examination to be objectionable in any way, they are not passed, but are held under objection till explanation is received. On receipt of the explanation the vouchers are either passed or rejected.

As an Account Department it has to tabulate the receipts and expenditure of the whole Raj under their respective heads and sub-heads, and to compile therefrom monthly and yearly statements of accounts.

As a Finance Department it has to prepare the budget statements of the estimated receipts and expenditure for the succeeding year, and to submit the same for the orders of the Maharaja at least three months before the year commences. It has to see whether the revenues are increasing or decreasing, and to inform the Government of the chief causes of such fluctuations. It has to suggest means for the curtailment of expenditure, and to advise the Government on all questions which directly or indirectly affect the finances of the State.

(b).—BRANCHES OF THE DEPARTMENT.

For convenience of work, the Department is divided into eight branches of which a brief account is given below :—

(1) *Main Branch,*—also called the Correspondence Branch. This is the controlling and directing office of the Department, and the Accountant-General himself presides over it, and looks into all important matters appertaining to it. All references from other Departments are disposed of here; all papers requiring the orders of His Highness or of the Minister are prepared here; all orders are received here; and all circulars for facilitating and improving the work of the Department are issued from this office.

(2) *Civil Audit Branch.*—The Assistant Accountant-General presides over this Branch, and all vouchers, excepting those relating to the Public Works and Military offices, are inspected here on the post-audit system. 63,332 vouchers were audited in the year under review, and Rs. 5,419 paid away by mistake were recovered. Fifty-nine new pensions were sanctioned during the year. The total number of Civil Pensioners at the close of the year was 268, who drew an aggregate pension of Rs. 51,326 a year.

(3) *Military Audit Branch*—All Military vouchers are post-audited here, except Silledari and Sibandi Supplementary pay-abstracts which are pre-audited. 5,003 vouchers were audited during

the year under review, and Rs. 1,342 paid away through mistake were recovered. Thirty-five new pensions were sanctioned during the year. The total number of Military Pensioners at the close of the year was 635, who drew an aggregate pension of Rs. 53,512 a year.

(4) *Public Works Audit Branch.*—This Branch exercises audit control over Public Works, Railways, Municipalities, and the Baroda and Visnagar Banks. No less than 31,586 vouchers were audited during the year under review. The accounts of the Baroda Municipality, the Baroda Weaving Mill, and the Gandevi Sugar Factory, were also audited by this Branch. But the Municipality is now a self-governing town ; the Mill has been sold, and the Factory has also been sold.

The out door work done by this Branch includes the inspection of His Highness's Railway accounts at Bombay and Ajmere. At the latter place the examination of the railway accounts was continued during the year, and small errors aggregating to Rs. 1,169 were discovered, and were mostly admitted by the Railway authorities. Similarly during the examination of Railway accounts in Bombay, errors amounting to Rs. 210 were detected for which credits were given by the Railway authorities.

Refund was claimed by the Baroda Government on account of terminals on foreign traffic on our Petlad and Mehsana railways. The claim was ultimately admitted, and a sum of Rs. 15,582, in all, has been credited to our railways. Similar credits to the extent of Rs. 12,140 have been given to our Kalol railways.

The increase of the lower class fare from 3 pies to 4 pies the mile on the Dabhoi Railway, made in the previous year, brought in some increase in earnings, but is a measure of doubtful expediency.

(5) *Inspection Branch.*—This Branch inspects accounts of all Departments except Military and Public Works referred to above. The multiplicity of the work of this Branch will be apparent from the fact that the accounts of the following offices were inspected within the year under report :—

Taluka and Sub-Divisional Revenue offices	21
Offices of Civil Courts	11
Offices of Magistrates	9
Police Offices	16
Medical Offices	12
Jail Offices	2
Municipal Offices	15
Customs Excise and Opium Offices	17
Religious Institutions	2
School Offices	65
Forest Offices	3
Registration Offices	9
Banks and Government Gardens	4
Total ...	186

The errors detected amounted to Rs. 3,378. Of this sum, Rs. 1,225 were recovered, Rs. 1,439 were written off on sufficient grounds, and Rs. 714 were pending disposal at the close of the year.

(6) *Compilation of Accounts Branch.*—The final accounts of the State are compiled by this Branch from the daily and monthly sheets received

from all Treasuries. The total Receipts and Disbursements of the year under review will be shewn further on.

(7) *Central Treasury.*—Mr. Anandrao Gobind Dighe continued to be in charge of the Central Treasury at Baroda, and did his work with his accustomed care and ability. The total receipts during the year under review, including adjustments in this Treasury, amounted to Rs. 265,17,483. And the total Disbursements came to Rs. 273,51,564. The cash receipts and disbursements came to nearly 65 lacs and 73 lacs respectively, giving a monthly average of over 5 lacs in receipts, and over 6 lacs in disbursements.

The transactions carried on with the Bank of Bombay, including its Surat, Broach, Ahmedabad, and Bhavnagar Branches, amounted during the year under report to about 80 lacs in remittances, and about 85 lacs in withdrawals.

(8) *Stamp Branch.*—This Branch is also under the superintendence of the Central Treasury Officer. The revenue from Stamps during the year 1904-05 was Rs. 4,11,898 against Rs. 4,41,473 of the previous year.

Water-marked Court Fee Stamps of higher values, for which there was no demand, were converted into smaller values. Adhesive Court Fee Stamps of small values were substituted for stamp papers.

General.—Much additional work was thrown on the Accountant-General as President of Departmental Examination Committees, as Member of

Committee for passing Rules and Regulations, as

f
r

f
f
n
o
y

ır
ır

Receipts.—contd.

No.	Description of items.	1903-1904.	1904-1905.
		Rs.	Rs.
17	Municipalities	95,150	20,072
18	Public Works Department.	1,18,479	1,03,361
19	Mint	114	500
20	Miscellaneous including Salt, Ferries, Police, Medical, Press, Army, Bank, General and Miscellaneous.	1,20,618	1,60.884
	Total ..	1,58,13,714	1,13,80,802

Disbursements.

No.	Description of items.	1903-1904.	1904-1905.
		Rs.	Rs.
1	Land Revenue	18,12,849	19,67,554
2	Other Civil Establishments.	1,15,080	99,001
3	Forests	54,607	63,989
4	Stamps	23,550	18,576
5	Registration	39,452	81,262
6	Tributes	.....	68
7	Opium	15,85,141	13,83,872
8	Railways.....	....	....
9	Mill	83,272	2,53,823
10	Palace	27,15,921	27,71,365
11	General Administration		
	1 Tour Expenses	1,556	....
	2 Central Offices	4,15,943	4,95,859
12	Judicial Department ..	3,36,755	3,10,232
13	Police	6,86,049	7,31,846
14	Jail	47,398	44,904
15	Education	6,54,033	6,74,011
16	Medical	1,69,817	1,63,874
17	Printing Press	78,838	92,772
18	Municipalities	3,16,008	1,51,666
19	Public Works	11,20,491	16,28,656
20	Army	21,84,146	21,60,191
21	DevasthanDharmadaya	2,78,676	3,03,706
22	Assamdars-Nemnookdars.	7,46,870	7,32,795
23	Extraordinary	99,420	1,16,186
24	Miscellaneous (including interest, miscellaneous &c.)	1,74,795	3,90,135
	Total ..	1,37,40,677	1,45,86,293

Causes of Increase in Receipts :—Forest shews
an increase of over twenty-two thousand Rupees in
1904-05, as compared with 1903-04, owing to the
greater sale of forest produce due to the careful
administration of past years.

Opium shews a revenue of over 16½ lacs in 1904-
05 as against less than 15 lacs in 1903-04. But
neither of these sums should be taken as the net
revenue from opium. The pass duty on opium sent
to Bombay for sale, and the cost price of opium sold
at Bombay and in the State of Baroda, are included
in the above sums. They amount to 10 lacs in
1904-05. The net revenue from opium in 1904-05
was therefore only Rs. 6,59,334.

Railways shew an increase in receipts by nearly
1½ lacs, owing to increase of traffic, as well as to
the absence of any purchase of rolling stock for the
Dabhoi system of railways.

The increase under head Education is due to a
grant of over Rs 32,000 received from religious and
charitable institutions.

The increase under other heads is trifling.

Causes of Decrease in Receipts :—Land Revenue
and Miscellaneous Revenue shew a vast decrease
of nearly 45 lacs, owing to the large remissions and
suspensions liberally ordered by His Highness on
account of the famine of 1904-05.

The decrease in Excise and Customs is apparent,
not real. The former is due to the fact that some
outstanding arrears, exceeding a lac of rupees, were
realized in 1903-04. The latter is due to the fact
that a portion of the Customs revenue has now been

allotted to Self-Governing Municipalities created in 1904-05.

The decrease in Stamps is possibly owing to scarcity and famine.

The decrease in Jail revenue is due to certain adjustments of convict labour made in the preceding year.

Lastly, the decrease shewn under the head Municipalities is apparent, not real. It is due to the fact, already mentioned, that the larger Municipalities have been made Self-Governing towns, and appropriate the local incomes for their local expenses.

The decrease under other heads is trifling, and calls for no explanation.

Causes of Increase in Disbursements :—Land Revenue shews an increase in disbursements owing to the appointment of a new Settlement Commissioner, and a revision in the salaries of the higher grade Revenue Officers.

The Mill shews a large increase owing to large purchases of materials. The Mill was sold within the year under report.

Palace shews an increase of over half a lac. The figures given by the Accountant-General regarding Palace expenditure include items of expenditure shewn in the Khangi Department accounts, as well as other items of special expenditure. Among these last may be mentioned a large amount of about six lacs, which was under suspense head against Javeri Uttamchand for Jewellery purchased by a previous Ruler, and was settled in 1904-05.

General Administration includes His Highness's
Tours and the expenses of Central Offices. The
tour expenses of 1904-05 are still shewn under
the head of Advance, and have not yet been
debited to the accounts. The increase in the
expenses of Central Offices is due to the appointment of a Revenue Minister, the purchase of record
racks for the new Record Office, and the establishment of the Court of Wards and other Branches of
the Revenue Department.

Police shews a large increase, mainly owing to
revision of salaries in the lower grades required
for more efficients work.

The Education Department shews an increase
of nearly twenty thousand Rupees, which brings
up the total expenditure on Education to nearly
6¾ lacs. Deducting educational receipts amounting to over a lac, the nett expense incurred on
education in this State exceeds 5½ lacs.

Public works shew a large increase, owing to
construction of buildings in Baroda, the purchase
of a site for building in Bombay, and other causes.

The heading of Devasthans shews an increase,—
some expenditure under that head having been
transferred from the Khangi Department. A large
increase is also shewn under head Miscellaneous,
due to the adjustment of a large sum required to
make up the full value of Babashai coins sold as
waste copper. The remaining items of increase
are trifling.

Causes of Decrease in Disbursements.—Opium
shews a large decrease of over two lacs. But,

as explained before, the figures for opium do
not shew the net receipts or expenditure. Out
of the total expenditure under this head for
1904-05 should be deducted Rs. 4,80,000 paid
as pass duty on opium sent to Bombay, and
Rs. 8,36,570 paid for the purchase of Opium juice.
The net expenditure or opium for 1904-05 was
therefore only Rs. 67,302.

The Judicial Department shews a decrease of
over 26,000 Rupees, as the post of Chief Justice
remained vacant for a time.

Municipalities shew a decrease of over a lac
and a-half, as Baroda and seven other towns
were made Self-Governing Municipalities, with
incomes and expenses of their own, which were
accordingly withdrawn from the general accounts.

Lastly the Army shews a satisfactory decrease
of nearly 24,000 Rupees. The other items of
decrease are of less importance.

XI.—EDUCATION.

(a).—ORGANISATION OF THE DEPARTMENT.

The Education Department continues to receive the special attention of His Highness the Maharaja. In no other Department has his liberality been more conspicuous; and in none are the results more tangible. The percentage of the revenues which the State spends on Education is over four, against about one per cent. in British India. And nearly one-half the boys of school-going age are actually under instruction in Baroda, a result which is seen in few other places in India.

The Department has continued under the control of Mr. Jamshedji A. Dalal, M.A., LL.B. Mr. Dalal has had a varied experience. Besides serving in the British Education Department, and as Principal of the Gujrat College at Ahmedabad, he has occupied the posts of District Officer, Census Superintendent, Famine Commissioner, Revenue Commissioner, and Naib Diwan in this State. He received the personal distinction of Khan Bahadur from the Indian Government on the 1st of January 1905.

The Department embraces in all 1,265 Educational Institutions. English is taught in twenty-two of these, viz., 1 Arts College, 3 High Schools, 14 Government Anglo-Vernacular Schools, 2 Grant-in-aid High Schools, and 2 Grant-in-aid Anglo-Vernacular Schools.

27

For purely Vernacular Education we have 1,243 schools in the State, or nearly 40 schools in each Taluka. This gives an average of one school for every two or three villages.

An important change has been introduced from the commencement of the current year. Gramyashalas or Village Schools, numbering 578, have been transferred to the newly formed Local Boards. All the Graded Schools, as well as the Compulsory Schools have continued to be under the direct management of the Education Department.

The total expenditure on Education in the year under report has been Rs. 6,48,028, and the receipts have amounted only to Rs. 87,015. These figures, however, do not include all the items included by the Accountant-General under the head of Education. The total expenditure according to his reckoning is Rs. 6,74,011, as stated above,—which comes to 5½ annas per head of population in Baroda, against about one or two annas in British India.

(b)—ENGLISH EDUCATION.

Baroda College.—This College is affiliated to the Bombay University in the faculties of Arts, Science and Law. It was first opened in 1882, and began only with a Previous Class, but has progressed step by step. It sends up students for the M.A. Degree, the B.Sc. in Science, and the first LL.B. Examination in Law. This combined privilege is not enjoyed by any other Institution in Gujrat, and our College has maintained its high reputation, both for excellence of teaching and for success at academic examinations. It continues to attract students from the Bombay Presidency, and even from Central India.

Besides the Principal and the Vice-Principal, the College Staff had 7 other Professors, 2 Fellows, one Sanscrit Teacher, and one Lecturer in French. The College Staff suffered two losses during the year under report. Mr. Tait, M.A., B.Sc., who had been Principal of the College for upwards of a quarter of a century, retired from the service of the State on 1st November 1904. He had endeared himself to his pupils, and his retirement was regretted by all who knew him. A sadder loss was sustained in the untimely death of Professor Jagjivan Shah, M.A., LL.B., who had occupied the chair of Logic, Moral Philosophy, and General Jurisprudence with credit for upwards of three years. He was a great favourite at the College, his career was full of hope and promise, and his early death caused wide-spread sorrow.

Mr. A. Beaumauris Clarke, B.A., of Jesus College, Cambridge, was confirmed in the post of Principal, vacated by Mr. Tait, and Mr. Aravind A. Ghose was appointed Vice-Principal in October 1904. Mr. Ghose was educated at St. Paul's School, London, and then at King's College Cambridge, where he secured First Class honors in Classical Tripos in 1892. He also competed for the Indian Civil Service in 1890, and secured a high place among

the Selected Candidates, but failing in a physical
test, he joined the Baorda State Service. Mr. Ghose
acted as Principal, and Mr. Tapidas Mehta acted
as Vice-Principal, during Mr. Clarke's absence on
furlough.

Professor Masani, M.A., B.Sc., who teaches
Biology and is also Director of the State
Museum, was deputed by His Highness to visit
the leading Museums and Scientific Institutions
in Europe, and left India with the Maharaja in
April last.

Dr. Kanga, M.A., B.Sc., L.M. & S., who, like
Professor Masani, is also a Chancellor's Medallist.
and a Fellow of the Bombay University, continued
to preside over the Physical and Chemical Labora-
tories. Professor Bhaskar R. Arte M.A., who
is a Bhau Daji Prizeman and a Jagannath
Shankarshet Scholar, continued to lecture in Sanskrit. Professor Naik, M.A., a Cobden Club Medallist, occupied the chair of History and Political
Economy. And Professor Nawabali M.A., from
Aligarh, continued his lectures in Persian in the
year under report.

There were 225 students on the College rolls
during the year, as against 206 during the previous.
year. Of these, 12 attended Science Classes,
while the number of Law students was 18.
Among the students, 140 took up Sanskrit for
their Second Language, 46 took up Persian, and
26 attended lectures in French. The average
annual cost of educating each pupil was Rs. 205,
as against Rs. 220 in the previous year.

The results of different examinations during the last two years are shown in the following statement :—

Names of Examinations.	Number of Students sent up.		Number of Students passed.	
	1904-05.	1905-06.	1904-05.	1905-06.
Previous	72	80	45	35
Intermediate arts.........	50	52	31	28
B.A.	30	33	23	19
M.A.	...	1	...	1
Intermediate Science....	2	4	2	2
B. Sc.	2	3	2	3
First LL.B.	19	15	11	13

The Baroda College has been endowed with about 22 Scholarships, of which no less than 17 have been supplied by the State; the other five are contributed by different funds. Three Scholarships of the value of Rs. 20 each, and named after His Highness the Maharaja, are reserved for Mahomedans, with the object of promoting higher education among that community.

The College also commands the use of a well-equipped Library, a physical and chemical and biological laboratory, and botanical gardens. A well built Boarding House is attached to it.

Prizes were distributed at the College by His Highness the Maharaja himself in the year under report.

High Schools.—Besides the Baroda High School, there are Government High Schools at Pattan and Amreli, and Grant-in-aid High Schools at Naosari and Gandevi. The following statement shews the results at the Matriculation Examination achieved by these five High Schools in the State :—

Name of the High School.	1903.		1904.	
	Students sent up.	Students passed.	Students sent up.	Students passed.
Baroda	59	41	64	32
Pattan.................	10	4	5	4
Amreli	5	4	6	4
Naosari	28	15	27	21
Gandevi	6	1	5	3

The Baroda High School continues to hold a high place among the schools affiliated to the Bombay University, and reflects credit on the Head Master Mr. Haṣabnis.

Anglo-Vernacular Schools.—There were 14 Government Anglo-Vernacular Schools in the year under report. Of these the (1) Petlad and (2) Visnagar Schools teach upto the Sixth Standard, and those at (3) Dabhoi, (4) Sojitra, (5) Vaso, (6) Kadi, (7) Mehsana, (8) Sidhpur and (9) Dwarka teach upto the Fifth Standard. The schools at (10) Padra, (11) Vadnagar, (12) Unjha and (13) Billimora teach upto the Fourth Standard; while (14) the Baroda Anglo-Vernacular School teaches upto the Third Standard only. Besides these fourteen Government Schools, there are two Grant-in-aid Anglo-Vernacular Schools at Naosari and at Vesma.

Attendance in the English-teaching Schools.— The total number of students in the different schools described above, in which English is taught during the last three years, is shown in the following tabular statement :—

Institutions.	Number of Students.		
	1902-08.	1908-04.	1904-05.
3 High schools............	930	1,007	1,126
14 Anglo-Vernacular schools	1,489	1,423	1,486
4 Grant-in-aid schools	525	498	483
Total	2,944	2,923	3,095

Adding to this number, the number of students at the Baroda College, we find that the total number of boys in English-teaching schools was 3,320 last year.

Scholarships.—Besides the three Mahomedan Scholarships, placed at the disposal of the Baroda College, referred to above, His Highness the Maharaja grants from his own private purse 54 other Scholarships, of the aggregate yearly value of Rs. 9,372, to different Educational Institutions both in and outside the State. Two of these are in the gift of the Elphinstone College Bombay ; while the Wilson College, the Fergusson College, and the Deccan College at Poona, have one each, ranging from Rs. 20 to Rs. 35, at their disposal. The College of Science at Poona, the Grant Medical College, and the Veterinary College at Bombay enjoy similar endowments from these funds for the benefit of His Highness's subjects. The

Baroda High School has been alloted four Scholarships from these funds, while there are thirty-seven
such Scholarships of the monthly value of Rs. 465,
distributed among the other schools. Besides
these amounts, a sum of Rs. 2,296 was also handed
over to the Deccan Association during the last
year, for the purpose of spreading education
among the Marathas.

Education in Europe.—Among the men who
have proceeded to Europe to complete their post
graduate studies with help from the State may be
mentioned, in addition to those named in the last
year's Report, the name of Dr. S. B. Jathar of Poona.
He is an L.M. & S. of the Bombay University,
and has gone to England to study Chemistry.
Other students were sent to England, America and
Japan, towards the close of the last year, or early
in the current year, to learn Mechanical Engineering
and other useful branches of knowledge.

Expenditure on English Education.—The expenditure incurred on account of English Education,
and the receipts of the several Institutions noted
above, are shown in the annexed tabular statement :—

	1903-04	1904-05
Expenditure......	1,53,965	1,52,711
Receipts.........	31,123	31,678

(c).—VERNACULAR EDUCATION.

The number of Vernacular Schools of all kinds, and of the pupils attending them, is given in the following statement :—

Year.	Government Boys' Schools.		Government Girls' Schools.		Village Schools and other Institutions.		Total.	
	Number of Schools.	Number of Boys.	Number of Schools.	Number of Girls in Girls' Schools.	Number of Institutions.	Number of students.	Number of schools.	Number of pupils.
1903-04.	498	44,723	94	12,731	652	21,173	1,244	78,627
1904-05.	496	46,897	94	12,817	653	22,435	1,243	81,649

The total number of pupils thus increased by 3,022 during the year under report, though there was a decrease of one in the number of institutions. All towns and large villages with over 1,000 inhabitants had schools, while many villages with less than a population of 500 had such institutions.

Government Vernacular Schools.—Of the 81,649 pupils, over ninety per cent. attended Government Schools, in which the average number of pupils was a hundred. But the money spent over these Government Schools, is approximately four lacs. The expenditure of about six hundred rupees on each Vernacular School is capable of some reduction. Another matter in which there is room for improvement is the transfer of teachers. The entire teaching staff in the State numbers about three thousand, and it was found on calculation, that over eighteen hundred transfers were made in the course of thirteen months. The transfer of three teachers out of every five, within the space of thirteen months, is unexampled in any Province in British India, and must be injurious to the cause of education.

Village Schools.—The total expenditure on the 578 Village Schools was Rs. 48,629, out of which Rs. 45,383 was contributed by the Revenue Budget, and Rs. 3,246 by the Education Department under the grant-in-aid rules. The average annual cost of each Village School was therefore Rs. 84 only. The Village Schools are opened in those villages where 16 children can be collected to attend them, and 16,320 children attended these schools in the year under report, as against 16,204 in the preceding year. The standards of education observed therein are lighter and more adapted to the requirements of rural villages. It has been stated before that these Gramyashalas have now been transferred to the control of the Local Boards. The Minister of Education keeps himself in touch with the educational work of the Local Boards, as he still continues to be responsible for the harmonious management of these schools, so as to carry out the general policy of the State.

Grant-in-aid Vernacular Schools.—There were fifty private schools in receipt of grants from Government under the Rules. Rs. 2,480 were thus granted to these institutions, which were availed of by about 3,150 pupils.

Infant Schools.—To reduce the burden of maintaining unwieldy primary classes in large towns and villages, the Departmental Rules enjoin the opening of Infant Schools wherever a teacher comes forward to teach little children in the First Standard and Below Standard classes. Nine such schools were maintained during the year under report; eight of them being in the Baroda District.

(d)—FEMALE EDUCATION.

The Female Training College and the connected Girls' Schools continued to be under the guidance and control of Miss Mary Bhor, a lady of considerable energy, ability and experience.

The number of girls attending the Girls' Schools (exclusive of the Female Training College), during the year under report, was 8,086 while the girls attending Mixed Schools were 5,027. The total number of girls attending schools was thus 13,113, or about 9 per cent. of the girls of school-going age. It should be remembered, however, that a large number of girls of the upper classes and of higher ages receive tuition at home, and we shall not be far from the mark if we put down the proportion of girls receiving instruction at over 10 per cent. of the total number of girls of the school going age.

Embroidery, Drawing and Practical Cookery are taught in the Girls' Schools at Baroda, Pattan, Naosari, Petlad and Visnagar. Lessons in music are also given in the first three schools, and in the Female Training College, thus affording the future Schoolmistresses a sufficient insight into their work. The Cookery classes have continued to do useful work and are popular. Plain needle work is taught in all the Schools, and Kindergarten materials are being supplied every year to the larger schools. Some of the Gujrati and Mahrathi Girls' Schools in Baroda have also facilities for teaching the Sanskrit to the advanced pupils. Several Scholarships, especially for grown up girls above certain ages, are also provided for in these schools.

The Female Training College was opened in 1882 for training women for the post of school mistresses. Widows and also wives of teachers receive instruction, and readily obtain appointments when they have completed the course of their education. The course prescribed is one for four years, and there are several scholarships to help the candidates during their preparatory career. There were 26 women under training in the last year, and seven of these obtained employment in the Department on their completing their course. Ten girls attending these classes were over 20 years of age. Three of the senior girls secured prizes of Rs. 15, 10, and 5 offered for public competition by the Gujrat Vernacular Society. Some of the pupil teachers, attending the practicing school, were instructed in brush work and blackboard drawing, kindergarten on the Fræbel system, paper-tearing and story lessons. A handsome donation of Rs. 1,500 was placed at the disposal of the Girls' schools by the Diwan in commemoration of the nuptials of the Yuvaraj Fattehsinh Rao; and prizes for physical exercises were distributed to the girls out of this fund. The total expenditure for this Training College was Rs. 5,426 during the year.

Zenana classes have also been continued for imparting education in reading, writing and household accounts, to such women as cannot attend ordinary girls' schools. There are six such classes attached to the leading girls' schools, and 140 women attended them during the year under review. They are examined by a Committee of ladies ; and 74 women passed out of 90 who attended. These classes meet for three hours in the afternoon, when women are generally free from their household duties. Four of these meet at Baroda, one at Naosari, and the sixth at Petlad.

(e)—Compulsory Education.

The experiment of Compulsory Education is being tried in the Amreli Taluka since 1893. Schools were opened in 10 villages in 1893, and the number rose to 52 in ten years. During the year under report there were 66 such Schools in 50 villages of the Amreli Taluka. There were 4 more Compulsory Schools under the Grant-in-aid system, while in 15 other ordinary schools the first three Standards were maintained under the Compulsory Education Rules, thus bringing up the total to 85 schools. Of these 22 were reserved for girls alone, the others being mixed schools for both boys and girls.

There were 2,799 boys and 1875 girls attending these Schools, against a total of 5,201 of the previous year. The decrease was probably owing to the famine of the last year. Adding to this number 1,215 children who have passed the compulsory age limits, but continue to attend the schools, we have a total of 5,879 pupils attending these Compulsory Schools, representing 11 per cent. of the population of the Taluka.

Fifteen per cent. of the total population may well be considered to be the proportion of the children of school going age between 7 and 15; and considering our lower limits of age, which are 7 to 12 for boys and 7 to 10 for girls, we may fairly claim that we have succeeded in placing the entire juvenile population of the Taluka under instruction.

The percentage of passes was over 66 in 25 of these Compulsory Schools, over 50 in 31, over 33 in 16 Schools, and under 33 only in 12 Schools. These results are tolerably good; but the tuition imparted in some of these Compulsory Schools came to the unfavourable notice of His Highness the Maharaja on the occasion of his visit to Amreli in January 1905, and shewed a lack of supervision. Steps have been taken to effect an improvement. The total expenditure to the State for purely Compulsory Education was Rs. 12,125 in 1904-05 against Rs. 15,083 of the previous year.

The idea of extending Compulsory Education to all parts of the State has been present in His Highness's mind for some years, and a law for this purpose was passed in July 1904. It provides for the application of the Act to those Talukas or localities to which the extension of the enactment is duly notified in the *Ajna Patrika*. The age limits for compulsory attendance for boys have been fixed between 6 and 14; and for girls between 6 and 12. Exemption from such compulsory attendance is granted to :—

(1) Children whose parents or guardians have an annual income below Rs. 150 or any other amount fixed by orders of the Maharaja.

(2) Agricultural children, whose parents may be paying an assessment to the State below an amount to be fixed.

(3) Children who are incapacitated by illness or permanent physical infirmity or mental defect for acquiring instruction.

(4) Children who are necessarily required to stay at home by the bedside of aged or ailing parents.

(5) Children who receive instruction at home, or have learnt the Compulsory Standards.

(6) Children who are living over a mile from any established school.

(7) Purdah girls, and children of such classes for whom separate schools are ordinarily provided for in the State.

The Fourth Standard has, for the present, been recognised as the limit of Compulsory Education. Parents and Guardians of children, between the limits of age fixed by the said enactment, failing to send them to school, are liable to a fine of one rupee for every month till the children are sent to school. Fines are also prescribed for absences &c.

The extension of the Compulsory Education system under this Act, to different parts of the State, is, in the current year, receiving His Highness's attention.

(f)—EDUCATION OF LOWER CASTES.

Another bold move, made by His Highness the
Maharaja, was to spread education among the
very lowest castes. The conception of this Hindu
Ruler is to raise and elevate those very classes
whose touch is now regarded as pollution by his
orthodox Hindu subjects. It was no use issuing
an edict for the removal of the barriers; an edict
would fail of success, and would only accentuate
the distinction. The Maharaja, therefore, decided
on the wiser plan of imparting a free education
to the lower classes, and thereby helping them to
raise themselves. These Antyaja classes, which
include, Dheds, Bhangis, Chamars and Khalpas,
form a population of 1,63,176 in the State; and
their children could not attend schools opened
for other children. In 1883, therefore, it was decided to open special schools for them, and to
supply them with books, slates and other requisites free.

The success which has been achieved after 22
years' work in this direction is still moderate; and
the reason is obvious to all who know the condition
of these classes. Nevertheless 1,715 children of
these Antyaja castes attended these classes during
the year under report, against 1,626 of the previous
year. This represents upwards of ten per cent.
of the children of the school going age; and if one
child in every ten among them is attending school,
the prospect is not quite discouraging.

The Antyaja children are taught absolutely
free; and scolarships of the value of Rs. 115,

per month are given to deserving students in the Fourth and higher Standards of of these schools. The results of the examination were satisfactory; 1,109 students were examined, and 555 passed against 144 in the previous year. A Girls' School at Baroda, attended by 68 girls of these low classes, is an institution which ought to inspire hope in the heart of every practical reformer.

(g)—EDUCATION OF FOREST TRIBES.

Boarding Schools for the boys of the Dhanka and other Forest Tribes have continued to work satisfactorily at Songadh, Vyara, and Mahua, in the Naosari District. A similar institution for girls is also being maintained at Songadh at State expense. The boys are taught reading and writing; and practical lessons in Carpentry and Agriculture are also imparted to them in a Model Farm attached to the Songadh Boarding House. Here they can make and repair ploughs and such other tools and implements as would be useful to them in agriculture. Various kinds of crops are being experimented upon in the Model Farm; mulberry trees are planted over about 40 bighas; and the pupils are instructed in the processes of Sericulture.

The Songadh Boarding School had the benefit of a visit, in November 1905, from Mr. Sly, Inspector General of Agriculture under the Indian Government; and a portion of his inspection remarks is quoted below :—

"I have been very much interested in visiting this experiment in the education of the

29

Dhankas, a backward aboriginal race. The scheme has evidently been carefully thought out. The system of education has been specially devised, and special inducements are given in, not only a free education, but free food and clothing. It is very satisfactory to learn that, whereas at first pressure had to be exercised to induce boys to enter the school, there are now more candidates than can be accommodated. * * * The farm is well managed on practical lines, and I find that the boys really do themselves almost all the practical work. I tested some of the boys in ploughing, in which they performed very creditably. The sericulture section is just being organized upon right lines with the assistance and advice of N. G. Mukerji, the Silk Expert of the Bengal Government."

The effect of education on these forest races, who were lately steeped in ignorance and addicted to drinking, has been surprising. They have started an association which they term the "An-Arya Hita Vardhaka Sabha," where lectures are given with the object of checking the vice of drinking, and of curtailing ruinous expenditure on occasions of funerals and weddings. Improvement is also observed in their social and religious customs, their manners, dress, and habits.

(h)—ORPHANAGES.

During the recent famine years, special arragements were made for housing, clothing, and feeding hundreds of children, who were abandoned by their helpless parents and guardians. And the question forced itself on our attention, as to what should be done with those children who were left on our hands. Many were reclaimed by their parents after the time of trouble was over, but a large number still remained unclaimed. His Highness the Maharaja, with his usual generosity, ordered that State Orphanages (Anath Ashrams) should be opened, one in each District, for taking charge of those orphans, as well as all children that might be discovered in future, without any relations or guardians to take care of them. An Act has been added to the Statute Book for the purpose, authorising the District Authorities to send all such destitute children to the Central Orphanage in the vicinity. The Dhanka Boarding Houses in Songadh were utilised for the purpose for the Naosari District ; and three other Orphanages were started in March 1902 for the remaining Districts. The Orphanage Act provides for the housing and feeding of these children, as well as imparting to them primary instruction, and a knowledge of various handicrafts which may prove useful to them in life.

The proposal of the Department to concentrate all the orphan boys in one Central Institution, and all the girls in another, and to locate them both at Amreli for the purpose of better supervision, is under consideration. The number of orphans, now maintained in the different branches, is given below in the form of a comparative table :—

Name of the Orphanage.	Number of Children.		
	Boys.	Girls.	Total.
Baroda...............	12	6	18
Mehsana..............	28	26	54
Amreli...............	53	33	86
Songadh Boys Boarding House	6	...	6
Do. Girls Boading House	...	1	1
Total	99	66	165

The total expenditure incurred on these Orphanages, during the year, was Rs. 7,358, the monthly maximum expenditure fixed per head being Rs. 4.

(i)—MUSIC SCHOOLS.

Another institution, peculiar to Baroda, is its Music Schools. The first School was opened in 1886 under the late renowned Professor of Music, Mowla Baksh, who had invented a notation for Indian Music. Pupils, trained in our schools, open classes in Bombay and other parts of India, and through them the music and notation of Mowla Baksh have acquired a wide celebrity.

The Music Schools of Baroda are now under the superintendence of Mr. Allauddin, one of Mowla Baksh's sons, who was sent by His Highness to Europe to learn the science there. There are Music Schools at Baroda, Naosari and Pattan, and special Music Classes are also attached to the Female Training College, some Girls' Schools in Baroda town, and at Naosari and at Pattan.

Besides instruction in vocal music, the students are also taught to play on the Fiddle, *Sitar* Harmonium and *Tabla*.

The following table gives the figures for the Music Schools for the year under report and the previous year :—

Name of the School.	Number of Pupils.	
	1903-04	1904-05
Baroda	106	147
Naosari...................	90	114
Pattan	44	54
Girl Schools..............	313	323
Total	553	638
Expenditure Rs.	5,203	5,287

(*j*)—Sanskrit and Urdu Schools.

There are nine Sanskrit Schools in the State, generally maintained by *Devasthan* funds or by the charity of private donors, and the expenditure from the State funds in the way of grants-in-aid comes to about Rs. 1,360 a year. These schools were at Baroda,[Sidhpur, Sinor, Petlad, Sojitra, Dwarka, Beyt, and Karnali. The total number of pupils was 421 during the year under report, as against 446 of the previous year.

Every year, examinations are held in the different branches of Sanskrit learning, such as the Vedas, Grammar, Logic, the Dharmasastras, the Vedanta and other Systems of Metaphysics, and the Puranas. As usual the examinations were held in August last year, and Rs. 357 were awarded to 24 persons. The total amount of Dakshina distributed, and of expenditure incurred, was Rs. 17,453 in the year under report. The State Library has a large collection of Sanskrit books and manuscripts.

There are altogether 39 Urdu Schools, especially for the Mahomedan subjects of His Highness, and these Schools are attended by boys and girls. A special Deputy Inspector is employed for inspecting these Urdu Schools. The total number of boys and girls attending these Urdu Schools during the last two years is given below:—

1904-04.		1904-05.	
Boys.	Girls.	Boys.	Girls.
4,175	468	6,460	447

2958 Mahomedan boys attended other schools, which gives a total of 9,418 or a percentage of nearly six to the total Mahomedan population in the State.

(k)—MISCELLANEOUS INSTITUTIONS.

Manual Training.—There were three classes for Manual Training during the year under report, attached to the Boys' Schools at Visnagar, Pattan and Kadi. The number of students who attended these classes were respectively 99, 128 and 184, against 106, 169 and 132 in the previous year. Where there is a Manual Training Class, the students have the choice either to attend these classes, or to take up the subjects of History and Geography in the fourth class of Boys' Schools. Drawing and Carpentry were the subjects taught in these classes as a training for the hand and eye. The proposal to extend these classes to three more schools is under consideration.

Drawing.—Drawing classes are attached to the High Schools at Baroda, Pattan and Amreli, and this subject is compulsory in all the classes except the Matriculation class. There are also about half a dozen drawing classes attached to different Vernacular Schools. A complete course of drawing is taught to students in the Technical Institute, as will be stated further on.

Night Schools.—The number of Night Schools was the same, *i.e.*, six, as in the previous year, with 134 pupils, as against 127. Two of these were in Baroda town, two in Baroda District, and two in Kadi District. The first two were Mahrathi, and the last four were all Gujrati. Those employed in service or other occupations avail themselves of these Night Schools, where they acquire sufficient knowledge to be able to read, write, and do small sums. The highest Standard taught in these schools is the Fifth. It is under contemplation to open more of these schools for the artisan classes.

Battalion Schools.—There were seven Schools for the Military servants in Baroda, one at Dhari, and one at Dwarka for the battalion stationed there. Three of the Baroda Schools taught Mahrathi alone, while Hindustani was added in the other four. There were 411 pupils in Baroda, 134 at Dhari, and 101 at Dwarka. All these schools shewed satisfactory results at the examinations held.

Agricultural School.—Twenty-nine pupils attend the Agricultural School, which is now placed under the control of the Director of Agriculture.

Associations.—Teachers' Associations, called *Jnana Vardhaka Sabhas,* hold meetings every Saturday for the purpose of having discussions on educational topics, and hearing lectures on literary and scientific subjects. Fifty such meetings were held, 14 in Baroda District, 20 in Kadi, 8 in Naosari, and 8 in Amreli, during the year.

Moral Text Books.—Attention is being paid to the imparting of moral and religious instruction to boys and girls. A small text book of moral precepts, illustrated by stories from ancient Hindu works, has been prepared by the accomplished and talented Mrs. Sharada Mehta, a graduate of the Bombay University, and wife of the House-Surgeon of the Dufferin Hospital at Baroda.

(*l*)—TECHNICAL EDUCATION.

The Kala-Bhavan, literally Temple of Arts, is a Technical Institute of great practical utility, and is one of the most notable instances of the Maharaja's unceasing endeavours towards progress and advancement. No more useful institution for encouraging industries and manufactures exists in this State, or perhaps in India.

The Technical Institute of Baroda was founded in June 1890, with classes for drawing, carpentry, and dyeing and calico-printing; and a class in mechanical engineering was added in the same year.

The Training College for men and the Agricultural classes, which were already in existence, were amalgamated with the Institute. Thus, in the first year of its existence, the Institute was provided with six different courses of instruction, each to extend over a period of three years, and was furnished with a library, a chemical laboratory, a physical laboratory, and other appliances. Workshops for the practical instruction of the students of the carpentry and mechanical engineering classes were also fitted up, along with a dye-house for dyeing and calico-printing. The subjects and methods of study have undergone revision in subsequent years according to new needs and requirements.

In 1891-92, the Maharaja sanctioned a sum of Rs. 50,000 towards the preparation of literary, scientific, and technical books in the Gujrati and Mahrathi languages. The work of preparing books was closed in 1896, with an additional grant of Rs. 15,000 to meet the liabilities already incurred.

In 1897, an important addition was made. A weaving class was opened with the object of introducing the fly-shuttle arrangement in the ordinary hand-loom in use in this country.

More ambitious work was undertaken after a visit of the then Principal to the Paris Exhibition of 1900; but much of this work, like nib and button-making, brush manufacture and pyrography, had to be abandoned subsequently. A class in watch-making was started in 1902, and has been continued.

Such has been the past history of this remarkable Institute, and the following brief account of its working during the year under report will indicate its present utility.

There were six schools under the Kala Bhavan during the year under report, *viz.*, those of Art, Architecture, Mechanical Technology, Chemical Technology, Weaving, and Watch-Making. The total number of students in the Kala-Bhavan rose from 233 to 364. Of these, 89 belonged to the city of Baroda, 99 to other places in the Baroda State, and 176 were outsiders. These last came mostly from the Bombay Presidency and the other Native States of Gujrat and Kathiawar; but 16 came from the Central Provinces, and 3 from so far as the United Provinces. 123 students sought admission into the engineering class, but for want of accommodation only 32 were admitted.

Besides the usual Kala-Bhavan scholarships of the aggregate value of Rs. 102 per month, 12 apprentice scholarships of Rs. 8 each per month, and tenable for three years, were awarded by the Director of Public Instruction of the Central Provinces to help students from that province to prosecute their studies in our Institute. There was also a scholarship of Rs. 7 granted by the Jain Swetambar Conference to a Jain student, one of Rs. 15 by the Porebunder State, one of Rs. 7 by the Manowadar State, and there were two scholarships of Rs. 9 and one of Rs. 7 by the Lakhtar State, available for students from these States studying at our Institute. Besides these, the firm of

Messrs. Leopold Cassella & Company of Germany
offered to send Rs. 45 per month to be distributed
as scholarships to the students of Calico-printing
and Dyeing, and the offer was accepted.

Out of 169 Candidates who presented for examination in the different schools, 11 out of 51
passed in Arts, 14 out of 28 in Carpentry, 54 out
of 57 in Mechanical Engineering, 8 out of 14 in
Dyeing, 7 out of 13 in Weaving, and one in Watch-
Making. 19 of our men out of 34 were successful
in the Engineer's Examination under the Bombay
Boiler Inspection Act, and obtained Engineer's
Certificates from the Government of Bombay.

Prizes and diplomas to the successful students
were distributed by His Highness the Maharaja
on the 25th of March 1905, prior to his departure
for Europe. Her Highness the Maharani also
graced the occasion with her presence, and a neat
little exhibition of students' work was got up for
the occasion.

One Gold Medal, two Silver and five Bronze
Medals, and four Certificates of Merit were awarded to the articles exhibited by the Baroda Institute
at the Industrial and Arts Exhibition held at
Bombay, in connection with the 20th Indian National Congress.

Industrial Schools.—In 1891-92 three Branch
Technical Institutes were opened at Kathor,
Petlad, and Pattan, and the Palace and the Public
Works Engineering Workshops were added to the
Central Institute at Baroda. The Branch Institute
of Petlad was transferred to Vaso in 1896, and

thence to Padra in 1904. The Technical Institute of Pattan was removed to Kadi in 1899. One practical and gratifying result of the Petlad-Vaso Institute was the opening of the successful Dyeing Factory of Petlad, of which mention has already been made in a previous chapter.

The numbers who attended these Industrial schools at Kathor, Vadnagar, and Padra were 86 in the year under report, against 83 of the previous year. Drawing and dyeing are taught in the Kathor and Padra branches, and carpentry and dyeing at Vadnagar.

The expenditure on the Kala-Bhavan and the Industrial schools last year was Rs. 52,679. The proposal to open some more industrial schools and commerical classes is under consideration.

Training College.—This College for Pedagogy was revived in June last, after an interval of 7 years, as a branch of the Kala-Bhavan. There were 66 admissions, 34 in the higher and 32 in the lower class. For accommodating these candidates two boarding houses have been opened under the direct supervision of the teachers. Fifteen scholarships of Rs. 7 per month are reserved for the teachers who avail themselves of this Training College.

It is necessary to mention that the present successful management of the Institute is largely due to the care and industry of Mr. Raojibhai M. Patel, its Principal. He was one of the young men who were sent to Europe by His Highness at State expense, and he studied mechanical engineering, cotton spinning and weaving, and the manufacture of textile machinery, at Bolton and Manchester. He became a Member of the Institute of Mechanical Engineers when in England, and returned to India in 1896. Since December 1902 he has been continuously in charge of the Technical Institute. Mr. Raojibhai has worked with ability, energy, and tact, and commands the respect of his pupils.

(m)—THE MUSEUM.

The Baroda Museum was established with the object of affording instruction to the people. The building was commenced in the year 1890, and completed in 1894. It runs from east to west, about 150 feet in length, and about 40 feet in breadth. It is a two-storied building, and contains an underground cellar.

The organization took place in July 1894. A European Director was employed for 12 months to give it a start, and, on the expiration of that period, Professor Masani was appointed as permanent Director, and occupies the post up to this day. With the liberal support of His Highness the Maharaja, the Museum has gone on steadily growing in importance; and in the last year was visited daily by 985 persons on an average.

It is divided into the Arts Section and the Science Section. The former contains an interesting collection of typical specimens of all arts and industries from almost all countries of the civilised world, specimens of fine and applied art which can be advantageously imitated by

Indian artists and craftsmen. The Indian arts are also more or less fully represented, and special care has been taken to collect and exhibit samples of the industrial arts of the Baroda State.

Among the arts specimens thus collected, the chief are silver, gold, brass, copper, bronze, iron, aluminium, electro-types and electro-plates, plain as well as engraved, inlaid and encrusted; ornamental leather work and lacquerware; carved, inlaid, and painted wood work; marble inlaying; rare pieces of old Chinaware, pottery and terracotta; porcelain and majolica of the finest description and latest make, such as the Royal Copenhagen, the Royal Worcester, the Royal Crown Derby, Doulton Ware, and the celebrated Limoges Sevres porcelain of France. The best glass work of the principal countries in the Continent of Europe has also been got together. A choice collection of pictures and paintings and some Indian musical instruments represent the fine arts. A large number of the specimens of the textile fabrics has also been collected and arranged in show cases specially allotted to them. Among the arts specimens, collected from the different art centres within the State, may be mentioned the Sankheda lacquerware, the silk Patolas and pottery of Pattan, sandalwood carved work inlaid with ivory from Billimora, brass work of Visnagar, silver work of Amreli, and blackwood carving of Visnagar and Unjha.

The Science Section represents almost all the branches of natural as well as physical sciences, namely, geology, mineralogy, palæontology, botany, zoology, ethnology, archæology, chemistry, and physics, the two last named being represented by a number of typical instruments and apparatus in mechanics, hydrostatics, light, heat, sound, and electricity.

The natural history gallery is sub-divided into invertebrata and vertebrata, the former containing dry and preserved animals of all orders, namely, protozoa, porifera, coelenterata, echinodermata, vermes, crustacea, mollusca, and in addition a large collection of shells.

The vertebrata class shows stuffed specimens and skeletons of the reptilia and batrachia. The ornithology is represented by skins of birds stuffed and mounted, as also skeletons, eggs, and nests of Indian as well as foreign birds. The extensive mammalian gallery has a splendid stock of mammals of all natural orders, namely, monotremata, marsupilia, edentata perissodactyla, artiodactyla proboscidea, hyracoidea, rodentia, insectivora, pinnipedia, carnivora, cheroptera, and primates, in stuffed and mounted specimens, as also skeletons, skins, mounted heads and skulls.

The botanical sub-section contains a herbarium of dried plants of almost all the natural orders met with in the Bombay Presidency, and artificial models of plants and fruits.

The anatomical room shows gypsum and papiers mache models of all parts of human and comparative anatomy, as well as a very instructive serie-embryological models in wax.

The economic gallery has a fine, large collection of mineral and vegetable medicinal drugs, as well as that of cereals, grown in the country, together with fibres, dye-stuffs, gums and other economic products.

The educational section contains object lesson cards and models of animals useful in the Kinder-garten system of teaching.

The ethnological gallery consists of an Egyptian mummy, a number of old arms, coins, medals, and ornaments, and a small but interesting series of spears, shoes, praying mats, combs, water bottles, pots and clubs, used by the semi-barbarous tribes of Somaliland.

The Director of the Museum, Professor Masani, proceeded to Europe with His Highness the Maha-raja to study the arrangements of the principal museums on the Continent. A large sum was placed at his disposal for the purchase of rare speci-mens of Arts and Science. Some of these have already arrived, and others are expected, and these will materially add to the usefulness of the insti-tution. Additions have also been made from the Bombay Industrial Exhibition of 1904-05, and from other places.

(n)—EDUCATION OF THE MAHARAJA'S CHILDREN.

Mr. T. H. French was in charge of the educa-tion of the Maharaja's children. Raj Kumar Sivajirao was preparing himself for the Bombay Matriculation Examination, and his work accord-ingly was mostly revision and the solving of ex-amination papers. He worked for 207 days in the year, about six hours every day, except Saturdays when he did three hours' work.

The school was held at Baroda till the end of March, when the children left for Europe. They then stayed at Eastbourne till the end of the year under report, Raj Kumar Sivajirao working privately at home, Raj Kumari Indira Raja attending a private school, Malvernhurst, and Raj Kumar Dhairyashilrao working privately and attending St. Christopher's School for games.

Raj Kumar Dhairyshilrao's studies were much interrupted owing to ill-health. He went to Darjiling in October, 1904, and did some work after his return to Baroda. In Europe he spent six weeks at Biarritz for his health, and returned to Eastbourne by the end of the official year.

In the current year Raj Kumar Sivajirao returned from Europe to attend the Matriculation Examination held in Bombay ; but unfortunately a high fever prevented his attendance for one day, and he was therefore unable to pass.

———

XII. MEDICAL.

(a)—Organization of the Department.

Dr. Shamsudin J. Sulemani, L.M., held the post of Chief Medical Officer. He joined the service of the State in 1876, and has served it faithfully and well during thirty years; and in 1899 the title of Khan Bahadur was conferred on him by the British Government. He was on leave from 9th May to 23rd June 1905, when Dr. Manekji Muncherji Gimi acted for him.

The strength of the Department continued the same as it was in 1903-04, with the addition of one Hospital Assistant.

The scale of pay of Hospital Assistants was revised to induce better qualified men to accept the appointment.

The pay of Medical pupils was also increased to attract better men.

(b)—Institutions.

The subjoined table gives an exhaustive list of all the medical institutions in the State open to the public, as well as the number of indoor and outdoor patients. The Lunatic Asylum and the Military Hospitals and Dispensaries are not shown here :—

Baroda City.

Institutions.	Indoor Patients.	Outdoor Patients.
Countess of Dufferin Hospital.	808	14,742
Jamnabai Dispensary........	....	38,581
Mahomedwadi Dispensary....	....	17,181

Baroda District.

Institutions.	Indoor Patients.	Outdoor Patients.
Dabhoi Dispensary	8	9,454
Petlad ,, ...	38	13,720
Anasuya Leper Hospital	171	382
Sankheda Dispensary	1	6,449
Sinor ,, ...	8	4,460
Saoli ,, ...	2	5,376
Vaghodia ,, ...	....	2,088
Karjan ,, ...	1	2,369
Padra ,, ...	3	6,937
Sojitra ,, ...	4	8,539

Naosari District.

Institutions.	Indoor Patients.	Outdoor Patients.
Naosari Civil Hospital	61	9,169
Gandevi Dispensary	....	7,090
Billimora ,, ...	2	3,977
Kathor ,, ...	2	4,460
Songadh ,, ...	9	3,923
Vyara ,, ...	....	4,784
Mahua ,, ...	....	4,281
Palsana ,, ...	....	3,508

Kadi District.

Institutions.	Indoor Patients.	Outdoor Patients.
Patan Civil Hospital	94	11,981
Kadi ,, ,, ...	42	7,544
Mehsana Dispensary	75	8,284
Visnagar ,, ...	107	5,912
Vadnagar ,, ...	1	7,058
Kheralu ,, ...	8	4,878
Vijapur ,, ...	2	9,234
Sidhpur ,, ...	8	7,971
Kalol ,, ...	5	7,661
Dehgam ,, ...	12	7,562
Chanasma ,, ...	1	8,807
Bechraji ,, ...	4	1,973
Harij ,, ...	....	2,105

Amreli District.

Institutions.	Indoor Patients.	Outdoor Patients.
Amreli Civil Hospital........	162	12,401
Dwarka Civil Hospital	11	7,123
Kodinar Dispensary	1	6,753
Damnagar ,, ...	1	4,980
Beyt ,, ...	....	3,737
Dhari town ,, ...	....	2,919

It will be seen from the above that the people
have largely availed themselves of the medical aid
so liberally extended to them, and the institutions
above noted continue to be as largely attended as
before. The figures given in the foregoing tables
shew new patients only, and a patient attending
for a number of days is shewn only once. The real
attendance in the dispensaries, day after day, was
therefore much larger than the above figures
would indicate; for instance, the Jamnabai Dispensary in Baroda City had an average daily attendance of 528 patients; the Mahomedwadi Dispensary
had an average daily attendance of 160 patients;
and the Countess of Dufferin Hospital had an
average daily attendance of 130 out-door patients,
and 56 indoor patients. Among the Taluka Dispensaries those of Petlad, Pattan, and Amreli were
the most largely attended, each treating over ten
thousand new patients annually.

The Countess of Dufferin Hospital treated the
largest number of indoor patients. Dr. Gimi is
in charge of this Hospital, and Dr. Sorabji Gazdar
acted for him for a time; while Dr. Sumant Mehta,
who has received his medical education in Europe,

was the House Surgeon. Among the Taluka institutions excluding the Anasuya Leper Hospital, the
Hospitals at Amreli, Visnagar, and Pattan treated
the largest number of indoor patients.

As regards sex, out of the total number of patients treated, about 50 per cent. were males, 20 per
cent. were females, and 30 per cent. were children.

(c)—PREVAILING DISEASES.

The most common diseases for which patients
were treated at the different medical institutions,
including the Military Hospitals and Dispensaries,
during the two last two years, are shown below :—

Names of Diseases.	Number of Patients.	
	1903-04.	1904-05.
Malarial fever	85,488	58,528
Worms	12,923	11,207
Dysentery	4,115	3,702
Diarrhoea	5,649	5,348
Venereal Diseases............	5,167	7,291
Rheumatic affections	9,569	9,545
Diseases of the nervous system	7,227	7,575
,, of the eye	29,517	29,168
,, of the ear	16,553	16,488
,, of the skin..........	27,687	26,551
,, of the lungs	661	973
Other Diseases of the Re-spiratory system.	15,005	14,629

It will be noticed that there was less of malaria
during the year under report than in 1903-04.
Perhaps this was due to scanty rainfall. In the
other diseases there is not any notable difference.

Eye diseases and skin diseases come next after
fever, and these three diseases brought a considerably larger number of patients to our medical
institutions than all the other diseases put together.

Plague was raging in all the Districts in a sporadic form. The number of towns and villages affected by it was 282, of which 45 had a mortality of 50 and over. At most of those 45 places, the disease was of a severe type. At the other places plague appeared in a mild form.

The total number of cases was 13,056, of which 9,374 proved fatal. The figures of cases and deaths during the year 1903-04 were respectively 19,982 and 14,946, showing that, during the year under report, the severity and extent of the epidemic was comparatively small.

The measures for relief adopted in previous years were continued during the year under report. Improved sanitation and free ventilation appear to be the only remedies. The material condition of the people has also some connexion with the spread of the disease, as has been remarked elsewhere.

(d)—CHEMICAL LABORATORY AND MEDICAL STORES.

Fifty-six Medico Legal cases, involving separate analysis of 213 articles, and 20 other miscellaneous cases, involving analysis of 361 articles, were investigated and reported on. Ninety-nine samples of water from different places were also examined.

The Medico Legal cases may be classified as below :—

Suspected Cases.	Number.
Human poisoning............	23
Cattle poisoning	5
Blood stains, &c.............	28

Dr. Sorabji Gazdar, who is the Chemical Analyser of the State, is also in charge of the Medical Stores. At the beginning of the year under report the value of medicines, &c., in stock at the depot was Rs. 59,678; and the cost of medicines, instruments, and appliances, bought during the year, was Rs. 33,152. The stores supplied to the Hospitals and Dispensaries of the State were ample and of good quality; and altogether His Highness provides for medical aid to his subjects on a very liberal scale.

(e)—LUNATIC ASYLUM.

The total number of lunatics treated during the year was 27 against 31 in the previous year. Of the 27, five were discharged cured, 3 absented, 2 died, and 17 remained under treatment. The total expenditure on account of the Asylum amounted to Rs. 2,785. The cost per lunatic was Rs. 103 per annum.

(f)—MISCELLANEOUS.

Ambulance Classes.—Ambulance classes were regularly held and lectures given. Dr. Dhanjishah Mehta compiled a book on the subject in 1901, and continued to deliver courses of lectures down to July 1904, after which the work was taken up by Dr. Sumant Mehta, House Surgeon of the Dufferin Hospital. Twenty-three candidates passed the examination test last year. Lectures on Home Hygiene were also given.

Obstetric Cases.—The number of obstetric cases, attended to by the midwife in the city of Baroda, was 163. Of these 19 were of abnormal and 35 of prolonged labour.

Befri Seed.—The Chief Medical Officer gave his opinion during the last famine that Befri seeds containing 21.1 per cent. of albuminoids, were nutritious like wheat or oatmeal. The Reporter on Economic Products of the Government of India confirms this opinion, and in his letter to the Resident at Baroda states that "the seed seems to be a good food."

Expenditure.—The dispensaries at Mehsana, Visnagar, and Bechraji were maintained, as before, from the funds of the Bechraji temple; and the Leper Hospital at Anasuya from the revenues of Amla village. Deducting these contributions, the expenditure of the Department was Rs. 1,61,397 against Rs. 1,69,804 of the previous year, as detailed below :—

Items.	Expenditure.	
	1903-04.	1904-05.
	Rs.	Rs.
Establishment	1,13,519	1,10,611
Contingencies	28,281	24,653
Medicines and instruments.	28,004	26,133
Total ..	1,69,804	1,61,397

The decrease in expenditure was chiefly due to the Municipal contributions received from B. class towns in the year 1904-05.

The annual increase of grants of Rs. 5,000 and Rs. 2,000, for medicines and contingencies respectively, has added to the efficiency of the institutions.

XIII. PUBLIC WORKS.

(a)—Constitution of the Department.

The constitution of the Department, as set forth in the report for 1903-4, continued unaltered during the year 1904-05.

Mr. Graham R. Lynn, M.I.C.E., was the Chief Engineer until October 1904, when he retired from service. Mr. J. R. Chico, L.C.E., acted as Chief Engineer from October 1904 to March 1905. On the 2nd March, His Highness appointed Mr. Chunilal Tarachand Dalal, L.C.E., as Chief Engineer.

His Highness the Maharaja, being desirous of forming a separate branch for the development of all irrigation projects throughout the State, appointed Mr. Vasanji K. Desai, L.C.E., as Executive Engineer for Irrigation, with the necessary establishment, in November 1904.

The services of Rao Bahadur Khandubhai G. Desai, L.C.E., (retired Executive Engineer of the P. W. Department, Bombay Presidency,) were engaged in December 1904, for a period of one year, to give his opinion on the irrigation projects prepared by our Engineers, to finish the incomplete projects, to prepare and develop new schemes, and to supervise the execution of the irrigation works in progress.

On account of the famine operations in Okhamandal, that Taluka was turned into a special Executive Division, and placed in charge of an Executive Engineer in direct communication with the Chief Engineer.

(b)—BUILDINGS AND SPECIAL WORKS.

The following important works were completed, or were in progress, during the year under report :—

Baroda District.—Some additions to the L. V. Palace, fountains in the terrace garden, servants' quarters, two bungalows near the palace, and two villas near the Chiman Bag. Also additions to the bungalows at Ootacamand, and a small bungalow at Bombay with stables and coachhouses. A market in Baroda town was also commenced.

The scheme for conveying electric energy from the central station at Baroda, L. V. Palace to Makarpura, a distance of 4 miles, was pushed on. This scheme is full of promise. The sectional sewage pumps of the city drainage are proposed to be worked by electric power ; and that power along the route of the transmission lines can be used to work motor pumps for irrigating farms and driving small factories. The use of small motors, ranging from $\frac{1}{6}$ H.P. to 1 H.P. or upwards, for working hand looms, is likely to promote home weaving industry. Necessary provision has also been made in the scheme for street lighting.

Kadi District.—The Villa at Pattan was in progress ; when completed it will be for the use of His Highness, and also of Officers on tour.

A bungalow for the Civil Surgeon at Mehsana, having an architectural frontage of classic style, and a bungalow for the Opium Superintendent at Sidhpur, were in progress. A record building at Mehsana was completed.

(c)—ROADS.

Amreli District—The Amreli—Kundla Road and the Challala—Dharangni Road were completed. The Damnagr—Dhasa Road and the Dhari—Challala Road were thoroughly repaired. The Dhari—Dalkhania—Sapness Road was also taken in hand, and the work was in progress at the close of the year. It has been stated elsewhere that the tolls levied on these roads have now been suspended.

Baroda, Kadi and Naosari Districts.—Railway lines run through these Districts, and there is less need for roads here than in Amreli. Nearly all the Talukas are intersected by such lines, or are within easy distance from railway stations; what is needed therefore is, in these last cases, to construct or improve feeder roads from the stations to the Taluka head-quarters. Smaller roads connecting villages with each other, or with the main lines of communication by rail or road, are now left to Local Boards.

(d)—TANKS AND WELLS.

During the year under report there was scanty rain; and, to relieve the distress from scarcity of water, many tanks were repaired and wells deepened. The following are some of them :—

Baroda District.—The Bhandraj tank and Dabhao tank in Petlad were excavated. Thirty-six tanks in Petlad taluka, and a few elsewhere, were deepened.

Five new wells were sunk in Petlad, 14 in Vaghodia, 2 in Saoli, and 5 in Baroda. 33 wells were deepened and repaired in Petlad, 39 in Vaghodia, 59 in Saoli, 11 in Baroda, and 1 in Padra. Thus, in all, 169 wells were either deepened and repaired or newly sunk.

Kadi District.—The Jamnapur, Charup, Chatiarda, Sidhnath, Dhinoj and Mooria tanks were excavated, improved or repaired.

Amreli District.—The Mota Ankadia tank in Amreli Taluka and the Dhamel tank in Damnagar Taluka were excavated.

The Bhimgaja tank project, as an Irrigation work in Okhamandal Taluka, was taken in hand, and the work started.

(e)—RAILWAYS.

All the four State Railways *viz*: (1) Dabhoi Railway, (2) Petlad Railway, (3) Mehsana Railway, (4) Vijapur Kalol Kadi Railway—were open for traffic.

Some particulars relating to each of them are given below :—

(1) *Dabhoi Railway System.*—The different branches of this line open for traffic were working as under during the year under report.

Dates of Opening.	Sections.	Mileage.
April 1873.........	Miyagam to Dabhoi	20·00
April 1879.........	Dabhoi to Chandod........	10·62
September 1879 ..	Dabhoi to Bhadarpur......	9·64
July 1880	Dabhoi to Goyagate	17·00
January 1881	Goyagate to Vishwamitri..	1·63
June 1890	Badharpur to Bodeli	12·77
July 1897	Vishwamitri to Padra	7·14
July 1903	Padra to Mobha	9·20
November 1904 ..	Mobha to Masor Road	6·49
	Total ..	94·49

The line from Mobha to Masor Road, an extension of 6·49 miles, was opened during the year.

The total capital outlay on this line upto the end of June 1905 was Rs. 24,44,044. The percentage of net earning on capital outlay during the year 1904 was Rs. 5·19.

(2). *Petlad Railway System.*—The branches of this line open for traffic continued to work as under :—

Dates of Opening.	Sections.	Mileage.
May 1890	Anand to Petlad	13·17
June 1901........	Petlad to Tarapur	8·33
	Total ..	21·50

The total capital outlay on this line upto the end of June 1905 was Rs. 11,22,562. The percentage of net earnings on capital outlay during the year 1904 was Rs. 5·71.

(3). *Mehsana Railway System.*—The branches of this system open for traffic continued to work as under :—

Dates of Opening.	Sections.	Mileage.
1887	Mehsana to Vadnagar	20·73
1888	Vadnagar to Kheralu......	7·00
1891	Mehsana to Pattan........	24·69
1891	Mehsana to Viramgam	40·21
	Total ..	92·63

Further extensions of this system are under consideration ; *viz* : (1) Visnagar to Vijapur, (2) Manud Chanasma to Bechraji, (3) Kheralu to Dabhora, and (4) Chanasma to Harij. The latter three branches were taken in hand during the year under report. Their total extension would measure about 48 miles.

There was a light rail road from Shedvi to Kadarpur, a distance of 7 miles, during the year under report. This line was extended to Kheralu. The earthwork was almost completed from Kheralu to Kadarpur to suit the metre guage line proposed to be constructed as far as Dabhora.

The earthwork of the Manud Chanasma Bechraji Railway was first taken up as a relief work, and was then let by contract, and 6,91,584 cubic feet of earth-work was done.

Some earth-work was done also on the third extension, *viz*: Chanasma to Harij.

The line from Visnagar to Vijapur was under survey.

The total capital outlay on this system upto the end of June 1905 was Rs. 34,17,153; and the percentage of net earnings on the capital outlay during the year 1904 was Rs. 6'03.

(4). *Vijapur Kalol Kadi Railway System.*—The branches of this line continued to work as under:—

Dates of Opening.	Sections.	Mileage.
June 1902	Kalol to Vijapur	29'44
July 1903	Kalol to Kadi	11'93
	Total ..	41'37

The total capital outlay on this line upto June 1905 was Rs. 13,18,476. The percentage of net earnings on the capital outlay, during the year 1904 was Rs. 3'00.

The total State Railway lines at present measure 250 miles, and the total capital investment on the same at the end of June 1905 was Rs. 83,02,235, giving an average of over Rs. 33,000 per mile. The average nett profit on the capital investment in 1904 was 5·25 per cent.

Besides the earnings referred to above, the State realized from its 1,600 shares of the Tapti Valley Railway (of the nominal value of Rs. 8,00,000), a sum of Rs. 22,400 during the year 1904, which gives an average of only 2·8 per cent.

(f)—IRRIGATION.

His Highness the Maharaja has devoted much attention to the subject of irrigation, and a large number of important works have been constructed or are still in progress. It must be admitted, however, that some of the larger works have not been as successful as was expected. This is partly due to the continuous dificient rainfall of the past seven or eight years, and in some cases perhaps to mistakes. It would be useful to note briefly what has been done in the different Districts.

Baroda District.—Six irrigation tanks have been constructed, and the cost of each of them is shewn below :—

	Rs.
Karchiya	38,566
Haripura	30,945
Lachras	6,664
Khokra	19,320
Sarsi in Desar	11,267
Kumbhari	12,577

A sum of a lac and twenty thousand in round numbers is spent on these six tanks. What is now wanted is to construct channels for bringing the water of these tanks to the use of cultivators, and to make administrative arrangements for supplying the water at a low rate. These steps are being taken in the current year.

A seventh tank at Muwal is an old tank which irrigates 1,600 acres of land.

The eighth irrigation work in the District is the Orsang Scheme. This is a project to dam the water of the Orsang river, and to use the perennial flow for irrigating lands. The dam which is 2,700 feet long is on a rock foundation, and six feet above the bed level of the river. The take off for the canal is in a rocky nulla on the right bank. The catchment area is about 750 square miles, and the canal from Jojwa to Akhtiyarpura is six miles in length. The cost up to date is Rs. 5,22,066, and a larger sum will have to be spent before the work is completed.

The present Chief Engineer proposes to widen the canal, and to build a reservoir at its end across the head of the Dhader river. He estimates, the capacity of the reservoir will be about 600 million cubic feet. He believes, it will be possible to irrigate 20,000 acres of rice land from the canal; and if any water is left in the tank at the end of the rainy season, it may be used for winter crops.

There are two other ambitious schemes in this District under contemplation. The first is the project of the Alwa Tank near Vagodhia, which is expected to impound 300 million cubic feet of water, and is estimated to cost ten lacs. And the second is to utilize the flow of the Hiran river, and to construct an impounding reservoir.

Kadi District.—The Kaderpur Tank is the most important irrigation work in this District, and has cost Rs. 3,68,000. The bund is 12,000 feet long and 27 feet high; the catchment area is 30 square miles; and the impounding capacity is 767 million cubic feet. It appears, however, that the work has been constructed on too large a scale, and the water supply, such as we have had in recent years, can fill a reservoir of the capacity of a hundred million cubic feet only. The present Chief Engineer proposes to allow all the upper parts of the tank to be cultivated, to store only a hundred million cubic feet of water, and to cut distribution channels which will irrigate 1,500 acres of land. Schemes for increasing the catchment area, and thus adding to the water supply, are reserved for future consideration.

The second most important irrigation work in this District is the Anawada Dam. It is a submerged weir, built across the Saraswati river below Pattan, with the object of arresting the underflow in the sand. The idea is to raise the water after the monsoon by removable weir shutters, and to lead the water thus arrested through a canal to irrigate a portion of the Harij Taluka. The Dam and some miles of the canal have been completed at a cost of Rs. 85,000, but in this case also, the expected supply of water has not come in these dry years, and will probably never be available. The perennial supply in the river disappears in sides of the Dam, and there is no water in the canal. The present Chief Engineer proposes to

33

put an under sluice in the Dam, and to lower and widen the canal. His idea is, that the canal can then feed a series of tanks, and lands in Harij Taluka can be irrigated. An additional sum of over a lac of rupees will be required to carry out this scheme.

The Dharusen Reservoir is an impounding reservoir, which has been constructed to utilise the flow in the northern drainage channel from Gotwar village in the cold season. It is expected to irrigate from 1,000 to 2,000 acres in the north of the Kadi Taluka. The head works are finished, and the canal remains to be done.

Naosari District.—Hitherto this District has not suffered from any serious famine. There are a few irrigation works under contemplation. The Umrat Tank is situated in the Naosari Taluka. It has a capacity of 69 million cubic feet, and is capable of irrigating 800 acres. The Bunderpada Weir and Canal is an old work, and is situated in the Songadh Taluka. It is fed by a small stream, and irrigates about 200 bighas. The Chikhli Weir is constructed in the Vyara Taluka across the Mindhola river, and irrigates 600 bighas. There are other projects in this division in course of investigation.

Amreli District.—The Singoda River project was a scheme to dam the river near Ghatwar by a masonry bund, and utilize the flow for irrigating the land on the left bank of the river. The catchment area was reckoned at 150 square miles, and it was anticipated that 3,000 acres could be irrigated. Rs. 36,312 have been spent on cutting a canal and constructing a Bungalow. But it is found that the river has not much perennial supply in the dry season. The present Chief Engineer proposes to reduce the estimated cost of the proposed dam by constructing it higher up, and to build a reservoir across the river in the Junagadh territory. Permission to make a survey has been obtained.

The Pichwi project was expected to impound 280 million cubic feet of water, and to irrigate 5,600 acres. Rs. 1,02,158 have been spent. But the catchment area is only 30 square miles, and looking at the deficiency of water in these parts, the present Chief Engineer proposes to reduce the first estimate and to make the reservoir smaller. With an additional expenditure of 1½ lacs he proposes to store 170 million cubic feet of water, and irrigate 2,500 acres only.

The Ankadia tank is a smaller work, estimated to hold 70 million cubic feet of water, and to protect dry fields. We have spent Rs. 23,368 on it up to the end of the year under report, and the work is in progress.

The Bhimgaja tank was estimated to hold 373 million cubic feet of water. But as the catchment area is only 21 square miles, we shall probably never get more than 105 million cubic feet. The present Chief Engineer accordingly proposes to reduce the work to that capacity, and the estimate will be reduced to about Rs. 50,000 only. Rs. 8,500 were spent up to the close of the year under report.

(g)—MISCELLANEOUS.

Water Lifts—With a view to ascertain the relative efficiency of the various kinds of water lifts in use, and also new inventions, a Committee was appointed with Mr. Abbas Tyabji, Judge of the Varisht Court, as President. The Committee's Report was received in December 1904, and the results of the several experiments made were published in the local papers, in order that the general public might take advantage of the information in selecting the kind of lift that might suit their requirements.

Harbour and Navigation.—The question of forming a harbour at Velan was first started in 1886. In 1894 the question was again moved by Mr. Robert Bruce Foote, then Geological Surveyor to His Highness's Government. The late Mr. Jagannath Sadashiv, A.M., L.C.E., then Executive Engineer of the Baroda Water Works, investigated the scheme and reported favourably on the same. In the famine of 1900, His Highness visited the place, and sanctioned the improvement of the harbour. During the year under report the project was again thoroughly investigated, and a comprehensive report with plans and estimates has been prepared. The matter is under consideration of the Chief Engineer.

The District Officer of Naosari suggested the improvement of the harbours at Naosari and Billimora, and a sum has been provided in the current year's budget for the purpose. The plans and estimates for both these works have been prepared, and the works are under construction.

(h)—EXPENDITURE OF THE DEPARTMENT.

The expenditure of the Department during the last two years is shown below :—

Nature of work.	Year 1903-04.	Year 1904-05.
1. Original works	14,02,682	11,57,223
2. Repairs	3,83,894	2,89,234
3. Establishment	1,79,361	1,94,711
4. Tools and plants..........	10,935	55,687
5. Petty Revenue Public Works.	30,750	78,444
6. Military Public Works ..	24,061	31,858
7. Famine Relief Works....	7,165	1,98,846
8. Refund	103	248
Total Rs. ..	19,88,951	20,06,251

The following table shows the expenditure incurred in each District during the year under report, as compared with that in the previous year :—

Districts.	Expenditure in 1903-04.	Expenditure in 1904-05.
1. Baroda City..................	3,67,749	6,85,526
2. Baroda District..............	8,71,768	2,13,106
3. Naosari District	1,25,594	91,289
4. Kadi District	1,21,922	1,76,025
5. Kadi Irrigation	1,37,653	31,615
6. Amreli District..............	1,77,387	3,75,951
7. Okhamandal Taluka..........	Nil	12,794
8. Gardens	1,86,878	4,19,945
Total Rs.	19,88,951	20,06,251

The Department also expended, on account of contribution works for other Departments, the sum of Rs. 2,94,188. Thus the total expenditure amounted to Rs. 23,00,439. The ratio of the cost of the establishment to the total outlay was 9·2 per cent.

XIV.—POLICE.

(a)—CONSTITUTION OF THE FORCE.

During the year under report, the Department was administered by Mr. Govindbhai Hathibhai Desai, B.A., LL.B., officiating Police Commissioner.

The sanctioned strength and pay of the Police force and establishment underwent a revision. The new sanctioned strength, excluding non-effectives, is 4,886 against 4,763 in the preceding year, and is distributed as follows :—

District.	Sanctioned strength excluding non-effectives.	Jail, Treasury, Guard and other duties.	Vacancies.	Number engaged in prevention and detection of crime.
Baroda........	2,031	928	81	1,022
Kadi	1,524	421	40	1,063
Naosari	765	259	98	413
Amreli........	566	225	12	329
	4,886	1,833	226	2,827

From the above table it will be seen that 2,827, or 57·86 per cent of the force, were employed on regular police duty, viz., that the duty of prevention and detection of crime. 4 men and 1 officer were entertained as extra police in the Amreli District on Famine Relief Works. No preventive police was appointed during the year under report.

Comparing the number of policemen employed on regular police duty with the area and population of the whole State, it is found that there was, on an average, one policeman for an area of 2·86 square miles, and for every group of 690 men.

Excluding non-effectives and vacancies from the sanctioned strength, there were, in the last year, 4,660 men and officers of whom 2,937, *i.e.*, 63·03 per cent. were able to read and write. The percentage in the preceding year was 54·79. This clearly shows that the number of those who can read and write is steadily increasing in the force.

There were 22 Judicial and 1,941 Departmental punishments during the year, against 13 Judicial and 1,451 Departmental punishments of the previous year. This increase is due to a stricter discipline having been enforced. On the other hand 185 officers and men were given money rewards in the last year, against 87 of the previous year.

The expenditure incurred on the Police during the last two years is shewn below:—

	1904-05.	1903-04.
	Rs.	Rs.
Pay and allowance	5,68,341	5,40,949
Arms and Accoutrements.....	32,377	14,057
Miscellaneous charges	35,078	41,409
	6,35,796	5,96,414

(b)—REFORMS.

The following are the most important reforms which were introduced in the Police Department during the year under report :—

(1) A new Police Code has been compiled and published in three volumes. It embodies all the rules and regulations necessary for the proper discharge of police functions.

(2) A special Police Drill Book has been prepared and published, embodying the latest improvements.

(3) An endeavour has been made to render the force more efficient by making accessible to all officers information about Criminal Tribes and Dangerous Gangs.

(4) Correspondence and writing work has been reduced to the lowest possible limits. The rules of the Revenue Department applicable to the Police have been clearly indicated.

(5) The pay of the Police has been revised and raised, so as to attract better recruits. The beneficial result of this arrangement is already apparent.

(6) The number of useless men is reduced. Of the 1,349 foot and 437 sowars handed over to the Department, about 117 foot and 50 swars have been maintained for performance of extra duty, and the rest have been returned to the Military Department.

(7). The dress of the force has been improved, and a Dress Regulation Book,
giving description and coloured plates
of the uniforms of officers and men, has
been published.

(8). His Highness the Maharaja has passed
orders regarding the admission of educated persons in the force, to a greater
extent than in the past.

On the whole the care and zeal with which
Mr. Govindbhai Hathibhai has administered the
Police force, and the success with which he has
kept down crime in a year of distress and famine
like 1904-05, are creditable to him and to the Department.

(c)—STATISTICS.

The subjoined table furnishes particulars with
regard to offences against person and property in
the four Districts of the State for the last year, as
compared with those of the preceding year :—

	Baroda.		Kadi.		Naosari.		Amreli.		Total.	
	1904-05.	1903-04.	1904-05.	1903-04.	1904-05.	1903-04.	1904-05.	1903-04.	1904-05.	1903-04.
Murder	21	14	10	15	4	3	3	5	38	37
Culpable homicide....	9	9	21	20	2	9	2	5	34	43
Grievous hurt	37	31	53	39	22	11	11	6	123	87
Rape	5	2	5	2	3	0	2	0	15	4
Theft................	474	405	643	535	116	119	116	96	1,349	1,155
Theft with house-breaking.	381	263	218	167	35	44	66	45	700	519
Robbery	45	28	57	40	4	11	7	7	113	86
Dacoity...............	5	6	8	6	0	0	0	1	13	13
Receiving stolen pro-perty.	16	20	10	24	3	1	6	3	35	48
Criminal breach of trust.	42	46	28	54	9	11	6	10	85	121
Mischief	70	42	19	21	0	2	6	4	95	69
Miscellaneous	172	114	443	511	94	47	47	28	756	700
Total ..	1,277	980	1,515	1,434	292	258	272	210	3,356	2,882

Offences against person.—There has been a decrease in culpable homicide during the year under report, as compared with the previous year, and an increase in other offences. The difference does not call for any explanation.

Offences against property.—There is an increase in theft and robbery cases, owing to the distress and the famine of the year ; but there has been a decrease in receiving stolen property and criminal breach of trust. Dacoity cases remain the same as in the previous year, *i.e.*, 13 during the whole twelve months.

The table given below furnishes particulars of other miscellaneous offences :—

	Baroda.		Kadi.		Naosari.		Amreli.		Total.	
	1904-05	1903-04	1904-05	1903-04	1904-05	1903-04	1904-05	1903-04	1904-05	1903-04
Rioting	16	0	34	40	5	20	3	5	58	65
Offences against coinage.............	3	4	10	2	1	0	3	1	17	7
Offences against marriage	29	23	16	5	3	6	12	4	60	38
Offences against justice.............	18	16	3	1	3	6	5	3	29	26
Miscellaneous	323	256	292	330	107	143	21	17	743	746
Total ..	389	299	355	378	119	175	44	30	907	882

It is satisfactory to find that during a year of famine there was no increase in rioting cases, but on the contrary a marked decrease as compared with the previous year. This happy result is due : *firstly* to the peaceful disposition of the people of India among whom grain riots are rare, *secondly* to the liberal measures of relief organised by His Highness's Government, and *thirdly* to the efficiency and good work of the Police. Offences against coinage and offences against marriage shew, however, a marked increase during the year under review.

The proportion of crime to the police employed on prevention and detection of crime in the State was 1˙5 cognizable offences to each policeman. The proportion of crime to population was 1 cognizable offence to every group of 600 men. In other words there was only one cognizable crime in an average village during the entire 12 months.

In addition to 4,263 cases reported during the last year, 385 cases were pending from the previous year. Out of this total, 272 were withdrawn, and 1,115 ordered by Magistrates to be struck off as false. The number of cases left for police enquiry was, therefore, 3,261. Of these, 2,572 or 78˙87 per cent. were committed to Magistrates, 218 or 6˙69 per cent. remained undetected, and 471 or 14˙44 per cent. were pending enquiry. The following table gives the details for the year 1904-05 and 1903-04 :—

Years.	No. of cases report during the year.	Cases of previous year brought under inquiry.	Total.	Cases struck off as false.	Cases withdrawn.	Number of cases for Police.
1904–05	4,263	385	4,648	1,115	272	3,261
1903–04	3,764	404	4,168	930	315	2,923

The proportion of 78'87 per cent. of cases being detected, and only 6'69 per cent. of cases being undetected, is so favorable to the Police that it might raise a suspicion that many hopeless cases are not registered. To judge work by percentages of successful cases is always attended with the danger that the Police endeavour to make out good percentages by not reporting bad cases. Such suppression of crime is not unknown in British India, and care should be taken against its prevalence here. The practice can be checked, firstly by judging the merit of officers by work done in particular cases rather than by percentages, secondly by constant watchfulness on the part of the Police Commissioner and all Superior Officers, and thirdly by taking severe departmental notice of every instance in which the suppression of crime is proved.

The subjoined table shews the disposal of the cases which the police dealt with during the year 1904-05 and 1903-04 :—

Cases.

Years.	Resulted in acquittal.	Withdrawn.	Resulted in conviction.	Remained pending at the end of the year.	Total number of cases sent to Magistrates for trial.	Percentage of convictions to cases sent to Magistrates excluding cases withdrawn and pending.
1904–05	631	113	1,532	296	2,572	70·83
1903–04	547	103	1,452	247	2,349	72·64

The number of persons arrested during the year, with those left under police enquiry from last year, was 5,334, of whom 4,288 were sent up for trial.

Details about disposal of persons committed for trial for the years 1904-05 and 1903-04 are given below :—

Persons.

Years.	Released in cases withdrawn.	Died after commencement of trial.	Escaped.	Pending trial at the end of the year.	Convicted.	Acquitted.	Percentage of those convicted after deducting the figures in columns 2, 3, 4, and 5.
1904–05	278	10	....	501	2,086	1,413	59·62
1903–04	203	4	....	441	1,916	1,211	61·27

The following table furnishes details with regard to property for the years 1904-05 and 1903-04 :—

Years.	Cases in which property was alleged to have been stolen which the police had to deal with.	Alleged value of the stolen property.	Cases in which property was recovered.	Value of property recovered.	Percentage of property recovered to property stolen.	Percentage of cases in which property was recovered to those in which it was stolen
		Rs.		Rs.		
1904–05	1,526	1,56,580	1,018	99,767	63·72	66·71
1903–04	1,218	1,28,807	844	78,381	60·92	69·29

The general results of police administration during the last two years are summed up in the following table:—

Years.	Percentage of conviction to cases decided by Magistrates.	Percentage of persons convicted to persons committed.	Percentage of property recovered to property stolen.
1904–1905	70·83	59·62	63·72
1903–1904	72·64	61·27	60·92

The table shews that in the matter of convictions the Police were less successful in 1904-05 than in the previous year ; but in recovering stolen property they were more successful.

XV.—JAILS.

(a)—District and Subordinate Jails.

Mr. Govindbhai H. Desai was in charge of the Jail Department during the year under report.

Besides the *Central Jail* at Baroda there were four *District Jails* in the State, *viz.*, one at Kadi, one at Naosari, one at Amreli and one at Dwarka.

The number of *Subordinate Jails* was reduced from 2 to 1. The only Subordinate Jail left was at Mehsana ; and the number of *Lock-ups* in the State rose from 38 to 39.

The Central Jail at Baroda and the District Jails of Kadi, Naosari and Amreli, are under the superintendence of the Civil Surgeons of these places. The District Jail at Dwarka is under the control of the Vahivatdar of that place, as there is no Civil Surgeon there. The one Subordinate Jail at Mehsana is also under the control of the Vahivatdar of the place. All Lock-ups are under the control of the local Vahivatdars and Mahalkaris.

The total number of persons received in all the Jails during the year under report was 5,219 against 4,980 in the preceding year. The increase of 239 is due to the greater number of offences, owing to the failure of the monsoon and the consequent scarcity in most of the Talukas. The total daily average in all the Jails was, however, only 915 against 1,040 in the preceding year.

Nearly 90 per cent. of the total number of convicts were Hindus, and about 10 per cent. were Mahomedans. The ages between 16 and 40 contributed the largest number of criminals as in the preceding year. About 10 per cent. of the adult convicts knew how to read and write. Agriculturists and labourers and private servants formed the largest portion of the Jail population. The offences which led to the greatest number of convictions were grievous hurt and theft. Most of the sentences were for periods ranging between a month and 6 months.

The total expenditure for the year under Report was Rs. 67,165 against Rs. 67,419 in the preceding year.

The total earnings from convict labour in all the Jails was Rs. 24,554 against 27,325 in the preceding year. The average annual cost per prisoner came up to Rs. 73 against 65 in the last year. The increase in the cost per prisoner is due to the higher value of food in a year of scarcity, and to the permanent guard and establishment charges being distributed over a smaller number of daily average number of prisoners.

(b)—REFORMS.

The following are the principal reforms introduced during the year under report :—

(1) The pay of jail officials and warders has been revised and converted into British currency.

(2) The powers of Jail Superintendents have been clearly defined, and unnecessary correspondence is thus checked.

(3) Jail records in all the jails have been arranged according to the new Record Rules.

(4) Intramural labour in the Central Jail at Baroda has been augmented.

XVI.—FAMINE RELIEF.

(a) PREPARATION.

Famine had been long unknown in Gujrat. The province, like Oudh, claimed the honour of being a Garden of India, where the crops were seldom known to fail. From this fancied security, Gujrat was awakened in to the sad realities of a prolonged famine which lasted from 1899 to 1902.

The rains were fairly good in 1903, but again failed in 1904; and the campaign of relief had to be resumed after what proved to be only a brief intermission.

The scantiness of the South-West Monsoon was watched with anxiety, both by the people and the Officers, and before the first week of September had passed, their worst fears seemed to be realised. His Highness the Maharaja personally watched these premonitory symptoms, and lost no time in organising a special Department for Famine Relief. Mr. R. C. Dutt, the Revenue Minister, was placed in charge of the Famine Relief Work; and Mr. Manubhai N. Mehta was placed under him as Famine Commissioner, to plan and organise the necessary relief operations.

The Monsoon failed over three districts out of the four which comprise the State. The situation was saved in Naosari and parts of the Baroda district by the downpour of September, but the Kadi and the Amreli districts received no portion of these showers. The total rain-fall, however, was deficient everywhere, as will appear from the annexed statement.

Name of the District.	Total average rainfall.		
	1899-1900.	1904-1905.	10 years preceding 1899-1900
Baroda	5·39	17·6	40·1
Kadi	3·75	9·80	25·10
Amreli	4·77	7·56	21·66
Naosari	18·62	25·40	53·65

Thus the rainfall, though better than in 1899-1900, was short of the decennial average preceding that year. Against an average of 40 inches in Baroda District, the year under report registered a deficiency of over 50 per cent. in all the Talukas except Sankheda and Tilakwada. The Kadi District had even a worse record. The annual average for the decade immediately preceding the drought of 1899 had been 25 inches; for the year under review it scarcely exceeded 9. The general deficiency of rainfall throughout the Kadi District thus exceeded 60 per cent. even after the September rains. But the Amreli District was the worst. The Talukas of Amreli, Dhari, and Damnagar had only about 5 inches of rainfall against an average of 21; while in the Okhamandal Taluka the rainfall was only 3 inches against an average of 19. The deficiency in Amreli thus exceeded 75 per cent., and a wide spread distress soon became inevitable.

His Highness's Government were alive to the danger which was impending. With the appointment of Mr. Manubhai Mehta, as Famine Commissioner, the strength of the Intelligence Department

35

was duly reinforced, so that no symptom of distress might remain undetected. The District and Taluka officers were charged with the duty of watching all the usual signals and sending weekly reports. Besides noting the increase in the prices of food grains, they were asked to watch the following facts :—

(a). Contraction of private charity as evidenced by the wandering of paupers.

(b). Shrinking of private credit.

(c). Feverish activity in the grain trade,

(d). Restlessness culminating in increased crime.

(e). Unusual and aimless wandering of people.

(f). Extraordinary migration of flocks and herds of cattle in search of pasturage.

The District Executive Engineers were warned to hold themselves in readiness with a workable list of relief works, and an adequate number of spare hands. Special establishments were sanctioned for preparing and maturing important irrigation and drainage projects, so that the outlay required for relief might not be wasted on unremunerative works of doubtful value. The Police and the Medical Departments were also told to be in readiness.

Tours of inspection were undertaken. His Highness himself, with a view to witness the condition of the crops with his own eyes, visited the Sankheda and Petlad Talukas, accompanied by the Revenue Minister and the Revenue and the Famine Commissioners, as early as the first week of September. The Diwan was directed by His Highness to visit the affected districts of Kadi, and included Pattan, Vadaoali, Sidhpur, Mehsana, Harij and Kheralu Talukas in his tour. In the following month the Diwan proceeded to Amreli, and visited the Talukas of Damnagar, Amreli, Dhari and Kodinar.

Early in November, the Revenue Minister, accompanied by the Maharaja's eldest son and the Famine Commissioner, again made a tour through the affected Talukas of Kadi District, He visited Mehsana, Visnagar, Sidhpur, Pattan and Kalol Talukas. All the revenue officials from the various Talukas were invited to meet him in a Conference at Mehsana, to discuss the requirements of their several charges, and to devise the necessary measures of relief. The Famine Commissioner was then asked to visit outlying villages and the Harij, Vadaoali and Kadi Talukas. And thus all necessary information was collected for settling the details of the relief campaign and opening relief operations.

The Famine Commissioner had, by that time, also finished his tour through the Amreli District. He proceeded to Okhamandal early in September in order to settle a programme of relief measures needed for that Taluka, which is usually the earliest to succumb. He then proceeded to Kodinar to organise the operations of exporting grass from the Gir forest to Okhamandal, and to examine the two irrigation projects at Ghatwar and Pichwi, which had been left incomplete during the previous famine. The Famine Commissioner finished his first round of tours with a visit to the Petlad Taluka, which had by that time been showing some symptoms of distress.

In January and February 1905, His Highness the Maharaja, accompanied by the Revenue Minister and the Revenue Commissioner, made a prolonged tour in Amreli and Kadi Districts, and saw the condition of his people in the Amreli, Dhari, Damnagar, and Mehsana Talukas. His Highness's tours were productive of very beneficent results, as the remissions of the land revenue demand, ordered immediately after, were the outcome of his personal observations.

The Famine Commissioner, meanwhile, had finished a useful work in revising the Famine Relief Code with the help of the Revenue Commissioner. The Code had been hastily improvised in 1899 to meet the pressing requirements of the year, and stood much in need of modifications in the light of the ampler experience obtained since. The valuable Report of the Famine Commission of Sir Antony MacDonnell had also been published, and no Code could be complete unless it took note of the conclusions arrived at by that important Commission. Sir Antony MacDonnell has made various suggestions regarding the different methods of exacting work from relief seekers, the allotment of tasks, the fixing of wages, the classification and the payment of labourers according to their age, sex, and physical condition, and the relief of their dependents on works.

The Famine Commissioner took note of all this in revising the Baroda Famine Code, which, it is hoped, will require little revision hereafter.

Early in October, when all hopes of any improvement in the situation were abandoned, the District Officers were instructed to formulate their proposals regarding the various measures of relief needed for the Talukas under their charge. These different programmes of relief received the careful consideration of the Maharaja, assisted by all the highest Officers convened in Council, and plans of action were laid down. The various measures of relief determined upon after these consultations are mentioned below :—

Prompt suspensions of the land-revenue demand.

Liberal remissions of both the current year's land-revenue, and of accumulated arrears.

Advances in the form of *Takavi* to cultivators on a large scale, both for the permanent improvement of their lands, and for enabling them to tide over the impending calamity.

Improvement of the drinking water supply.

· Arrangements to meet the scarcity of fodder.

Relief works.

Gratuitous relief.

His Highness the Maharaja sanctioned an aggregate amount of Rs. 27,33,985 for these measures. Out of this sum, Rs. 16,51,800 were meant for the numerous relief works approved of in the Public Works programme, and Rs. 10,82,185 were allotted to the various items on the Civil Agency programme.

(b)—SUSPENSIONS OF LAND-REVENUE.

Instructions had been issued to the District Officers to collect statistics of the outturn of crops in the different Talukas by personal observation as early as October, and their proposals regarding the suspension of the land revenue demand were submitted to His Highness the Maharaja by the end of November. These were carefully considered by the Maharaja, assisted by the Chief Officers of the State, and the following decision was then arrived at.

His Highness suspended the entire revenue demand, for the current year, besides all the past arrears, in all the Talukas of the Amreli District, except in two groups of villages in the Kodinar Taluka, where only six annas in the rupee of the annual demand were to be realized. The entire agricultural population of the Okhamandal Taluka, except the Waghers who have to pay only a nominal assessment on their Salami land, were included in this measure of suspension. The Kadi District came next. Different rates of realization were fixed for the several Talukas according to their respective needs for relief; and an average of six annas in the rupee of the annual demand was fixed for realization, while all the past arrears were entirely suspended. In the Baroda District the realisation of all the past arrears was entirely suspended, and the current demand was wholly or partially suspended in the more afflicted rice-growing Talukas of Vaghodia and Saoli, and in the Chorashi villages. In the Petlad and Siswa

Talukas entire suspension was allowed in about 85 villages; the remaining being called upon to pay eight annas in the rupee in Petlad, and four annas in Siswa. In the District of Naosari a suspension of three-fourths of the accumulated arrears of the past was allowed in the backward Talukas of Velachha and Vakal.

In ordering these suspensions His Highness's Government at the same time adopted measures:—

(a) To have an early and wide publicity given to the orders, so as to leave no room for corruption;

(b) To substitute a rough and general inquiry by groups of villages, in the place of individual enquiries regarding the outturn of crops in each holding;

(c) To do away with all differentiation between rich and poor cultivators, in villages where suspension was ordered;

(d) To include holders of alienated land and inamdars in the same privileges as were vouchsafed to Khalsa land.

These orders for the suspension of the land revenue had a very wholesome effect, inspired confidence in the people, and stimulated local credit. They had also the effect of preventing the migration of numbers of cultivators, and keeping them attached to their soil.

(c)—REMISSIONS OF LAND REVENUE.

One beneficent result that ensued from His Highness's personal observation of the distress of his people during his tours was the policy of liberal remissions inaugurated this year.

The rules in force regarding the grant of remissions pre-suppose individual inquiry into the circumstances and the paying capacity of each cultivator. Such a procedure was however unsuitable to the circumstances of the last year. The past arrears had swollen to a very large figure, and some summary method of wiping out the bad debts of the cultivators had become absolutely necessary. A summary method was accordingly adopted. Statistics of the accumulated arrears of the past were collected, and a standard of the *paying capacity* of the tenants was fixed for each District or part of District. All arrears in excess of this standard was ordered to be struck off, and the balance was left to be realised by equal instalments spread over eight years.

Thus for the Amreli District, His Highness was pleased to order the remission of all arrears exceeding 18 months' revenue demand, which was accepted as the paying capacity of the tenants of that District. This, together with one-fourth of the current year's revenue demand, which in all aggregated to nearly four lakhs of rupees, was summarily wiped off from the State accounts. Similarly an eighteen months' revenue demand was fixed as the standard of the paying capacity in all the less affected Talukas of the Kadi District, and arrears of past revenues in excess of that amount were ordered to be written off. For the mere afflicted tracts of the Kadi District, however, all arrears in excess of only *one year's* revenue demand were ordered to be summarily wiped off. Besides these remissions of the past arrears, the whole District was allowed a remission of 3/16ths of its current year's revenue dues. In the Baroda District, one-fourth of the current year's revenue demand was entirely remitted in the whole of the Vaghodia Taluka, and in certain specified villages of the Saoli, Baroda, Dabhoi and Padra Talukas. With regard to past arrears, the Vaghodia Taluka was relieved of the whole amount in excess of *one year's* revenue demand, which was accepted as the standard of paying capacity for its ryots. It was raised to eighteen months' demand for certain specified groups of villages in the Saoli, Baroda, Tilakwada and Dabhoi Talukas, and to two years' demand for other groups of villages in the same Talukas as well as in Sankheda and Sinor. On the other hand, no remission was allowed to the rich cotton growing Choranda Taluka, or to Petlad and Siswa Talukas which had been recently settled, or to the District of Naosari.

Including the remissions sanctioned under the operation of ordinary rules, the total amount remitted came to about 29 lakhs, as shewn in a previous Chapter.

(d)—Advances to Cultivators.

His Highness's Government makes an annual provision for *Takavi* loans in the Budget, both for the sinking of wells and for other improvements of the soil. Under improvements of the soil are included the work of field terracing and the raising of embankments for rice cultivation; but the

36

most frequent use for which such advances are
taken is the sinking of irrigation wells. An advance of two lakhs of rupees is made every year
for the sinking of such wells; and the sum is
repayable by easy instalments spread over 30 years,
and carries no interest for sums below 500 rupees.
Out of the above sum Rs. 1,00,000 were allotted to
Kadi, and Rs. 50,000 to the Amreli District, during
the year under report. This amount was however,
largely supplemented by additional and special
grants from the Famine Relief Funds; Rs. 50,000
being allotted to Kadi, a like amount to Amreli,
and Rs. 26,000 to Okhamandal.

Numbers of cultivators were thus enabled to sink
wells in their holdings, and to raise some amount
of rabi crop for the maintenance of their family
and their cattle; while large numbers of labourers,
who would have otherwise crowded to relief
camps, found occupation in their own villages.

The extent to which the cultivators availed
themselves of these liberal advances, offered for
well-sinking, is indicated in the following table:—

Name of District.	Number of wells made.				Amount advanced.
	Permanent wells.	Temporary wells.	Repairs.	Total.	
Baroda........	21	..	38	59	14,090
Kadi..........	647	..	67	714	1,36,405
Amreli........	405	38	229	672	90,426
Total ..	1073	38	334	1,445	2,40,861

Thus the largest amount was absorbed by Kadi,
where no less than 714 wells were sunk or repaired

with these *Takavi* advances. In the Amreli District, the largest number was constructed in Okhamandal Taluka, where Rs. 25,735 were advanced for
278 wells. Temporary wells were undertaken in
the Amreli District alone where the hard and rocky
nature of the soil adds much to the cost of permanent wells.

In order to encourage the sinking of wells, His
Highness's Government promised a remission of all
the wet rates, ordinarily levied on the use of well-
irrigation, in all the Districts. A remission of the
rates charged in the Padra Taluka for the use of
wells was also specially sanctioned by His Highness. It was further proclaimed that no fines
would be levied for unauthorised cultivation in
unoccupied waste lands. Encouraged by these
concessions, and by the example of those cultivators
who successfully sank wells with the help of *Takavi*
advances, other cultivators, who had private
means of their own, came forward and spent a
goodly sum of money in sinking wells without any
State help. The following table gives the numbers
of wells sunk by private capital, and the amount
spent on them :—

Serial No.	Name of the District.	Number of wells undertaken.				Amount Spent.
		Permanent wells.	Temporary wells.	Repairs.	Total.	
1	Kadi	853	725	26	1,104	90,255
2	Naosari ..	51	17	9	77	15,850
3	Amreli	5	29	20	54	3,151
	Total ..	409	771	55	1,235	1,09,256

It will thus be seen that while an advance of nearly 2½ lakhs was made by the Government, a further sum of over 1 lakh was spent by the people themselves in the construction and repair of wells.

The policy of sinking irrigation wells at State expense, which was experimentally tried during the famine of 1900, has proved by experience to be unsound. The cultivator is always able to make wells for himself much more cheaply than the Government can make for him. Most of the Government wells sunk in the previous famine in the Damnagar and Dhari Talukas have run dry ; and they all stand in need of repair and further excavation, which means further Government outlay. We have only to provide the agriculturist with the necessary advance, and he will construct the necessary wells, and take care of them for all time to come.

Other objects for which *Takavi* loans were given are mentioned below. The cultivator, in times of scarcity, finds it necessary to provide himself with seed corn, with cattle and manure, with well-gearing, and other agricultural requisites. Large amounts were sanctioned for such purposes. The loans were advanced on very easy terms, and were offered at the commencement of the distress, so as to keep the rayat bound to his holding.

Special concessions were also sanctioned, relaxing the usual limitations and safe-guards imposed on such loans, to make them more acceptable to the cultivator. Interest was foregone on all loans below Rs. 500; periods of repayment were enhanced

by one year ; joint security on the principle of co-
operative credit was largely accepted in the place
of separate individual sureties; and the restrictions
on the granting of loans to borrowers, who were in
arrears for land revenue for a previous loan, were
temporarily suspended. Two or more loans to one
and the same borrower for one single object were
allowed ; and the minimum limit of such loans was
much reduced to make them largely acceptable.
Elaborate inquiries as to previous incumbrances on
the land of the borrower were avoided; and the disposal of applications were accelerated.

The subjoined table indicates the extent to
which these loans were availed of in the different
districts :—

Object of the loan.	Baroda.	Kadi.	Amreli.	Total.
	Rs.	Rs.	Rs.	Rs.
Wells	10,440	70,066	88,434	1,68,940
Bullocks	27,954	1,20,618	22,200	1,70,772
Seed-grain	1,559	18,158	25,585	45,302
Well-gearing	51	6,158	15,025	21,234
Fodder	16,267	13,762	2,420	32,449
Land Improve-ment	80	23	...	103
Miscellaneous ..	6,014	10,645	8,505	25,164
Total ..	62,365	2,39,430	1,62,169	4,63,964

To these may be added Rs. 15,765 advanced
with interest according to the ordinary rules, and
the total advances actually made by the State
came to Rs. 4,79,729.

(e)—SUPPLY OF DRINKING WATER.

The question of the scarcity of drinking water became serious during the year under report. The water level in the wells went down as early as October 1904, and the miseries of a water famine had to be carefully provided against. The Famine Commissioner invited statistics from all the different Talukas regarding their water supply, and large sums were placed in the hands of the District Officers for the excavation of wells for drinking water. Special boring tools, capable of penetrating to deep strata of water, were ordered from Europe and America; and the sinking of temporary pits and the burrowing of hollows in the beds of tanks and rivers were resorted to, where salt water was tapped by deep boring. Cattle troughs were also provided, and large wells with perennial supplies of subsoil water were sought out. Taluka Officers were also empowered to sanction small temporary wells up to a cost of Rs. 50, wherever they were required for a population of a thousand.

Early in the hot weather, the Famine Commissioner proceeded upon on extensive tour, which lasted for close upon three months, and visited village after village to see that no avoidable distress was permitted to remain unnoticed. He expedited the construction of wells in most of the parts he visited, so as to provide against the water famine which was apprehended to assume its worst form in the summer.

It is worthy of note that a very large number
of these wells were entrusted, not to contractors,
but to the villagers themselves, or to Village
Boards or Local Boards then under formation, and
no single case of failure or mis-management by
these bodies came to light. Much money was thus
saved, and the people worked for themselves.

The following statement shows the amounts
sanctioned for the different Districts, and the
number of wells sunk or improved for the purposes
of drinking and other domestic uses, during the
year under report :—

Serial No.	Name of the District.	Amount sanctioned.	Wells undertaken.			Total.
			New.		Repairs.	
			Lined.	Unlined.		
1	Baroda ..	84,840	37	6	179	222
2	Kadi	1,03,015	35	54	109	198
3	Naosari ..	73,623	51	4	159	214
4	Amreli ..	6,646	1	5	58	64
	Total ..	2,68,124	124	69	505	698

Out of the above sum, about Rs. 1,14,618 were
actually spent during the year under report, the
remaining amount being carried forward for dis-
bursement on the completion of the works in the
current year.

In the Baroda District, the Petlad, Saoli, and
Vaghodia Talukas shewed early symptoms of a
scarcity of drinking water. The rocky soil of
some of the villages in the Saoli and Vaghodia

Talukas proved a great hindrance to the sinking of wells, and it was in these villages that the scarcity of potable water was most acute. In Rahakui village, the rocky bed of the well defied all boring tools and blasting operations, and the villagers had to fetch water in metal tubs by carts from a distance of two to three miles. In Kamrol, a well was sunk upwards of 80 feet, and yet the boring tools could not reach the subterranean water. Special boring apparatus had to be ordered for these rocky strata, and the difficulties of the villagers were not entirely removed.

In the Naosari District, three sets of boring tools were used where there was much scarcity of potable water in the Velacha Taluka. Special wells for Bhangies and other low classes had also to be provided. These people are not allowed to use wells reserved for the general use of villagers, and, in the programme of wells above referred to, wells for these depressed classes were included.

In the Kadi District, much was not attempted at first in the way of the improvement of the water supply till the Famine Commissioner visited it again in May 1905. The money provided for the purpose was left mostly untouched, and it was feared that some of our population would migrate into neighbouring British villages in search of water. Prompt measures were required and were adopted. Rs. 54,000 were placed in the hands of Sub-Divisional Officer of Kadi; Rs. 34,000 was allowed to the Pattan Sub-Divisional Officer, and Rs. 10,000 to the Visnagar Sub-Divisional Officer.

These officers were directed to undertake the requisite number of wells in the Talukas within their Sub-Divisions, and the works were commenced at once. Some were completed within the year under report, and the rest have been completed in the current year.

In the Amreli District acute scarcity of drinking water was apprehended in Okhamandal and Beyt. Five new wells were ordered to be sunk in the island of Beyt, which suffers from a special disadvantage. The sea surrounding the islet taints the sources of supply in the wells, and makes the water too salt for human drink. The people of Beyt have often to shift the sites of their wells in search of new springs of untainted water, and their difficulties recur from year to year.

(f)—SUPPLY OF FODDER.

One redeeming feature of the famine of 1904-05, as compared with the visitation of 1899, was, that sufficient fodder had been raised by the cultivators for their cattle. During the previous famine, even before the earlier months of the distress were over, large numbers of milk and plough cattle had perished for want of fodder. The mortality among these dumb creatures was frightful, and the months of October, November, and December saw waggon loads of hides and bones exported from the land. The Autumn of 1904 presaged no such carnage. There was sufficient stock of fodder, either laid by from the surplus of past years, or raised from the stunted food grains which were not ripe enough for human

27

consumption. The Baroda Government had not, therefore, to face a fodder famine except in some few tracts ; and the amounts deemed necessary for loans, for the purchase of grass, were therefore proportionately small for the different Talukas. Rs. 53,000 were sanctioned for Kadi, Rs. 21,000 for Amreli and Okhamandal, and Rs. 18,000 were allotted for a like purpose to the Petlad and Padra Talukas of the Baroda District. The comparatively low rate of mortality among the cattle also explains the low figures of advances given for the purchase of new bullocks.

Information was collected from all the Talukas, early in the cold weather of 1904, regarding their fodder reserves. It was then ascertained that the only Talukas which apprehended a shortage were Okhamandal, Damnagar, and Amreli in Amreli District, Pattan, Kadi, Sidhpur, Vadaoli, Harij, and Mehsana in Kadi District, and Petlad, and Padra in Baroda District. Notifications were published in the *Ajna Patrika* as early as the 4th November 1904, promising remission of assessment for all lands on which grass or other fodder for the consumption of cattle would be raised by cultivators. The same notification permitted and encouraged them to grow grass on unoccupied waste lands, wherever there was any facility for irrigation. The fodder so raised was also declared immune against any process of distraint at the instance either of the Government or of private creditors. This concession was extended to the whole of the Amreli District, and to the Western and Central

Talukas of the Kadi District. These measures were not without a wholesome effect. 79,384 Bighas of land are reported to have been brought under cultivation on account of this privilege, and about 5,98,705 maunds of fodder for the use of cattle were raised thereon.

Moreover, all the pasture lands under the control of the Forest Department, and situated in the Songadh and Vyara Talukas of the Naosari District, as well as in the Dhari and Kodinar Talukas of the Amreli District, were thrown open for free grazing to all the subjects of the State. Kodinar had about 17 inches of rain during the year under report, twelve of which fell within 24 hours. The fall, though unevenly distributed, had left that Taluka in a better condition than the rest of the District, especially as regards fodder. Large numbers of cattle had come to the grazing reserves even from outside the Baroda State. This was promptly stopped, so as to safeguard the supply for our own cattle. The grass grown in Dhari and Kodinar, besides supplying local needs, met the requirements of Okhamandal and Damnagar Talukas. Cattle from distant villages in Amreli were taken to the Dhari Hills during the earlier months, and a large quantity of grass, cut and stacked there, was allowed to be taken *gratis* to the outlying villages in head-loads throughout the year. Pasture grounds and *Bids*, which are usually farmed out by the Revenue Department, and which had not already been put up to auction, were thrown open to free grazing.

The quantity of grass and fodder grown in the Saoli and Vaghodia Talukas in Baroda was so abundant during the year under report, that the grass cutting operations supplied remunerative labour to workmen in both of these Talukas throughout the year. The labourers in these two Talukas, which were otherwise sorely affected owing to the entire failure of their staple rice crop, were able to keep themselves away from the Relief Works opened by the State, entirely on account of these grass operations. The Dhari and Kodinar labourers, similarly, could afford to ignore the Relief Works, on account of their continued employment on the more remunerative work of cutting grass in the jungles. The abundance of fodder thus helped both man and beast to remain independent of State help to a considerable extent.

The Saoli and Vaghodia grass also helped the cultivators of the Petlad and Padra Talukas to find fodder for their own cattle. No State-Depots of grass were established; it was thought better to leave the people free to purchase grass from any quarter they liked, than to send them down to a few State-Depots, where the management is generally expensive and corrupt. The people were only helped with *takavi* advances; Rs. 13,821 were lent to the Petlad cultivators, and Rs. 4,304 to the Padra people, to enable them to make their own arrangements with the grass dealers in the Saoli and Vaghodia Mahals.

Similarly, though there was an acute scarcity of fodder in the Western and Central Talukas of the Kadi District, the cultivators, even there, were allowed to make their own arrangements. Rs. 9,400 and Rs. 3,000 respectively were advanced to the Kadi and Pattan Talukas for the purpose. Our experience in recent famines has taught us that, in respect of irrigation and drinking wells, as well as in the matter of fodder and seed corn, the people shift for themselves better if we make the requisite grants to them, than if we try to make all detailed arrangements for them with a grandmotherly care.

The following statement gives the amount of loans advanced for the purchase of grass in the different Districts in the famines of 1900 and 1905.

Name of the District.	Amount of Takavi for the purchase of grass.	
	1900.	1904–05.
	Rs.	Rs.
Baroda	29,865	16,260
Kadi	3,369	13,762
Amreli	9,895	2,420

Measures were devised to import grass from Kodinar to Okhamandal. Rupees 2,000 were accordingly sanctioned for cutting grass in Kodinar and exporting it by sea to Okhamandal; and a sum of Rs. 11,000 was also sanctioned as advance to the Okha ryots to enable them to purchase the grass. The whole operations cost Rs. 6,232 to the State, while the proceeds of the sales at Okhamandal amounted to Rs. 6,350.

(g).—RELIEF WORKS.

Programmes of works for the Kadi, Amreli, and Baroda districts were settled in December by the highest Officers of the State, met in Council, and were approved of by His Highness the Maharaja. Two sets of programmes were prepared; one was for immediate use, and consisted of works whose detailed plans and estimates were already sanctioned or were ready for approval; the other was intended to be a sort of emergency programme, and included works which were being projected, and which could be taken up in case of any emergency or dearth of other eligible works. The principles on which these Famine Programmes were settled had been deduced from the lessons of past experience, both here and in British Territory. (1). Works ordinarily provided for in the Annual Budget of the Public Works Department were freely resorted to, and were admirably adapted as Test Works in the early stages of the distress. (2). Next to them, preference was given to works commenced, but left half-finished, during the last famine. (3). Similarly, repairs to works already executed, as maintenance of roads and railway embankments, were given a preference over works involving an altogether fresh outlay. (4). Amongst new works, priority was allowed as far as possible to remunerative works. (5). Then came works of a protective or preventive value. (6). Lastly works of local utility, or required under special circumstances, or considered useful for backward or forest tribes, were included in these lists of eligible relief works.

Test Works :—By the latter end of September 1904, when the failure of the monsoons had made a famine inevitable, Test Works were at once ordered to be opened in the Amreli and Okhamandal Talukas. Most of the road repair works, provided in the ordinary Annual Budget, were thus utilised to gauge the extent of the distress. The Bhimgaja Irrigation project, as it had been lately modified, seemed to be full of promise, and the work of breaking and collecting metal on the site of the proposed head-works near Gopi was sanctioned as a further Test Work.

The numbers on these Test Works in Okhamandal exceeded 600 per day by the middle of October, and they were ordered to be converted into full Relief Works from the 1st of November. In Amreli, the Test Works did not attract labourers till the middle of November, but the numbers rose to 200 by the end of December.

In the Kadi District, the first Test Works started in the middle of October had to be closed, as they failed to attract labour ; but there was demand for work later on, and the works had to be resumed. The Famine Commissioner ordered the starting of the Thol Tank for the Kadi Taluka, the Muna Tank for the Pattan Taluka, and the Dasawada Tank for the Sidhpur Taluka. The Harij Sub-Taluka was also provided with a useful irrigation tank work at Gowna Jamanpur. The daily average on these works in the Kadi District, in the aggregate, attained the figure of 500 by the closing week of December; and some of them were converted into full Relief Works at the commencement of the new year.

In Baroda, acute distress had been averted in most of the Talukas by the September rains; but Petlad and the rice growing Talukas of Saoli and Vaghodia had to face a total failure of crops, and relief measures soon became necessary. Test Works were ordered to be opened at Manghrole and Pachrania in Petlad Taluka, and at Vasna in the Siswa sub-Taluka, by the middle of December; and within less than a week the Manghrole work alone mustered about 700 men. This indicated acute distress, and two other works were forthwith started in the southern villages, which also attracted upwards of 100 labourers each.

In order to prevent the Test Works from being unduly attractive, the task of labour exacted was stringent, though not repellant. There was no minimum wage or dependant's dole assured to any workman; dependants, whether infants or aged and destitute relations, were given no extra wages; and payment was made strictly by results. These safeguards were quite sufficient to send away those who could afford to earn their livelihood elsewhere. The prices of food did not at any time evince any ¦sign of a sudden upheaval; and the wage scale based thereon was consequently never unduly attractive. But labour alone was recognised to be of the essence of the test; neither a *distance* test nor a *compulsory residence* test was insisted upon. Both these tests are open to grave practical objections. In Petlad Taluka for instance, the Vaso people are proud of their position among their neighbours and kinsmen, and will rather die in their own village than resort to work in distant centres as common laborers. Similarly, the Thakardas of the Kadi and Kalol Talukas will suffer any privation rather than appear as laborers, spade in hand, in the neighbouring villages where they have matrimonial connexions. Moreover, an obligation to attend only a distant work carries compulsory residence on the work in its train. This necessitates the formation of Relief Camps, Health Camps, Relief Hospitals, and all the costly paraphernalia of large Relief Works. Such a compulsory residence, besides, has the disadvantage of taking the labourer away from his home, his agricultural live stock, and his farm. He has to neglect his cattle and leave them behind, and he has to carry his infant and aged relations with him, or leave them to die.

Tests Works were not unduly prolonged; and, with the new year, Relief Works were in full swing in almost all the Talukas affected by the famine.

*Irrigation Works :—*Among new and remunerative works precedence was naturally allowed to large Irrigation Reservoirs and Dams, as well as Drainage Channels, which had a remunerative as well as protective value. Some parts of the State suffer from a lack of irrigational facilities, while others are damaged by annual inundation. If Irrigation and Drainage works be successfully constructed in these parts, much of the evil is likely to be removed. It was necessary, however, to proceed with due caution.

The Commission of Sir Colin Scott-Moncrieff has held that the Province of Gujarat is not quite suited to Major Irrigation Works of a large magnitude. The volume of waters, flowing in the majority of the rivers after November, is far too low to be of much value for any considerable area of *Rabi* crops. On the other hand, large and costly storage works, calculated to impound the copious monsoon supplies, have their own risks. A large volume of water is likely to be wasted both by percolation and evaporation in the sun burnt plains of Gujarat. It is the light sandy loam of the *Gorat* soil that is supposed to profit best by irrigation, and it is only the rice crop which is likely to be most benefitted by large irrigation works. All these circumstances have to be collectively viewed before the chances of success of a proposed irrigation work can be judged.

Measures were adopted in 1904-05 with caution. A special Irrigation Department was opened under Mr. Vasanji Desai to work out the details of irrigation projects ; and the services of Mr. Khandubhai G. Desai, a retired Executive Engineer of the Bombay Presidency, were also engaged for a year, for advice and consultation in the maturing of schemes. Lastly, the services of Mr. Chunilal T. Dalal, who has successfully constructed some of the largest of tanks in Southern India, were obtained from the Mysore Government, as

Chief Engineer of the State. It is believed that, with the cautious advice of these officers, the works that we now undertake will have a high protective efficiency, if not also a remunerative value. The Bhimgaja Reservoir in Okhamandal, the Shatrunja Dam and the Ankadia and Bhandaria Tanks in Amreli, the Dhamel Tank in Damnagar, and the Pichwi and Singoda Projects in Kodinar were all referred to these officers out of the Amreli Programme. They were also requested to mature and investigate the Vadnagar feeder cut, the Umta and Anawada Canals, the Thol and Khakharia as well as the Jamanpur Tanks, and the Harij Reclamation Bund in the Kadi District. Of the works in the Baroda Programme they had to consider the big Alwa Scheme, which is proposed as a supplementary storage work to complete the Orsang project. They were also asked to investigate the full potentiality of the ambitious Jhankhari Scheme in the Naosari District.

Only slow progress could be made with these preliminary enquires, made with due caution. The only schemes that were handed over to the Famine Commissioner for execution during the year under report were (1) the Bhimgaja Dam in Okhamandal (2) the Ankadia Tank in Amreli, (3) the Dhamel Tank in Damnagar, and (4) the Minor Irrigation tanks in Petlad Taluka. These were all proceeded with as Famine Relief Works, and substantial progress was made during the year. The Ankadia Tank had close upon 3,000 labourers as the daily average in June, and one of the works in Petlad had upwards of 2,000 in March, and the works are well nigh finished. The Bhimgaja Dam has also made a satisfactory progress, and it is likely to be finished in the current year.

Railways.—Next to Irrigation schemes the construction of Railways occupies a prominent place in the Famine Programmes of the State. The Baroda territories have been intersected by a net work of small railways which, besides being very useful, are also fairly paying. It is true that Railway works do not possess any pre-eminent fitness for the purpose of famine relief. Their earthwork alone forms the kind of unskilled labour which is suited to the capabilities of the relief seekers. A disproportionately large amount of their estimated expenditure is taken up by skilled labour, such as is required in the building of bridges and masonry culverts; and another large outlay has to be incurred abroad in the purchase of rails and the rolling stock. But the construction of metalled roads on the sandy soil of Gujarat is not a less expensive undertaking; and the annual cost of their maintenance is so prohibitive that Railways on the narrow and metre gauges prove more economical in the end. Accordingly, we had included in our Famine Programmes the Nar-Vaso line, the Becharaji and Harij lines, the Vijapur-Vadnagar line, the Kheralu—Dabhoda line, the Amreli-Chital line, and the Jamnagar—Dwarka line.

Some of these lines, however, could not be undertaken pending negotiations in the Political Department; and only the construction of the Becharaji and Harij lines was taken up in the year under report. They were seriously commenced in the month of May, at the fag end of the working season. The Railway authorities took an unduly long time in marking the lines ; and the works had to be let out to contractors to attract labourers by the promise of higher wages than what the Relief Code allowed. The works made slow progress within the year under report; and the number of relief seekers did not justify the commencement of other lines.

Roads.—The construction of roads is considered an eligible Relief Work, wherever they are capable of serving as feeders to Railways, or as high ways for traffic between one Taluka town and another. They are selected on the ground of their securing an easy access to celebrated places of public resort, or serving the requirements of important towns. They are also chosen for their use in securing markets for the agricultural products of the rural villages and outlying districts.

The roads selected in Baroda and Kadi Districts did not attract many relief seekers. Large classes of people were helped by advances to work in their own fields, or in the sinking of village wells, and many of them were also occupied in the more remunerative operation of grass cutting. But better progress was made with regard to roads in the Amreli District. The Damnagar-Dhasa road was thoroughly repaired, as also the Chalala-Dhari road. The Amreli-Kundla and the Dhari-Dalkhania roads, which had been left incomplete during the previous famine, were resumed this year; and the small strip between Chalala and Dharagni, which had been omitted before, was completed, so as to make the chain of communication between Khambha and the Chital Railway Station complete. In the Okha-mandal Taluka no new roads were undertaken; only the important roads connecting Dwarka with Beyt were kept under repair. So also in the Kodinar Taluka only repairs to the Velan, Dholasa, and Ghatwad roads were undertaken for the purposes of relief.

Tanks.—Village works are a necessary part of all relief operations. They afford relief to backward classes whom it is difficult to draw to relief centres, and they are also suitable for those whom their social status prevents from going long distances as labourers. Village tanks are also admirably adapted as Relief Works on the approach of the monsoon, when the cultivator has to be brought nearer his own home, in order that he may be able to resume his agricultural pursuit with the breaking of the rains. Many of these tanks are capable of being turned into a system of minor irrigation works, each discharging its surplus water into the one lying next below, and being fed by drainage channels from further up the country. These tail-tanks, when linked up with each other, are capable of retaining the necessary amount of water for purposes of irrigation in times of drought, and have a highly protective value in rich rice-growing tracts. They also leave a rich silt in their beds for being cultivated in the dry months with *rabi* crops. The tanks in the Kadi and Kalol Talukas, as well as in the Petlad, Saoli and Vaghodia Talukas, are all capable of this two-fold use, and were included on that ground in the Relief Programme.

About thirty tanks were repaired in the Petlad Taluka alone during the year under report. Of these, the most important were at Dabhao, Bhadkad, Bhanderaj, Mangrol, and Malawada. All of these tanks command a large amount of rich *Kyari* soil, which was going out of cultivation owing to the neglect of the tanks. A similar tank, which belongs to the Inamdar of Dewa, was also repaired at his instance by the Government from the Inamdar's funds. Mention may also be made of the important tanks of the towns of Sojitra, Vaso, Dharmaj, Siswa, Vatadra, Ramol, Changa, and Kasar, which were thoroughly repaired, so as to be of use to the town-folk, besides irrigating the rice-lands at their command.

The Desar tank in the Saoli Taluka, as well as the Devalia tank which is calculated to feed the Alwa reservoir in the Vaghodia Taluka, were also opened as Test Works ; but had to be closed after some time.

In the Kadi District, most of the tanks repaired were situated in the Pattan and Sidhpur Talukas. The Charup tank work was opened as early in December 1904, so as to serve the needs of both these tracts. Subsequently the Muna, Jagral, and Jakha tanks were commenced. The Jamanpur and Piplana tanks were also begun to relieve the pressing needs of Harij Sub-Taluka.

The Kakoshi Circle of the Sidhpur Taluka claimed our equal attention during the year under report. The population consists largely of industrious Moomans and of thriftless Thakardas. The contrast between these two opposite types is very striking in these Kakoshi villages. The well irrigated and well cultivated fields of the Mooman alternate with shabby patches of neglected lands belonging to the Thakardas. These latter wanted looking after, and works had to be opened for them from the earliest months. The Dasawada and Mundwada tanks, as well as tank works at Vadhna, Hisor, and Chandalaj, gave them relief, and were finished during the year.

The Thakardas, inhabiting the Khakharia villages of Kadi and Kalol, stood in need of equal care. Sentiments of family and social pride prevented them from being seen at work in distant villages. They preferred to earn their living by carrying firewood to the Ahmedabad market, to appearing as hewers of wood and drawers of water in the neighbouring village of Thol, where a tank was started. The Thol tank commands about 2,000 bighas of very rich rice lands, and has a highly protective value, but had to be closed before the end of the year. The scheme of the tank is being revised and modified, and will be resumed at an early opportunity.

There were also tank works at Saij in the Kalol Taluka, Chhatiarda in Mehsana, Jetpur in Vadaoli, and the Dehgam Town tank, which attracted a fair number of labourers throughout the period they were kept open. The Dhinoj tank in the Vadaoli Taluka, and the Ranuj tank in Pattan, were also taken in hand during June and July, and much work was done. The Kheralu tank and the Vijapur tank, however, which were opened as Test Works, had to be abandoned as soon as they were started for want of labourers. The Balasar tank in the Kadi Taluka also failed to draw labour. No tanks of any importance were executed in Amreli and Naosari Districts.

It will be seen, from what has been stated before, that the relief afforded to sufferers during the year under report consisted very largely in advances made to the cultivators for sinking wells, improving their fields, and extending cultivation, and only to a limited extent in regular Relief Works. Tens of thousands of people found occupation in their own fields and villages out of the advances made by the Government, and our Railways and Irrigation Works, our Roads and even our Tanks did not therefore attract large multitudes. His Highness's Government looks with satisfaction on this phase of the Famine Relief measures of 1904-05. The advances made

The system of payment, pursued on these Relief Works, has been what the Famine Commission of ﹍﹍ has called the "Intermediate modified piece-work system," or payment strictly by results with a limited maximum but no guaranteed minimum. Payments were daily made, and the system of punctual payment and prompt measurement was admirably worked. Travelling auditors were appointed, and they visited the works from time to time. The wage scale was kept sliding according to the prevailing prices, and was duly notified to the workmen. The average wage amounted five pice for an adult male, four for an adult female, and three for children above seven. It once rose by a single pice, but never fell below the above average. Payments were made to the headman of each gang, so that the Officers were able to make payments every evening.

The tasks exacted were previously fixed after consulting the District Executive Engineers. With the approach of the monsoons, and the reversion to their village works, these tasks were raised by one fourth on all the works in the Kadi and Amreli Districts, so as to make them deterrent, and induce the people to return to their agricultural pursuits. Works in the Baroda District were all closed by the middle of July; and in the Kadi District they had to be wound up owing to the torrents of rain that fell in the third week of that month. They had to be continued for some time longer in the Amreli District, owing to the scanty rainfall of that District, and also with a view to push on the to the cultivators in this State are generally safe, and are easily recovered in good years; they give employment to men and women without degrading them to labourers on Relief Works; they are carried on by villagers in their own villages and require no regular Relief Camps; they permanently improve the cultivation of the State; and lastly they are carried on by the people themselves without the interference of Relief Officers. For all these reasons, our endeavour has been to foster and extend this kind of relief by means of advances to villagers, and to provide State Relief Works only for those who could find no sort of employment elsewhere, and came to our hands. And the Government have marked with pleasure that the numbers of those who thus came to regular Relief Works were never very high; and that multitudes found relief in their own homes and villages out of the advances made by the State.

Figures showing the number of workers on the regular Relief Works are given below. The highest number was reached in June when the total for the month exceeded five hundred thousand, giving an average of 17,000 per day.

Month.	Baroda City.	Baroda.	Kadi.	Naosari.	Amreli.	Total.
August	..	..	..	..	..	..
September..	..	..	..	..	5,236	5,236
October	..	..	..	..	21,346	21,346
November ..	1,419	..	2,764	553	19,094	23,829
December ..	2,503	8,132	14,620	5,709	33,790	64,755
January ...	2,037	32,719	30,750	4,787	49,583	1,19,896
February ..	2,903	61,572	32,432	..	51,695	1,48,602
March	5,029	90,792	36,595	..	71,443	2,03,859
April	2,621	1,29,632	58,660	..	1,30,397	3,21,310
May	1,122	1,99,519	90,629	9,956	1,59,487	4,60,712
June	384	1,91,096	1,53,660	10,479	1,57,126	5,12,736
July	118	66,304	76,794	1,038	2,20,164	3,64,418
Total..	18,136	7,79,766	4,96,894	32,522	9,19,371	22,46,689

The system of payment, pursued on these Relief Works, has been what the Famine Commission of 1901 has called the "Intermediate modified piece-work system," or payment strictly by results with a limited maximum but no guaranteed minimum. Payments were daily made, and the system of punctual payment and prompt measurement was admirably worked. Travelling auditors were appointed, and they visited the works from time to time. The wage scale was kept sliding according to the prevailing prices, and was duly notified to the workmen. The average wage amounted five pice for an adult male, four for an adult female, and three for children above seven. It once rose by a single pice, but never fell below the above average. Payments were made to the headman of each gang, so that the Officers were able to make payments every evening.

The tasks exacted were previously fixed after consulting the District Executive Engineers. With the approach of the monsoons, and the reversion to minor village works, these tasks were raised by one fourth on all the works in the Kadi and Amreli Districts, so as to make them deterrent, and induce the people'to return to their agricultural pursuits. Works in the Baroda District were all closed by the middle of July; and in the Kadi District they had to be wound up owing to the torrents of rain that fell in the third week of that month. They had to be continued for some time longer in the Amreli District, owing to the scanty rainfall of that District, and also with a view to push on the

Ankadia and Bhimgaja tanks. The work of the Bhimgaja Dam was treated throughout as an ordinary work, and ordinary market wages were paid.

(h) GRATUITOUS RELIEF.

Gratuitous Relief forms an important item of the measures devised for the relief of distress in every famine. Such relief has to be provided for the aged, the infirm, and the destitute, who are all thrown upon the bounty of the State with the contraction of private charity and the shrinking of family incomes. The distribution of village doles, and the housing of destitute incapables in poor houses, are the acknowledged forms of gratuitous relief in times of famine. Directly the period of tests and trials is over, and the presence and extent of distress are ascertained, the opening of full relief works has to be largely supplemented by the starting of village doles and the opening of poor houses in towns.

During the year under report, five hundred thousand units of such destitute people were relieved by the bounty of the State. One-half of these were supported by the distribution of village doles, and an equal number relieved as dependants of labourers on relief works. No poor-houses were opened.

Dependants on minor works were entered on the list, of village doles, and were thus admitted to the benefits of gratuitous relief. An extra pice was given to mothers with infant in arm. Care was however taken that no undue laxity was allowed

to creep in as regards the admission of dependants on large works. The Officers in charge of such works were required to explain whenever the percentage of dependants to actual labourers exceeded twenty-five. All distant kinsmen, and foreigners coming with the workmen, were thus detected and sent away.

It is gratifying to note that the numbers in receipt of village doles were kept under reasonable limits in all the Districts, the only Talukas which returned any appreciably large numbers being Petlad and Amreli. Indeed, it was once apprehended, that this form of gratuitous relief did not reach all those who really deserved it. The Famine Commissioner undertook a house to house inspection in the villages he visited during his tours ; and it was very assuring to find that few deserving people had been omitted from the lists of village doles. Some remissness was found in the Pattan Taluka where the list of recipients was inadequate, and the mistake was promptly corrected.

The total expenditure on gratuitous relief did not exceed Rs. 16,300 during the period under review. Out of this, Rs. 6,760 were spent on the relief of dependants on works, and Rs. 9,540 on village doles. The number of persons relieved is shown in the statement given below. The largest number was reached in June, when over a hundred and twenty thousand, or 4000 *per diem*, obtained gratuitous relief.

Dependants on Relief works and those
gratuitously relieved.

Name of Month.	Baroda.	Kadi.	Amreli.	Total.
1	2	3	4	5
August	....	....	.....	....
September......	....	....	....	....
October	....	....	....	....
November	....	....	1,319	1,319
December	....	....	1,629	1,629
January	800	5,482	9,521	15,803
February	10,299	13,768	12,192	36,259
March	17,638	10,951	17,269	45,858
April...........	32,422	18,109	26,471	77,002
May	45,489	25,308	27,852	98,649
June...........	48,990	42,218	33,854	1,25,062
July	34,009	25,634	38,491	98,134
Total ..	1,89,647	1,41,470	1,68,598	4,99,715

There are also permanent charitable institutions
in the State where doles are given in all seasons.
There are several such religious and benevolent
institutions in Petlad, Pattan, and Kadi, and in
Amreli and Kodinar. They relieved large numbers
of poor helpless people by distribution of alms as
well as cooked rations. The Orphanages opened
in Baroda, Amreli, and Mehsana, during the last
famine, continued to feed and house helpless

children; and the institutions were kept open to
receive all the waifs and strays that might be
thrown upon State help for support. Maternity
or lying-in arrangements were made in all the
Relief Dispensaries attached to the large works;
and several cases of confinement were reported
from the Relief Camps attached to the Damnagar-
Dhasa road, the Dalkhania road, and the Vankia
and Ankadia works in the Amreli District.

Gratuitous Relief from the State was also supplemented to a great extent by private charity. The
most notable instances of the kind were the charitable contributions on the Dharmaj and Siswa tanks
in the Petlad Taluka, the Sadavartas maintained
by the Mahant Inamdar at Sidhpur, and similar
institutions at the well-known shrines of Dwarka
and Beyt. In Amreli and Dhari, also, decent collections were made in kind from the contributions
of grain-merchants; and most of the village
doles were distributed out of these private funds.

(i)—EXTENT OF THE FAMINE.

Prices of food grains.—The prices of food grains
did not rise to any abnormal pitch at any time
during the year. Though there was an upward
wave in the opening weeks of the drought, the
highest prices did not go beyond 25 per cent. above
the usual average. The prices of *Jwari* and *Bajri*,
which may be regarded as the staple food in use
amongst the poor, ranged between 28 to 24 lbs. a
rupee; and the resulting wage to an adult male
on the Relief Works averaged from five to six pices
per day. The prices of food grains continued to

remain steady, and there was nothing like a feverish activity in the grain market.

Distress in Baroda.—In the Baroda District the Talukas of Petlad, Saoli and Vaghodia were the only tracts which were severely affected. The loss caused by the failure of the rains was much intensified by the heavy frost of the cold weather that followed. Valuable standing crops of tobacco were blighted in the Petlad Taluka, and other irrigated garden crops were also damaged by the frost. The wheat crops suffered from rust over a large area in this Taluka; irrigation became difficult and costly as the level of the water in the wells sank low ; and the supply of fodder grew scanty. This explains the large numbers of Petlad men on the several Relief Works opened in their midst. The monthly total of units relieved reached the maximum figure of nearly two lakhs in the month of May, showing a daily average of more than six thousand. The Saoli and Vaghodia Talukas, which are poor and backward even in ordinary years, were also seriously affected ; but the grass cutting operations saved them. The necessities of other Talukas proved their opportunity. The Vaghodia Works failed to attract labourers ; and the Desar Tank work in Saoli was allowed to be continued with ordinary piece work wages, but failed to attract more than a small number of women and children.

- *Distress in Kadi.*—In the Kadi District the western and central Talukas suffered most as in the past. The treeless and waterless tracts of

Harij, Vadaoli, and north-west Pattan, were scenes of desolation from the commencement of the drought, and were the first to succumb. Parts of Sidhpur, Mehsana, Kadi, and Kalol, were also affected. Visnagar and the eastern Talukas of Vijapur, Kheralu, and Dehgam, were better off.

The Harij people managed to obtain some nourishment from the roots of a coarse variety of grass, which they dug up, threshed, and pounded into flour. The other western circles of the Pattan Taluka were also reduced to the same pitiable straits. The people had often to maintain themselves on the wild *keras* which grew on the brambles and hedges that enclosed their fields. The *keras* found a good market in the towns of Pattan and Palanpore, and brought some means of livelihood to their owners. Relief Works were opened in these parts at a very early stage of the drought, and they continued to attract large numbers throughout the period of distress. The Thakardas of the Kadi and Kalol villages were averse to attend Relief Works, as stated before ; but they managed to earn a living by the sale of firewood in the markets of Ahmedabad. Their women and children were largely engaged in collecting *gundas*, a sort of wild berries in which the district abounds. These berries are either used for human consumption or are given to milch cattle ; and their sale proceeds served to supplement the earnings from the sale of firewood. In the eastern Talukas of Dehgam and Vijapur, the mango and the mahua fruit served as nourishing food among the poor people. The numbers of relief-seekers throughout the District reached their maximum in June, when the monthly total of units relieved aggregated to over a lakh and a half, giving an average of five thousand per diem.

Distress in Amreli.—The Amreli District suffered most. The people of Okhamandal Taluka had suffered from a succession of years of scarcity, drought, and famine. The other Talukas of the District were also hard hit, as the people had no respite since the great calamity of 1899. The Relief Works opened in the Amreli, Damnagar, and Okhamandal Talukas attracted large numbers from the commencement; the maximum being reached in the months of May and June. The Dhari and Kodinar Talukas were less affected, and the grass cutting work gave them a means of subsistence. The numbers of relief-seekers throughout the District reached their maximum in July, when the monthly total rose to nearly two and a quarter lacs, giving a daily average of over seven thousand.

Emigration:—During the year under review 5,257 persons were reported to have left our territories in quest of labour outside the Raj, most of them from the Pattan, Vadaoli, and Harij Talukas. These people left their villages in October and November, under a panic, before they had any time to concert measures for self-help or seek for relief from the State. The Famine Commissioner, during his first tour in November, persuaded the people to stick to their lands and their homes, and seek for State relief which was being liberally offered. He also inquired into the causes of the early emigration that had set in, and found it to be only of a temporary character, and induced by panic caused by the memories of the previous famines. A majority of the people from the Vadaoli Taluka had gone to the Ahmedabad Cotton Mills for labour; while the Harij and Pattan people seemed to have been attracted by the prospects of remunerative labour on the canals of Sindh. Some of them had friends and relations in that Province, and had proceeded there to help them in irrigating their fields, or to go shares with them in cultivating lands with the canal water. The people were also attracted to the neighbouring Kankrej Taluka in the Palanpore Agency which abounds in wells, and therefore afforded them an ample field for labour. Most of these emigrants were agricultural labourers, and few of them had any lands of their own in our territories. Occupants of holdings remained attached to their lands and their homes, and resorted to the State Relief Works when they felt the pressure of distress. The flow of emigration was effectually checked in December, and completely stopped with the new year.

Immigration.—On the other hand 1,978 people were reported to have come into our territories, both from British India and from other Native States, in quest of labour.

As provided in the revised Famine Relief Code, these aliens were in no case refused admission on the Baroda Relief Works. They were duly attended to, and their wants relieved; and they were subsequently identified, collected into gangs, and returned to the Districts from which they had come. The Famine Commission of 1901 had complained that, because some of the Baroda subjects had sought relief on the British Works in progress at Broach and other districts of Gujarat in 1899-1900, they seriously "hampered the British Administration of Relief, and greatly affected the mortality in the British Districts." The famine of 1905 shews that the complaint was baseless. No subject of His Highness's Government sought relief on any British Relief Work in 1905; and the advent of foreigners did not hamper the Baroda Relief Administration in the least, nor added in any way to the famine mortality of the Raj. Such migrations in times of scarcity and distress are inevitable; the subjects of one Government are not prevented from having their friends and relations in another by any geographical limits. Baroda and British territories are so interlaced that such migrations cannot be stopped, and need not be stopped. It is the want of preparedness or mismanagement of famine operations, and not the migration of foreigners, that is responsible for high mortality in some years.

Crimes.—The return of crimes for the year under review shows an increase of 474 in the whole Raj, as compared with the return for the preceding year. The total number of offences in

1904-05 was 3,356 against 2,882 of the previous year, as shewn in a previous chapter.

Public Health.—The state of public-health continued to remain satisfactory throughout the year ; and there was nothing like the terrible mortality witnessed in the year of the great Famine 1899 and the subsequent years. The rate of mortality rose so high as 54·4 in 1899, and did not shrink below 48·2 in the subsequent year. During the year under report the death-rate was 24·7. And it is satisfactory to record that in 1904-05 *not a single death occurred in the numerous Relief Centres or in the Camps of Dependants, nor was a single case of death by starvation reported in the State.* Serious fears were entertained about the out-break of cholera in an epidemic form during the hot months, owing to the extreme scarcity of drinking water ; but fortunately they were soon dispelled, and the state of public health in the three summer months from April to June was even better than before. Large Works and Concentration Camps were broken up with the advent of the rains, and the labourers sent back to the Village Works nearer their homes.

Cattle-mortality :—It is equally gratifying to note that there was no excessive mortality of cattle during the year. The total death-rate per *mille* per annum was only 31, as compared with 575 in 1899, 78 in 1900, and 43 in 1901-02.

(*j*)—Expenditure on the Famine.

The total expenditure, incurred till the end of the year, in carrying on this campaign against the famine, is tabulated below, and compared with the expenses incurred in similar calamities in the past.

	Head of Expenditure.	1899-1900.	1900-1901.	1901-1902.	1904-1905.
1	Gratuitous Relief	1,57,833	1,57,413	1,14,598	5,850
2	Special Takavi for wells ..	15,16,525	12,23,808	3,14,686	6,66,531
3	Grants for Cattle	7,176	1,571	400	52
4	Grain Compensation ..	4,09,638	1,77,480	..	558
5	Public Works..	20,21,742	14,65,472	10,91,896	2,01,198
6	Supervision charges ..	1,57,295	2,50,619	77,305	35,850
7	Miscellaneous	3,35,029	2,24,422	5,09,931	79,053
	Total ..	46,05,238	35,00,785	21,08,811	9,89,067

The famine of 1905 was far less severe than those of 1899, 1900 and 1901; but making every allowance for that, His Highness's Government may well congratulate itself on the thoroughness and success with which the operations of 1905 have been carried out, and the care with which the expenditure has been controlled. Against an expenditure of over a *hundred lacs* incurred in the three years' famine, the total expenditure in 1904-05 was within *ten lacs*. And out of these ten laks, over six and a half lacs, Rs. 666,531, represent advances which have benefited the cultivation of the State, and which we expect to recover without difficulty if the present hard times are succeeded by a number of fairly prosperous years.

The only other item in the above table that calls for any remark is the cost of supervision incurred by the employment of additional establishments. The figure returned under this head by the Accountant General amounts to Rs. 35,850, which gives a rough average of about 3½ per cent. on the entire outlay. This sum is made up of Rs. 26,277 spent by the Civil Departments, and Rs. 9,573 on the supervision of Relief Works.

The actual expenditure incurred on Relief Works amounted to Rs. 2,52,687, of which Rs. 2,01,193 were audited by the end of July last, and have been shown in the statement given above. This, when added to Rs. 9,541 spent in village doles by the Civil Agency, gives a total of Rs. 2,62,228 as the entire expenditure, including unaudited items and suspense accounts.

It may be remarked that the incidence of expenditure per unit relieved was 1 anna 6½ pies, which tallies approximately with the incidence of expenditure in the Bombay Presidency during the great famine of 1899-1900, which was one anna six pies for the entire relief given to each unit who availed himself of State help in any form.

Conduct of Officers.—In concluding this account of the Famine Relief operations of 1904-05, it is necessary to add that the success of these operations is largely due to the thoughtful care and the untiring industry of the Famine Commissioner, Mr. Manubhai Nandshankar Mehta. He was appointed to the post, under the general supervision and orders of the Revenue Minister, by his Highness the Maharaja as early as September 1904 ; and he prepared himself for his work by a study of Sir Anthony Macdonnell's valuable Famine Commission Report, as well as the Reports of the previous famines in this State. Mr. Manubhai helped in revising the Famine Code of Baroda, and took an important part in all the deliberations which led to the preparation and final adoption of our Famine Relief Programme. From the first appearance of the signs of distress, and throughout the trying months when the famine was at its worst, Mr. Manubhai made prolonged and extensive tours through all the afflicted Talukas, seeing everything with his own eyes, and regulating and controlling all operations on the spot. It is due to his quiet unpretentious work, his watchful care, and his ceaseless industry, that the relief operations were conducted efficiently as well as economically, and were completely successful in preventing loss of life.

Mention should also be made of the good work done by Officers of the Public Works Department in carrying out the onerous duties imposed upon them, and in dealing with large numbers of relief seekers and dependants who came to our Centres. Mistakes made here and there were promptly corrected, and on the whole the work entrusted to the Department was ably and efficiently performed.

More difficult duties were imposed on the Revenue Officers of the State, the Revenue Commissioner, the District Officers, the Naeb Subahs of Sub-Divisions, and the Vahivatdars of Talukas. To all these Officers the Famine Relief operations meant a large increase of work in a year when extra work of various kinds had already been added to their ordinary duties. It was during this year that Village

Panchyets, Taluka Boards, and District Boards were organized, and a complete system of Local Self-Government was built up. It was in this year, also, that an Income Tax on a uniform scale was introduced throughout the State, assessments were made in towns and villages with the help of representative men, and numerous old taxes on different castes and professions were abolished. And lastly, His Highness's orders of remission of the Land Revenue at different rates in different Talukas required detailed and prolonged calculations and enquiries, which had to be completed within the year. In no preceding year, perhaps, were such multifarious duties added to the ordinary work of the Revenue Officers as in 1904-05 ; and it speaks well of the zeal, the industry, and the working capacity of the entire Revenue Service of the State, that all these manifold duties, and the work of Famine Relief, were discharged efficiently and well. In a few cases mistakes were made, or undue delay in the performance of some duties was observed. But these were promptly remedied, and on the whole the work of Revenue Officers during this trying year has been efficient and successful.

SUPPLEMENTAL NOTE.

Duration of Civil Cases.—After the present Report had been sent to the press, the question of the average duration of Civil Cases in Baroda State received the full consideration of the Council at two meetings. And the Council found:—

That taking the work of the last three years into consideration, the work of the Baroda Courts compares favourably, in respect of duration of cases, with that of the Courts in the Bombay Presidency, if the cases disposed of by the regular Small Cause Courts in Bombay be excluded from the calculation; and that even if these cases be included, the work of the Baroda Courts does not compare unfavourably with that of Bombay.

That the high average of 291 days for 1903-04 in Baroda was mainly owing to the disposal in that year of between two and three hundred old and long pending cases. Excluding these cases, the average duration comes down to 139 days.

That the method of reckoning the duration of cases is different in Bombay from that in Baroda; that the same Courts try Civil and Criminal Cases in this State; that the service of processes outside the State involves delay; that the Limitation Act 1897 and the Registration Act of 1902 brought in a large influx of cases which affected the averages of subsequent years; that the Officers of the Baroda Judicial Service have not the same practical experience of judicial work at the commencement of their career as the Officers in Bombay; that there were special reasons for the long duration of cases in some particular Courts; and that the Judicial Department were taking steps to reduce the long duration of Appeal Cases.

Local Cess Demand and Collection for 1903-04. The figures given in page 73 of the Report do not include the Local Cess amalgamated with the Land Revenue in certain Talukas. The accounts have been separated from 1904-05.

Lightning Source UK Ltd.
Milton Keynes UK
UKHW020734261118
332983UK00008B/548/P